PUBLICATIONS
OF THE
ARMY RECORDS SOCIETY
VOL. 8

THE BRITISH ARMY AND
SIGNALS INTELLIGENCE DURING
THE FIRST WORLD WAR

The Army Records Society was founded in 1984 in order to publish original records describing the development, organisation, administration and activities of the British Army from early times.

Any person wishing to become a Member of the Society is requested to apply to the Hon. Secretary, c/o The National Army Museum, Royal Hospital Road, London, SW3 4HT. The annual subscription entitles the Member to receive a copy of each volume issued by the Society in that year, and to purchase back volumes at reduced prices. Current subscription details, whether for individuals living within the British Isles, for individuals living overseas, or for institutions, will be furnished on request.

The Council of the Army Records Society wish it to be clearly understood that they are not answerable for opinions or observations that may appear in the Society's publications. For these the responsibility rests entirely with the Editors of the several works.

THE BRITISH ARMY AND SIGNALS INTELLIGENCE DURING THE FIRST WORLD WAR

Edited by
JOHN FERRIS

Published by
ALAN SUTTON
for the
ARMY RECORDS SOCIETY
1992

First published in the United Kingdom in 1992
Alan Sutton Publishing Ltd · Phoenix Mill · Far Thrupp · Stroud · Gloucestershire

First published in the United States of America in 1992
Alan Sutton Publishing Inc · Wolfeboro Falls · NH 03896–0848

British Library Cataloguing in Publication Data
Ferris, John Robert
British Army and Signals Intelligence During the First World War
I. Title
940.4

ISBN 0-7509-0247-7

Library of Congress Cataloging in Publication Data applied for

Typeset in 11/13 Ehrhardt
Typesetting and origination by
Alan Sutton Publishing Limited.
Printed in Great Britain by
The Bath Press, Avon.

Contents

Introduction

The great American cryptanalyst, William F. Friedman, once noted that 'interests of national security and domestic tranquility' led all states to pursue a 'policy of silence' about their codebreaking organisations.[1] Such a policy has certainly shaped the present case. Historians have paid little attention to the signals intelligence service of the British Army during the First World War; it is not easy to redress the balance.[2] The bulk of the relevant records have been destroyed or else retained indefinitely by Her Majesty's Government. Only a careful search of the papers of several British departments of state, of associated military forces and of British and allied officers, can produce even a fragmentary run of documents on the topic. Yet this evidence leads to a startling conclusion. Signals intelligence affected the British Army during the First World War no less than in the Second.

Intelligence does not win wars: but it does shape their course and in an odd fashion. As E.T. Williams, the head of intelligence for the 21st Army Group during the Second World War, noted:

> Perfect Intelligence in war must of necessity be out-of-date and therefore cease to be perfect. We deal with partial and outmoded sources from which we attempt to compose an intelligible appreciation having regard to the rules of evidence and our soldierly training and which we must be prepared constantly to revise as new evidence emerges. We deal not with the true but with the likely. Speed is therefore the essence of the matter.[3]

The aim of intelligence is to minimise uncertainty about the enemy and to maximise the efficiency of the use of one's own resources. As the intelligence branch at General Headquarters (GHQ) Iraq noted:

> When you know the location of every hostile regiment, it is self-evident that it becomes impossible for the enemy to take you unawares at any point. Hence your reserves, which would otherwise have to be kept in hand to meet surprises, can be

I

reduced to the lowest possible minimum and every ounce of your weight can be applied from the outset exactly where you know it will tell most heavily.[4]

In order to achieve such an aim, intelligence services must provide current, reliable and effective information while commanders may yet act on knowledge. The collection of such material is difficult enough, yet this is only the start of the problem. Pieces of intelligence tend to be fragmentary and controversial; their value is rarely self-evident. Inferences must be derived from each piece and collated with those drawn from others. Such information can be assessed in many ways, varying with one's perceptions and preconceptions. The best intelligence on earth is useless without an efficient link between the organs which collect, evaluate and act upon it. Flaws are possible anywhere along the chain – and when one link breaks so will the whole. Accurate intelligence may not be collected or assessed properly. It may not reach a commander in time to act. A general may be physically unable to profit from good intelligence or mishandle the attempt to do so.

The role and the value of intelligence also varies with the nature of the armies and the operations at hand. A good army can win with bad information, a poor one lose with excellent intelligence. Exactly the same piece of intelligence may lead an able force to victory and an incompetent one to disaster. Intelligence may also have different consquences when small and mobile forces operate over large spaces than when during a slow paced campaign of attrition. Consider the nature of intelligence in the different theatres of the Great War. Almost invariably in Russia, Palestine and Iraq and to a lesser extent on the Western Front during 1914 and 1918, force to space ratios were low, flanks often open and breakthrough and sometimes exploitation possible. An army could concentrate its strength against the enemy's weakness, outmanoeuvre or annihilate a defender – or place its reserves in prepared positions exactly where the foe planned to attack. Throughout these campaigns, the weight of intelligence also lay heavily in one side's favour. Under these circumstances, intelligence contributed to victories on an epic scale, just as it did in the Second World War. The Western Front between 1915–17, conversely, was characterised by dense force to space ratios, elaborate defensive systems and firepower which could kill but not move. Breakthrough was extremely difficult to achieve; exploitation impossible. Both sides also possessed intelligence services of high and roughly equal skill.

Each simultaneously penetrated the other's intentions and capabilities, thus rendering surprise a rare phenomenon. Thus intelligence cancelled out much of its own effect: but not all of it. In this campaign of attrition, intelligence presided over a realm of small advantages which collectively served to wear down one's foe more quickly than oneself. This increased one's chances for final victory, and reduced its price.

During the Great War at sea, one source of secret information was predominant, signals intelligence. Conversely, armies had many overlapping, interdependent and complementary founts of intelligence, each of which met part but not all of their needs. Commanders wanted information on the enemy's intentions, dispositions, perceptions, capabilities and order of battle. The intelligence section at the GHQ of the American Expeditionary Force (AEF), for example, sought 'to describe the enemy's forces, to determine the locations of his units, discover his intentions, and where and when he would carry them out. In addition to this, intelligence warned our troops of how the enemy would act and, when it was possible, why'.[5] None of this material was easy to acquire. In 1914, like every army in Europe, the British one was badly prepared for this task. It learned through experience and with effect, although its performance was probably no better than that of the armies of Austria-Hungary, France, Germany and the United States.

The British Army, like its peers, collected intelligence through three different means. First, combat units, by reconnaissance, observation and the capture of prisoners and documents, acquired most tactical information and frequently helped with the largest of concerns. This was the basic source of military intelligence. Second, agent networks traced enemy troop movements through Belgium and Palestine, but offered little other material. Here, Britain's performance was marked by luck, skill and success. Finally, three specialist organisations under military discipline provided intelligence through technical means. Two of these acquired virtually all the useful information on narrow but crucial topics and little else: aircraft photographs on the structure of the enemy's rear defences and the dispositions of combat units there, 'flash spotters' and 'sound rangers' on the location of its artillery pieces for the guidance of counter-battery fire. The third, intelligence derived from the foe's communications, illuminated a wider issue, the enemy's operational and strategic intentions and capabilities.[6]

Signals intelligence involved the interception of messages; traffic analysis, or the inferences derived from observation of the procedures

3

of communication circuits; the solution of codes and ciphers; signals security; and signals deception, the endeavour to mislead the enemy about one's own intentions and capabilities. Most of these techniques were developed only during the Great War itself, which was the dawn of modern signals intelligence. Although for centuries the interception and solution of messages had affected the course of campaigns, their value had been constrained by the nature of communication systems. Except in unusually fluid circumstances, despatch riders could not routinely be captured, nor field telegraph cables frequently tapped. One could not often intercept enemy messages, which limited one's ability to break its ciphers. Between 1896 and 1914, however, the rise of a new and uniquely flexible medium of communications created the precondition for modern signals intelligence. All radio traffic could be intercepted. Hence, one could read all the enemy's wireless messages in plain language and acquire information from the structure of its communication system. This heightened ability to intercept traffic also enhanced one's chances to solve ciphers.

Before 1914, no European army came fully to terms with the crytological consequences of the radio age, because none of them expected wireless to be used routinely in war. They all held that effective communications would be maintained through telegraph, telephone and despatch riders, with radio serving simply as a tertiary mode of signalling. In Europe, no army developed cryptographic systems that allowed wireless to be used with a high degree of security and effect – here the French were most successful – while just one army, that of Austria-Hungary, possessed a signals intelligence service. In this context, the British Army was marginally above the norm. Its radio service was of mediocre efficiency while its procedures for signals security were primitive – which is to say, average. Conversely, it had an elementary grasp of the techniques of cryptanalysis, some expertise in the solution of foreign codes and the interception of radio messages, and the intention to attack enemy traffic during wartime. In these spheres, only Austria-Hungary was better placed and France equally so. India, moreover, possessed one of the only two armies on earth with a codebreaking agency. Unfortunately, the enemy against which it was prepared, Tsarist Russia, became an ally in August 1914.[7]

The opening months of the Great War witnessed a peculiar situation regarding signals and signals intelligence. Any defender in a developed area, whether France or East Prussia, could communicate rapidly and securely by land-lines. In order to signal at all, any army in hostile territory had to use radio to an unexpected degree. Since ciphers were cumbersome to use and speedy transmission was the order of the day, every attacker continually sent crucial messages in clear. Generations of historians have sneered at the Russian Army for doing so before the battle of Tannenburg. Yet in France the German Army did precisely the same, with identical results. During September–November 1914 French and British forces intercepted at least some 50 radio messages in plain language from German divisions, corps, armies and army groups. These provided otherwise unavailable insights into the collapse of enemy command and the yawning gap in its line during mid September 1914. Victory on the Marne was no miracle. Over the next two months similar en clair transmissions (combined with solutions of encoded German traffic) warned the British Expeditionary Force (BEF) of the precise time, location and strength of six full scale attacks on its front, each involving four or more German corps.[8] Without this material, the BEF might well have lost the race to the sea, or even have been destroyed. At no time in this century has signals intelligence affected campaigns more significantly than at the very hour of its birth, in 1914.

For the rest of the war, signals systems and intelligence were involved in a symbiotic relationship. On the Eastern Front radio always remained a major form of communication whereas in the Middle East it acquired prominence only around late 1915. By December 1914, conversely, armies on the Western Front ceased to rely on wireless and turned to elaborate telegraph and telephone systems. This did not, however, spell the end of signals intelligence on that front. In mid 1915 France and Germany, and finally Britain, discovered that some of the traffic from the telegraph and telephone cables used on the front could be intercepted. By mid 1916, moreover, all armies in the west recognised that radio was needed to maintain efficient front-line communication. Consequently, wireless became an increasingly common means of signalling within corps, particularly between spotting airplanes and artillery units. Even here, however, radio was used far less frequently than in the Second World War. It was rarely utilized by higher echelons.[9]

Signals intelligence fed from communication systems and, like all parasites, sapped the strength of its host. The purpose of these systems was to maintain command and control. Their success shaped that of operations. In the west during 1915–17, all communications on the front line collapsed in battle, as cables were cut, runners killed and carrier pigeons shot down and eaten by one's own hungry men. The inability of the higher echelons of every army to signal with their own units contributed to many debacles and largely because of signals intelligence. Only radio and field telephones could maintain rapid communication on the front line. They also gave the enemy intelligence. Armies sought to minimise this danger by limiting their use of these forms of communication. They often stripped telephones from their battalions, precisely where these were most needed, while the reluctance of personnel to face the lengthy process of enciphering messages hampered the adoption of radio until the armistice. As a senior British wireless officer noted in 1917, 'Ciphers have always been the bugbear of wireless. People don't like, or they have not the time, to do the encyphering. The result is that messages are sent by some other means than that which requires ciphers or code, such as runner'.[10] By 1918 radio was technically in a position to solve many of the problems of signals in the field, the 'stranglehold' of signals security throttled its use.[11] Signals intelligence affected operations not merely by providing information but also by hampering communications and command.

The degree to which armies used means of communication which could be intercepted governed the scope for signals intelligence. Their skills in the art shaped its value. During 1914–17 on the Eastern Front and 1916–18 in the Middle East, Austria-Hungary and Britain outmatched their adversaries. In the west, one side sometimes lagged in matters of defence or led in offensive ones. Germany, for example, surpassed other armies in intercepting traffic on field telephones as Britain did between artillery and spotting aircraft. The French Army, perhaps, outstripped the rest in the techniques of cryptanalysis. The armies of the west, however, probably gained and lost in roughly the same fashion through these techniques.

Signals intelligence centres on the race between codebreakers and codemakers; the latter start with a heavy handicap. The sole purpose of cryptanalysts is to attack codes. Security, however, is only one requirement in military communication. In the days before machine cryptography, ciphers could be rendered secure only at the price of crippling signals. In 1918, for example, experts using two different versions of the British Army's 'field cipher' required four and 13 minutes respectively to encipher, transmit and decipher a message of 14 words.[12] When inexperienced operators handle heavy loads of traffic during emergencies, the use of complex systems can easily lead to transmitting errors which compromise security and operations. Indeed, when ordered to use such systems, personnel in the Great War tended to ignore either these commands or the use of radio. A careful balance had to be drawn between the needs for 'simplicity' and 'security'.[13] Ultimately, every army placed usability above secrecy – which was the correct decision in principle. No army, however, found an efficient margin between these criteria. They all hampered their own communications without helping security.

Armies could choose between three forms of codes and ciphers. The first was a plain code, by which an arbitrarily selected group of letters or numerals were substituted for plaintext words or phrases. The second was a plain cipher, by which each individual letter in a message was replaced by another. If additional security was desired at the cost of speed, such a message could be enciphered again ('reciphering' or 'double encipherment'). The third was a superenciphered code, by which a message was encoded and the code groups were then enciphered. Each system had distinct strengths and weaknesses. Plain codes were easier to use than ciphers and in one sense more secure. In practice, the compromise of one encoded message would not immediately betray the whole system. Once a single enciphered message was solved, conversely, every one encrypted by that keyword (the arbitrary means which governed the value of letters for a series of messages on a given cipher system) would necessarily follow. Thus, a lucky guess about one signal would automatically uncover the meaning of many more. A trivial message which compromised a cipher key could immediately betray the content of crucial orders. A superenciphered code was more secure and more difficult to use than plain code or cipher. All forms of code, however, suffer from one fatal flaw in war. In order to be used they must be widely distributed, hence are liable to be captured and once so have no security in themselves. Plain code becomes plaintext and superencipherment, simple encipherment. A compromised keyword can also be replaced more easily than a captured codebook.

Each system embodied a different balance between security and usability. When choosing among them, any organisation had to account for its own particular needs in these regards, and particularly for the ratio between its trained enciphering personnel and the volume of its traffic. Here armies faced extraordinary problems. Far more soldiers than sailors or diplomats had to handle codes and ciphers and to use easily intercepted means of communication. As the War Office wrote in 1919:

> The construction of Field Ciphers demands a much more thorough knowledge of the science of cryptography than do the average diplomatic codes. The latter are all more or less elaborate variations of certain defined and well known methods. There is no objection, moreover, to these methods being cumbersome to use as the encipherers and decipherers are experts and normally have time at their disposal. Ciphers for the Field, on the other hand, are far more liable to compromise. They must be simple and quick to use as they are frequently employed by untrained officers, and when time is precious. They depend, therefore, for security entirely on the ingenuity of the methods of construction and not on elaborate systems, which are unsuited for field work.[14]

Whereas navies and foreign offices utilized complex and often superenciphered codes, armies adopted simpler systems. Initially in the west and invariably in the Middle East, armies relied on plain ciphers, reciphering their most important traffic. In the west from 1917, simple codes became more common than ciphers. By 1918 elementary superenciphered codes gradually entered service.

On the Western Front, the British Army normally used worse cryptographic systems in the field than did its allies and its enemy. These were less secure without being easier to handle or less usable without being safer. During 1918, for example, the British Army relied primarily on four cryptographic systems for front line traffic. Two of these, the Playfair cipher and the fourth edition of the 'B.A.B. Trench Code', were cryptographically weak and known to be compromised. The only tolerably safe system possessed by the Army, the two versions of the Field Cipher, were exceedingly complex to use. Beyond this, British units and formations often created their own codes – which were easy both to use and to break. The British Army, moreover, proved remarkably slow in developing new cryptographic systems. Although it began to study new and effective code systems by January 1918, only just before the Armistice did the Army begin to bring them into service. During 1918, conversely, the American Army introduced 23 editions of 4 different trench codes; the German Army used two different cipher and two code systems (one of which went through 29 different editions for the two German armies on the American front alone).[15] In formal terms, these German and American cryptographic systems were more secure and no less usable than those of Britain. Surprising as it might seem, however, the inferiority of British cryptographic systems proved to be a minor problem: between 1916 and 1918 no army's codes and ciphers used on the front remained secure for long. In 1918, various errors in usage quickly compromised both of these German code systems and probably the American ones as well. For Britain, as for all armies on the front, the only effective security device was not to use radio at all.

In general, British signals security equalled that of any army – which is not to say much. Simply to establish effective communications for mass armies in such difficult conditions was a great achievement. No army simultaneously established an effective system of signals security. Since the offensive aspects of signals intelligence advanced so rapidly and radically, the proper defensive procedures were hard to define. Since so many personnel used signals, these were even harder to enforce. This left ample room for the exercise of signals intelligence.

Codebreakers were assisted by the frequent capture of the enemy's systems and the continual errors of operators, such as repeating the same message in several codes.[16] They also stalked their prey through first principles. Codes and ciphers could conceal the sense of a message but could not escape the structure of language: a particular grammar, a statistical frequency of the recurrence of letters, and common connections between letters or parts of speech. Codes and ciphers were broken by attacking their relationship to these underlying patterns of language. Successful codebreakers combined the pedantry of the grammarian with the logic of a linguistic philosopher and the flair of the chess grandmaster. Intelligence authorities at the War Office had clear ideas on the ideal background to produce men with the

right kind of brain to do this work. For research of this kind requires an active, well-trained and scholarly mind; not mathematical, but classical. . . It is of course undeniable that there may be a few men who, without having had university training, or without having acquired a great reputation for palaeographical work, nevertheless are well suited for this work. But there is no method of discovering such people. Therefore the only test applicable is that of scholarship.

When once you have got together two or three men of the right class, they will soon map out the work of themselves. It is for this

9

reason among others that detailed instructions of how to deal with the solution of codes would really be of little use, for whole volumes on the subject would be useless to the wrong kind of man, and the right man must and will prefer to work out his own line: and in so working become an expert.[17]

This assessment had strong points and weak ones. It downplayed useful sources of cryptanalytical expertise, whether a grasp of mathematics or a social position outside the charmed circle. The emphasis on classics as the school of thought, on learning through practice rather than theory, on the man of the right kind, were all characteristic of the culture of the British élite. This formula, however, also abandoned part of that culture, such as the reliance on amateurs, the abhorrence of experts. Nor was it entirely misguided. Classics (an eduction based on the traditional humanities, particularly Greek and Latin literature and philology) and palaeography (the reconstruction of texts, often fragmentary or corrupt in nature, and/or written in unknown languages) provided a perfectly sound background for cryptanalysis during this period. Indeed, palaeography may well have been the best possible academic background for a classical code-breaker. That narrow social base, moreover, provided some of the world's best cryptanalysts between 1914–45.

Whereas codebreakers at least purported to view their own success as stemming from hard work and common sense, outsiders viewed them virtually as magicians. Cryptanalysts certainly tested the limits of military tolerance. After the war, one British officer noted 'the necessity for great swiftness in arriving at a solution whenever the Germans suddenly presented us with the problem of a new code, ringing the changes upon the alphabet in this respect until it might have seemed that no one in the world could discover what the letters meant'. This was done by the

Decipherers, and a rummier set of fellows I never came across in all my born days. It was not in the smallest degree possible to teach these wonderful fellows a scrap of discipline. You had to treat them as geniuses, and to expect from them the most erratic behaviour. There was one officer amongst us who knew exactly how to treat them. He was always telling them that they were pitting their brains against the German brains, and that it was up to them to show the world that British brains were a darned sight better material than anything under a thick-boned German skull.

They answered to that. They were men of all ages, one of them had been a schoolmaster, another was a stockbroker, a third was a designer of ladies' hats – a very rum bird – and the fourth was a solicitor's clerk. They lived together in a dirty little rabbit hutch, smoking their pipes all day and all night, the hut being frightfully untidy, like themselves, and I don't think they looked upon washing or shaving as a part of their day's serious work. But they were the most amazingly brilliant fellows – both as linguists and as mathematicians. As soon as a new code came along they pounced upon it like vultures on their prey, and stuffing their pipes with tobacco, and muttering the new letters over and over again as they felt in their pockets for a match, they would wrestle with that new problem until they had made it as clear as daylight. Some of these codes angered them because they were so easy – problems to be solved in an hour or two. But some of them were real hard nuts to crack, and then these decipherers were in the seventh heaven. However, if my memory serves me rightly, there was never a new German code, baffling as they always appeared to us, which those four men did not solve within thirty-six hours.[18]

Codebreaking developed at different periods on the various fronts.[19] Between 1914–17 the Austro-Hungarian Army solved many important Russian and Italian cryptographic systems; no one else in those theatres had much success. From late 1916, the British Army continually broke most of the Turkish and German ciphers used in the Middle East.[20] The enemy was much less efficient at this task. In the west, the British and French armies solved some German ciphers in October–November 1914. This, however, did not become an important and consistent source of intelligence until late 1916/early 1917 – when every army on that front practised this art with, it appears, roughly equal success. The quality of information derived from this source also varied. In the Middle East and Russia, codebreakers often solved messages from the top of the enemy's command – thus uncovering the most significant of its intentions. On the Western Front during 1917–18, they acquired material primarily from within corps. According to a senior French cryptanalyst, this typically provided the following material.

If we open the archives (of French military codebreaking) at random we find that from the 5th to the 15th of December, 1917, four division movements were discovered by special information before any other means were used, and soon verified by examination of prisoners; 32 regiments, the situation of which were known, were identified anew; a radiogram of December 10 reports the presence of an "Eingriff" (sic. "Angriff") (counter-attack) division to the north of St. Quentin. Another, of the 10th, reports the presence at a point on the front of General von Erp, commanding the Three Hundredth and Forty-Second Division. A message of December 15th gives warning of a German surprise attack at the Abia farm; our troops, being warned, repulsed the enemy. A communication of the 5th mentions a change of call letters of the German wireless telegraph stations and gives the equivalent of the new ones and the old ones.[21]

Such traffic provided useful information on the enemy's dispositions, along with the occasional coup regarding its intentions. Its greatest value, however, precisely as with 'Ultra' in the Second World War, was to determine the enemy's order of battle. According to the head of intelligence of the AEF, in 1917–18 'frequently, as many as two-thirds of the identifications of enemy divisions along the front became known due to the ability of the Allies to decode intercepted wireless messages'.[22]

Problems of evidence hamper any attempt to determine in breadth and depth the influence of this source of intelligence on military operations. In the case of the Middle East, for example, it is fairly easy to address this issue for the periods between October 1916–July 1917 and November–December 1917, and extremely difficult for the remainder of 1917 and most of 1918. It is hard to determine so elementary a matter as how many encoded or enciphered German messages on the Western Front were broken during 1917–18. British records include solutions of perhaps 200 such messages, normally prefixed by the codeword 'Wave'.[23] This source, however, clearly provided much more material than that. From the spring of 1917 until the end of the war, the radio monitoring personnel of each British Army intercepted around 150–200 German messages per week. On occasion, individual allied stations intercepted 120 German radio messages each day.[24] In 1917 alone, British codebreakers solved several hundred encoded German messages.[25] In that year, according to William Friedman, 'the text of one week was sufficient to break into a new (German) code, and by the end of three weeks, messages were being read by us as quickly and almost as completely by the code-officers as by the enemy'. The French reconstructed some 30 front-line codes (and/or editions of codes) of the German Army during the war. In 1918, the Americans, British and French together continually penetrated one of the two main German trench code systems, had much success with the other, and sometimes solved both of the two cipher systems used near the front lines.[26] If one makes the safe assumption that British codebreakers were roughly as successful as their American cousins, during 1918 Britain should have had current effective access to just under half of the encoded radio traffic within German divisions every day. In the American case, this produced about four 'stencilled pages of text' per day. Given the larger size of the British Army, which was rather more often engaged in battle, I(e) probably produced two or three times more such pages on average. It certainly shared the fruits of the Allied success in reading half of the enciphered radio messages between German divisions, corps and armies on 10 days when 'heavy traffic was transmitted' – precisely during the major battles of 1918.[27]

Codebreaking is not the only form of signals intelligence: on the Western Front it was no more important than three others. The first was the interception of field telephone and telegraph traffic. Here Britain suffered one of its gravest failures in signals intelligence of this century. Once the German Army became aware of the problem and the prospect in 1915, it quickly established efficient security and interception systems. Through these means it gained much and lost little, because of the incompetent British response. By July 1916 on the Western Front Britain had only five listening sets (called 'I Toc' or 'IT' – intelligence telephone – sets). It failed to take even elementary steps to safeguard traffic within the 'dangerous zone', that area in which telegraph and telephone messages could be intercepted. According to one signals authority, these failures were 'so unnecessary as to border upon the criminal'.[28] Only German records (which are reported to have vanished forever) can define fully how much they gained from this source. Captured prisoners and documents and the testimony of several British intelligence and signals officers, however, indicate that this source had devastating consequences. Throughout 1916, it provided first-rate intelligence on the British order of battle and dispositions. Captured documents indicated that by March 1916, the identifications of the British order of battle produced by the German listening (or 'Moritz') sets 'equalled the total obtained by all other means' and that through this source the Germans identified the deployment of 70 per cent of the British units on the front during the entire battle of the Somme. The fragmentary records suggest that 'Moritz' also warned of the precise time and place of at least many and perhaps most of the divisional attacks launched during that battle. The Germans intercepted at least one operations order for an attack by an entire corps in time to act before the British did. Tactical surprise was intended to safeguard all of these assaults. Failures in signals security destroyed this shield. While this offensive would have been a debacle in any case, this failure increased its scale.[29]

This disaster, however, also sparked the birth of British signals intelligence on the Western Front. In particular, GHQ France quickly overcame the problem with field telephones. By late 1916, each British corps had on average two IT sets, compared with the German four.[30] Although these provided tactical intelligence which held thousands of lives in its sway, the great aggressive days of 'IT' were over. Its primary purpose became defensive – the policing of one's own telephone traffic. Here Britain quickly reached the German level and then surpassed it through the use of the 'Fullerphone'. This device transmitted telegraphic traffic via a weak electrical current over telephone lines. Such messages were extremely difficult although not absolutely impossible for the enemy to intercept; telephone traffic remained as vulnerable as before. In 1917–18, some 23,400 'Fullerphones' were allocated to the British Army. These technical improvements had disproportionately significant operational consequences. German GHQ, lacking the reliable agent networks of its British counterpart, relied far more heavily on listening sets for order of battle intelligence. This source was increasingly less effective for that purpose.[31]

At precisely this time, another type of signals intelligence rose to the fore. Artillery dominated the war of attrition. The effect of its fire hinged on direction from aircraft, which was conducted primarily by radio, and through simple codes. By 1918, at any rate, these German codes 'rarely escaped detection (by the British) for more than a few hours'.[32] The interception and analysis of this traffic provided tactical intelligence and disclosed the dispositions of enemy aircraft and artillery – a powerful clue to its operational intentions.[33] During mid 1915 Captain Lefroy of the radio unit of the Royal Flying Corps (RFC) and later the chief of signals interception in the Middle East, carried out some pioneering traffic analysis against such messages. His lead was only sporadically pursued before the autumn of 1916, when it was followed by the head of the wireless section at GHQ, Captain Ferdinand Touhy, enthusiastically supported by the chief of the RFC on the Western Front, Hugh Trenchard. This intelligence served exactly the same function as radar during 1940. It guided RFC fighters onto the spotting aircraft of the enemy while the latter were at work, which was otherwise hard to arrange. Some squadrons, on standby to act on this information, routinely disrupted German spotting missions and destroyed enemy aircraft.[34]

Although American authorities regarded the British as the leaders in this field, the latter's success is difficult to quantify.[35] One informed, although possibly biased, British authority indicates that through this method, 80 per cent of the enemy's spotting aircraft over an unspecified time and place were 'found by our machines and either destroyed or compelled to abandon their registration' and that during March 1918, on the Fourth Army front alone, 30 enemy spotting aircraft were shot down.[36] While the latter claim seems plausible and indicative of the general state of affairs, the first one is exaggerated. The remaining, albeit fragmentary, British evidence suggests that this means of signals intelligence simply reduced by 10 per cent to 20 per cent the time spent in registration by enemy airplanes and marginally increased their aggregate losses and significantly heightened the rate of success of intercepting RFC squadrons.[37] All this, in any case, was useful and not the end of the story. Between October 1917 and March 1918, British codebreakers solved the traffic of 577 out of a total of 639 German spotting missions along the British front in time to give effective warning to troops about to be bombarded, thus hampering the effect of German artillery.[38] All told, this form of signals intelligence crippled the enemy's power in the campaign of attrition. During the First World War, this source had an effective lifespan of two years, between mid-1916 to mid-1918. It lived and died with the trenches. For Britain, however, this source was also the root of a new form of signals intelligence, which has retained great importance and received little scholarly attention ever since: traffic analysis.

During the Great War, every army assigned radio stations and personnel on a semi-permanent basis to particular formations. The structure of their communications replicated that of command. All stations within a division, corps or army signalled far more frequently within than without these groups. All headquarters' stations had a conventional procedure and pattern of communication with those at lower, adjacent and higher levels of command. Through traffic analysis, one could determine which stations were attached to what formations and communicated with which others. The normal structure of signalling revealed the enemy's organisation and dispositions. Intercommunication between various stations indicated the existence of a group of them and thus the members and the boundaries of a specific command. The fact that their signalling centred on one station, which used a given procedure, disclosed the location of a headquarters. Through direction-finding and the observation of the unique key-signatures of individual radio operators, one could identify the stations and personnel which belonged to specific formations. All the sub-units within a division remained attached together for long periods, which to a lesser extent held true with divisions and corps and with corps and armies. Thus, the identification of one battalion would almost certainly determine the location of a division, usually of a corps, often of an army. Variations from this 'standard of normality'[39] offered equally crucial intelligence. The movement of stations heralded reliefs or reinforcements and also reflected the enemy's strategic intentions. The sudden appearance in a new sector of a single radio operator who was known to work with an élite formation might indicate that a major action was imminent there. So too could changes in the routine practices of enemy wireless units. German stations, for example, invariably moved to the rear a few days before major withdrawals and often adopted specific procedures just before an attack.

No army was prepared to withstand traffic analysis: before 1916, for example, none changed its radio call signs regularly or assigned them randomly.[40] During its first two years of life, traffic analysis had the greatest and easiest success in its entire history. During 1917–18, this may well have been the single greatest source of operational intelligence available to every army on the Western Front. William Friedman wrote that in 1917, 'the entire enemy Order of Battle could be secured from goniometric data alone. No comment upon the importance of this information is necessary'.[41] The fragmentary British evidence which survives neither supports nor refutes this assessment. It indicates, however, that on a normal day in 1917, traffic analysis determined the location of around 50–60 per cent of the German divisions and artillery groupings on the British front.[42] American traffic analysis apparently remained roughly this successful in 1918.[43]

Traffic analysts, however, were not infallible. Any army could mislead them by exploiting the guesswork inherent in their trade. It could vary the call signs of some wireless stations and enforce radio silence on others. It might change the patterns of its traffic, by having stations break up communication within their groups while signalling frequently with others, or by maintaining normal patterns of wireless traffic in zones where assaults were to be launched while increasing levels elsewhere. Traffic analysts, none the less, could be gulled only through systematic and sophisticated tactics: one slip might compromise the whole. These techniques became at all effective on the Western Front only in 1918. Even then, one could merely camouflage the movements of several corps for a few days, or prevent the enemy from detecting preparations for attack over a limited time and space.[44] Of course, that could be decisive if the date was 8 August 1918 and the place, Amiens. The increasing uncertainty which surrounded traffic analysis, however, placed yet another weapon in the arsenal of signals intelligence: deception.

In 1918 a mobile campaign became possible on the Western Front because the war of attrition had finally been won and lost – by both sides simultaneously. The bulk of British, French and German divisions had lost much of their offensive and defensive capacity. The American Army was too small and inexperienced to dominate the front. A few élite formations, however, particularly the *Stosstruppe* and the Australian and the Canadian Corps, could smash through enemy defences, although their powers of exploitation were miniscule. Throughout most of 1918, none the less, any defender could crush any attack and annihilate the enemy's limited strength in storm troops – if it could determine where the assault would come. Major offensives aborted from the outset only when the defender knew their location and time in advance. Surprise was a characteristic of virtually every successful attack of 1918.

Surprise, however, is not the natural condition of warfare. It requires cunning manipulation or an unprepared opponent, preferably the two in tandem. On the Western Front between 1915 to 1917, surprise was extremely difficult although not entirely impossible to achieve. During late 1917, conversely, attacks by several German corps at Riga, Germano-Austrian ones at Caporetto and a British Army at Cambrai entirely surprised the defenders. In 1918 every army sought to acquire that opportunity and deny it to the enemy. The German Quartermaster General, Erich Ludendorff, wrote that 'In battle the one who gropes most in the dark is at a disadvantage. The precaution for the concealment of our measures and for misleading the enemy can therefore by decisive'. Once both sides had embraced this philosophy, the nature of the struggle shifted: as the German Ninth Army noted, 'warfare has become more than ever the realm of the uncertain'.[45]

The techniques for surprise, however, were biased in favour of the side with the initiative – thus multiplying the operational advantages which gave it that position. The aims were generally to confuse the enemy, and particularly to conceal the movement of reinforcements just before an assault. Typically, throughout 1918, a defender could not locate the enemy's reserves – between 10–20 per cent of its forces – in rear areas. The defender could usually detect preparations for major operations, but neither invariably nor with complete certainty; and the side with the initiative, simultaneously prepared for several major attacks up and down the front. Even if a defender could determine the correct sequence and locales of enemy attacks, surprise might still occur if it miscalculated the strength of the assault formations, or their style of tactics, or merely, in Ludendorff's words, 'the actual day and hour of the attack.'[46] If an attacker could double without detection its strength (especially in élite formations) on a ten mile sector for three days, cheap and dramatic breakthrough was possible. A defender who could locate only 80 per cent of the enemy's divisions stood next to disaster. One who could uncover the enemy's intentions was well on the road to triumph. The achievement of surprise hinged on many interdependent factors, such as heightened security conciousness among one's own troops and refinements in physical camouflage and the registration of artillery. First of equals among these, however, were signals security and deception. This, incidentally, is not a permanent condition of deception. Signals deception was so important in 1918 simply because signals intelligence, especially traffic analysis, was so remarkably powerful.[47]

Surprise required the concealment of one's operational intentions and capabilities, which was precisely the home ground of signals intelligence. This, the greatest single threat to surprise, had to be neutralized, and through two interlinked means, signals security and deception. In 1917–18 all armies sought to improve their security. Those of Britain and Germany, however, most emphasised deception. They alternately led the world in this endeavour, with the scales of the balance wavering continually between them. Their techniques became surprisingly sophisticated: not until 1943 would these again be matched. So to mislead the Italians before the battle of Caporetto and the western allies before the 'Michael' offensive of March 1918, Germany created phantom armies through signals deception.[48] Britain intended to do the same for its projected operations of 1919, under the control of that master of misdirection, Colonel Richard Meinertzhagen. Germany ultimately pursued a more ambitious policy of deception but, because this proved extraordinarily difficult to execute, its approach was no more effective than the simpler and more easily sustained one of Britain. The latter, indeed, was strikingly similar to the style of operational deception adopted by the British Army during 1944–45.

In any case, under the right circumstances, elementary techniques of signals deception could provide an extraordinary degree of surprise. Consider the most successful example of operational deception on the Western Front in 1918. In late July, following the brilliant and crushing French defensive victory at the second battle of the Marne, British GHQ prepared to launch a major attack under the aegis of the Fourth Army. The Australian and the Canadian Corps, supported by British and French divisions, would storm the Amiens sector, on the southern edge of the English line. In order to do so the Canadian Corps would have to be redeployed from the First Army, in southern Flanders. This could be more easily wished than realised. As General Rawlinson, the commander of the operation noted, 'The essence of the whole plan was secrecy. Wherever the Canadian Corps was identified by the enemy he would certainly expect an early offensive. The first problem, therefore, was to camouflage the movement of the Canadians'.[49] Detection of British intentions would be doubly sure if the Canadians could be found alongside the Australians, that other most deadly corps in the west. The German Army correctly regarded the Dominion formations as being 'the best attack divisions' possessed by the allies.[50]

A combination of German miscalculation and British security and deception solved the problem. From 18 July until 7 August, the German Army was preoccupied with a major French offensive in the Marne sector, and with a further onslaught which 60 French and American divisions were expected to launch in late August. While the German Army also anticipated a British offensive, it grossly under-estimated the quality and quantity of British (as against Dominion) troops. It believed that Britain possessed only some 17 divisions in reserve; and that these formations alone could engage in major offensive operations.[51] Ludendorff subsequently noted with surprise that British 'sector divisions, as experience has shown, are capable of participating in an offensive even after having been in the line for a comparatively long period of time'.[52] In future, merely 5–7 British reserve divisions 'can be considered ample for a new large-scale attack, since the Britisher taxes his sector divisions to the utmost. The British may be expected to make reckless use of all their forces in order to exploit the present situation'.[53] The failure to appreciate these facts before 8 August had created that situation. In effect, the Germans underestimated British offensive capabilities by one half. Before the battle of Amiens, moreover, they also misunderstood British intentions. Until July 1918, German traffic analysts had easily traced British dispositions and deployments. By then, British signals security was radically improving, and thus also the ability to conceal British operations. Without knowing it, the Germans had lost their enemy.[54] They were uncertain where the British would attack but seem to have regarded Flanders as being one of the most likely areas.

The British Army, meanwhile, through the interrogation of prisoners of war and observations of enemy deployments, correctly appreciated that the Germans expected an attack in Flanders. On 24 July, the British First Army, based in that sector, noted

> It is important to keep up this idea and to confirm the enemy in his suspicions; the measures being taken by us (ie. the First Army) being allowed to die down as soon as there is definite prospect of being able to carry out offensive operations on any part of the Army front, so as to lull the enemy into a false sense of security at the very time when we are beginning to think of a possible offensive.[55]

That formula underlay British operational deception for the next four months. In this case it was executed through simple means. The physical movements and (almost certainly) the radio traffic of the entire British Army were shaped to indicate activity throughout Flanders and quiet around Amiens. The Australian Corps conspicuously maintained a defensive posture in the Amiens sector until just before the attack, when it secretly massed its strength on a narrow front. The Canadian Corps moved alongside the Australians under the cover of extraordinarily thorough security precautions. It simultaneously despatched its radio stations from southern to northern Flanders to carry out normal transmissions, where a small body of troops conducted the aggressive raids typical of Canadian forces. Later, captured German soldiers and orders indicated that the enemy had remained entirely unsure both of the location of the Canadian Corps –

which was thought to be virtually everywhere except Amiens – and of the time and place of the British onslaught.[56] The attack at Amiens achieved absolute operational surprise, as regards time, place, strength and style of attack. It broke the nerve of the German Army and its high command.

While deception and its signals aspects were not uniformly effective, they occurred before every major attack of 1918. Success in this sphere was usually a precondition for surprise. These practices also pointed toward the future. After the First World War, Ferdinand Tuohy noted that

> The evolution of "Intelligence" has been quite distinct. To begin with, one concentrated almost entirely on finding out what the enemy was doing. Finally, one saw to it that the enemy was thoroughly well deceived and hood-winked into making false deductions. This final development of "Intelligence" will rule supreme in any future war; things will verily not be what they seem. When an enemy wishes to attack at any one point he will make all his outward and visible preparations in some other sector, whereupon the opposing "Intelligence" will tumble to the deceit being attempted and say: "Ha! ha! he thinks he is taking us all in by making all that show up North! Of course he's going to attack us down here where all seems to be so quiet!"
>
> To which reasoning "the other fellow," planning the attack, will in turn tumble and proceed to attack up North where all the display has been![57]

Not a bad prophecy of Operations 'Fortitude' and 'Mincemeat', when the enemy knew of British deception but could not escape the spider's web.

During the Great War, the British Army's record in the development and use of signals intelligence was far from perfect. Between January 1915 and July 1916, in particular, it paid little attention to the matter. This embittered the pioneers of British military signals intelligence, and led to disaster regarding the security of field telephone traffic in 1916.[58] After July 1916, however, the British Army overcame these problems. Signals intelligence was recognised as an increasingly valuable and uniquely reliable form of information. By 1918, for example, the British Second Army noted that the 'special nature of Wireless Intelligence called for very close liaison' between I(e) and the personnel responsible for assessing the enemy's order of battle. Simultaneously, according to a well-informed American source, British GHQ regarded signals intelligence on the enemy's dispositions and order of battle as being 'always correct and , . . by far the most valuable identifications of divisional positions and intentions outside of actual capture of a prisoner. They are even more valuable in a way because they anticipate coming events before prisoners can be obtained'.[59]

A reasonably efficient system emerged in which such material was collected by signals personnel who were generally controlled by intelligence officers.[60] This information was assessed by the latter and then distributed to operations staffs and commanders. In Palestine and Iraq, commanders and senior staff officers personally read much of the raw material. In France, conversely, signals intelligence entered the elaborate and by no means inefficient structure by which GHQ Intelligence assessed the mass of incoming information. All told, the British Army handled signals intelligence as well as did any other army of the Great War. In more general terms, the British Army experienced many intelligence failures during this war. Its performance, however, was no worse than that of any other military institution of this conflict, and better than most. Its failures are outweighed by its successes. Tragically, during the interwar years much of this expertise was lost. Only by late 1942, and after many bitter lessons, did the intelligence service of the British Army begin to regain its efficiency of 1918.

Signals intelligence was the smallest organisation of the British Army during the Great War which collected information through technical means. By mid-1916, around 75 personnel and by the armistice 1300 were involved in that labour. In 1917–18 approximately 250 men served with listening sets, 600 in the eleven 'Wireless Observation Groups' (WOGs) in the field and an uncertain number, perhaps 200, with their equivalents under the War Office's control in the United Kingdom.[61] Perhaps 25 per cent of the radio personnel of the British Army (excluding those attached to the RFC) worked full-time in the interception of enemy wireless traffic. The allocation of so many operators to this task crippled the use of wireless for British communication, yet these personnel could not even monitor important categories of traffic – such as plain language messages on the front line during 1918.[62] About 8 per cent of the Army's 'Intelligence Corps' worked as codebreakers and traffic analysts in section 'Ie', which derived intelligence from 'enemy wireless sources, codes and cyphers'.[63] Throughout 1917 11 officers and some other ranks worked with Ie in the Middle East. I(e) at GHQ France swelled from 10 officers and 36 other ranks in August 1917 to 14 and 58 by November 1918, while another 2–3 and 10–20 respectively served with each Army in France and GHQ Italy.[64] This strength was augmented by perhaps 85 personnel in the signals intelligence sections of the War Office, MI1(b) and MI1(e).[65] By the standards of the day, this was a large strength: it exceeds the numbers of Royal Navy and American Army personnel involved in signals intelligence, and, perhaps, matches that of the French Army.[66] Conversely, by 1945 ten times as many members of the British Army conducted similar work.[67]

The aim of this collection is to cover all the major elements of British signals intelligence on the front. It focusses on the highest levels of field command – corps, armies and GHQs – to the exclusion of other echelons, whether divisions or the War Office. The sections are ordered by subject, although this ranking is sometimes arbitrary – the line between signals security and deception, for example, or aircraft intelligence and traffic analysis, was not entirely clear cut. This aim has been easy to achieve in some cases. The documents clearly reveal the process by which signals intelligence was collected, analysed, distributed and affected operations in general. It has, however, proven difficult to address a central issue – the specific effect of such material – for two reasons. Whenever intelligence affects operations, a host of documents are produced: original reports from all sources, assessments of this material by staff officers and commanders, and papers regarding a battle. Only a volume equalling this one in size could include all of the documents relevant to any major operation – were these available. This, however, is rarely the case. For the British and Indian Armies in the Great War, such a full range of material survives only regarding France in 1914 and Iraq during 1915–16. The influence of signals intelligence can be traced with precision only in France during 1914 and the Middle East during 1917. A selection of documents from the latter case has been included so as to illustrate this issue.

The nature of the evidence has also affected this collection. Unlike the case with its naval equivalent, most of the records on the Army's signals intelligence from the Great War are not publicly available. The surviving material falls into three general categories. First, original reports from the organisations which collected signals intelligence, whether MI1(b), codebreakers at Army headquarters, 'IT' sets or traffic analysts, are extremely rare. (The main exception to this rule is the intelligence produced by MI1(e) about German bombing raids on the United Kingdom.) Second, a somewhat larger range of documents exists on signals deception, aircraft intelligence and the organisation and techniques of the signals intelligence service. Finally, much material survives on three matters from the Western Front – weekly summaries of traffic analysis reports in 1917–18 and material pertaining to the interception and security of field telephone traffic between 1916 and 1918 and to signals security in general during 1918. This volume reproduces a large proportion of the surviving documents from the first category, a smaller part from the second and a tiny portion from the third. Some captured German documents on these matters have also been printed, so to provide a basis of comparison and to illuminate the enemy's side of the story. Inevitably, a volume of this size cannot include all the relevant or interesting documents. It reproduces only a sample of the material on the signals intelligence service of the British Army. This however, will throw new light on Britain's military experience during the First World War.

The author is indepted to the copyright holders for permission to publish certain documents from the papers of Gerard Clauson and Guy Dawnay, both held by the Imperial War Museum, and from the Philip Leith Ross papers at the National Army Museum. All documents from the ADM, AIR and WO series fall under Crown copyright and appear by permission of the Controller of Her Majesty's Stationery Office. All documents from the RG-9 series fall under the copyright of the Canadian government and appear by permission of the Public Archives of Canada. I am grateful to Christopher Andrew, Brian Bond, Ian Brown, David French, Michael Handel, Elizabeth Herbert, Morgan Herbert, Anne Marie Link, David Kahn and Yigal Sheffy for assistance at various stages of this manuscript. I am particularly indebted to Evelyn Sobremonte and Laureen Quapp for typing the manuscript. This collection is dedicated to my brother, Douglas.

I
Field Telephones and Telegraphs: Intelligence and Security

These documents refer to the work of an entire branch of signals intelligence. Document One discusses the security of British field telephone and telegraph traffic during 1916. It reveals how a succession of minor slips can compromise the greatest of secrets, such as one's order of battle and operational dispositions and intentions. Documents Two and Three discuss the evolution of British security procedures between late 1916 and early 1917, when the standard precautions which governed the field until the armistice – indeed, until 1945 – were in place. Signals security, however, was established only through rigorous and complicated procedures which seriously hampered communications. Document Four, a British assessment of German procedures in security and interception, shows the enemy's lead in the field during 1916 and allows one to compare and contrast German and British approaches to the problem. Document Five, an excerpt from the only surviving record of a British or Dominion listening set unit, shows the complex technical and organisational problems involved in this work, which was, moreover, extraordinarily risky. Intercepting personnel routinely resided in no man's land – at greater risk than infantrymen in their trenches. Document Six is one of the few British or Dominion reports on field telephone security to survive from 1917–18. While this demonstrates that perfect security had not been established, the scale of the problem had declined. Intelligence primarily of tactical rather than operational value was compromised through this source, along with snippets of material on one's order of battle. Security had conquered intelligence, but at the price of command. The 'listening set' offers the classic example of one consequence of signals intelligence: a form of interception so successful that it cripples its host, and hence itself.

I

Memorandum by First Army, 27 October 1916

INDISCREET USE OF TELEPHONES NEAR THE FRONT

(a) *History of Listening Sets*

Listening sets have been in use by the French and Germans for nearly a year; by the British for 8–9 months, although no definite organization was established until April. Many experiments were tried by all 3 Armies before satisfactory results were obtained.

By means of these Listening Sets it is possible to intercept messages and telephone conversations, through induction or earth leakage,[1] up to a distance not yet definitely known, and varying according to the nature of the soil, but certainly up to 2,000 yards and probably considerably further in favourable conditions.[2]

(b) *Instances of misuse by our troops*

Apart from valuable information obtained about the enemy, our listening sets have intercepted many messages and a good deal of telephonic conversation on our own lines close to the front, containing much military information which would have been of considerable value to the enemy. Among such are the following instances:–

On First Army Front

(1) "Tell the officer only one patrol is going out to-night."
(2) A message mentioning the 24th Division.
(3) "I had to meet a party of Canadians"; (23rd October, 1916).
(4) Reference to "5th Canadian Infantry Brigade Pioneers" (22nd October, 1916).

The last two messages gave away the arrival of the Canadian Corps on our front.[3]

(5) "10th Royal Fusiliers. AAA. Please be at C.O's orders at 10 a.m."

(6) Various messages re: reliefs, giving positions of trench mortars, machine guns, etc.

Fronts of Other Armies

(1) "Why did witness not attend at BOESCHEPE on Seventh? Division demand report?"

(2) "What battalion is in line now?" – "The 10th Inniskilling."

(3) "You have challenged South Wales Borderers to a football match to-morrow, haven't you?"

(4) "This is the Brigade line". "Which Brigade?" Oh, "I can't tell you that – who are you – any way?" "This is a T.P." "Oh a test point". "Yes, for Divisional signals" "Oh right, we work to 22nd Brigade".

(5) "Daily strength return. Officers 19, O.R., 1065." Trench strength Officers 14, O.R., 845."

(6) "48th Infantry Brigade. Wire following officers, etc."

(7) "Please reply to my B M 309 by to-night's D.R.[4] – 36th Divisional Artillery."

(8) Many messages re formations, i.e. battalions, brigades, Divisions and Corps; re. reliefs, artillery fire, positions of batteries, billets, railheads, etc.,

(9) Most important information regarding raids, bombardments, mine explosions and attacks has been discussed on our telephones near the front line. In one case a whole set of orders was dictated by a Division to a Brigade at an Advanced Report Centre; in another an artillery observing officer discussed on the telephone from the front line how his battery or batteries could best co-operate with the attack that was shortly to be made – this was an attack of great importance.

(c) *Information known to have been the enemy*

It has been ascertained from captured German maps that, on 5th March 1916, out of 24 identifications on that portion of the

British front, 12, i.e. 50%, had been established by the listening apparatus.

It has been ascertained, both on the SOMME and on the French front, that the Germans have obtained much valuable information re raids, reliefs, bombardments, attacks, etc., from their interception of our indiscreet telephone conversations.

(d) *Orders issued and necessity for obeying them*

Strict orders have been issued from time to time with a view to preventing the enemy from obtaining information from telephones on our front, and a great improvement has taken place; most of the worst irregularities have been due to changes of Divisions, and have occurred when troops were still new to our Front. Things are, however, still far from perfect, and I wish to draw attention to the urgent necessity for enforcing the following rules:–

Information on the following points will neither be given nor asked for by telephone or "buzzer"[5] near the front line trenches:–

(a) Names of commanders, officers, headquarters, units, places, positions, map references. (This covers all references to O.P.'s,[6] M.G. emplacements,[7] Headquarters, Dumps, railways, T.M. emplacements.[8]

(b) Movements of troops, such as patrols, reliefs, transport, batteries, aeroplanes, etc., arrival of reinforcements.

(c) R.E. indents,[9] ammunition returns, casualty returns, burial returns, situation reports, strength of units.

(d) Positions of our troops, rest billets, training schools. Special care must be taken when repeating Corps or G.H.Q. situation reports.

(e) Impending operations such as *raids, artillery* or *trench mortar bombardments (retaliatory or otherwise), aeroplanes, mines, gas.*

(f) Effect of the enemy's artillery fire, trench mortar fire, hand grenades or gas; in fact, any effect of the enemy's operations against us.

(g) Observations of the enemy's movements, any references to prisoners or deserters, or statements made by them.

In addition to this, all unnecessary gossip and communication by telephone or "buzzer" must be stopped. If unnecessary conversations are permitted, time is wasted; our listening apparatus become jammed, and such conversations will constantly contain information of value to the enemy.

Absolute silence, except in cases of urgent military necessity, must be kept during the "Silent Hours"; these should be changed frequently.

Adequate measures must be taken to ensure the insulation of our wires.

Any disobedience of these orders must be punished with severity, by the most rigid disciplinary measures.

(e) *Information obtained by our own "Listening Sets"*
The following are a few instances of valuable information obtained by our apparatus:–

(1) That the Germans believed we were going to make a raid, alarmed the Battalion, evacuated the front line, and called up their reserves. Our guns were able to make good use of this information.

(2) One of our listening interpreters near NEUVILLE ST. VAAST overheard a German conversation about "work" beginning at 3 a.m., and, the matter being discussed in rather a peculiar way, the interpreter warned the Brigade Major that a raid seemed in contemplation. Steps were taken to meet the raid, which was beaten off with considerable enemy loss.

(3) Re reliefs, mine explosions, strength of companies etc.

Most of the German messages are sent in cypher, and several of these have been deciphered.

In general, the Germans take the strictest precautions, and it is extremely difficult to intercept their conversation at most places, whilst information of military value is rarely given. They use metallic circuits near their front line, and the strictest orders exist on the subjects to be mentioned on the telephone. Codes are used for all messages of any importance.

WO 95/167

2

Memorandum by Brigadier-General, General Staff, X Corps, 23 July 1916

Xth Corps G.X.246.
NOTES ON COMMUNICATIONS
To be read in conjunction with X Corps letter G.X.189 of
16/7/16

1. *Overhearing*

Several circulars have recently been issued on the subect of overhearing of our Signals by the enemy, and there is in consequence some doubt as to what restrictions are now necessary regarding the use of the telephones in the forward area under present circumstances.

Full details of the German system of overhearing are not yet available but there is clear evidence that it is extensively used, and may be effective over an area of 2 miles from our front line.

To entirely forbid the use of telephones within this zone would entail undue delay in the communication system, with possibly serious results.

At the same time it is necessary to take all possible precautions to prevent the enemy overhearing our messages, and these precautions must depend on the situation.

Where stationary conditions exist as on the front of the Northern Division, it must be assumed that the enemy has listening apparatus properly installed close to our front line, but in the OVILLERS sector it is most improbable that this exists.

A telephone circuit can only be considered reasonably safe when it is truly metallic, and quite free from earth leakage. Where these conditions cannot be assumed in the forward area danger of overhearing must always be assumed.

The following instruction will therefore be observed:–

(a) *As regards Northern Division Front*
(1) *Telegraph*
    Telegraph lines run from Division to each Brigade in line.
    As long as single current sets or Fullerphones can be used

on these circuits the latter may be considered safe for telegrams. If these circuits fail it is not 'safe' to send important messages by alternative buzzer route.

(2) *Telephones*

Good telephone circuits to each Brigade exist, but owing to the lines across the marsh being frequently cut by shell fire, there is always danger of earth leakage and they will therefore not be used for conversations which may be of value to the enemy.

Lines forward of Brigades cannot be considered safe for telephone or buzzer, but telegrams may be sent by fuller phone when latter become available. Except on emergency only such conversations (sic) can be of no value to the enemy will be permitted over the telephone.

Lines from Battalions to Companies will not be permitted, but one good forward route should be established in each Battalion sector up to front line which will be maintained, and kept ready for use in emergency, or as a "jumping off point" in the event of an advance being made.

A system of bells ringing from Companies to Battalion H.Q. for S.O.S. purposes will be installed. A bell indicator with Central Battery at Battalion H.Q. is recommended.

(b) *South Division Front*

On each Brigade front a point has been selected to which an armoured twin cable has been run. These points are X.14.a. central for Right Brigade, and X.8,c,1/o for Left Brigade. As long as the cables to these points remain undamaged the circuits may be considered safe for telegraph or telephone, and the points will be used as collecting stations where important messages will be received and sent from or to Brigade H.Q.

Forward of these points lines will be run to Battalions, but owing to the difficulty of maintenance these circuits cannot be regarded as safe, and will only be used on emergency or for messages which cannot convey information to the enemy. It is not desirable to run lines from Battalions to Companies.

(c) *Artillery O.P. Lines*

These are a source of great danger, but their use from the front trenches is frequently necessary. During operations it is generally impossible to run out metallic circuits, or to maintain lines in anything approaching a safe condition.

Stringent instructions will be issued that O.P. lines are only to be used for conversations absolutely necessary for direction of fire, and nothing must pass over the line which could convey information to the enemy.

(d) *General*

The definition of the term "on emergency" as applied to sending of messages in the forward area has frequently been a source of difficulty in the past.

Hard and fast rules restricting the use of telephones have prevented important messages being sent; again messages have been sent "on emergency" when circumstances obviously did not warrant this.

The decision as to whether circumstances warrant an important message being sent by telegraph or telephone over a dangerous line must rest with the Commander on the spot.

It is the duty of Signal Officers, and especially Brigade Section Officers[10] to keep their Staff informed as to the condition of forward lines and report at once when they have reason to believe that a circuit has become unsafe.

Brigade Section Officers should also ensure that when a Battalion goes into the line the Commander and Adjutant are aware of the condition of the lines in their sector and the precautions necessary to prevent messages being overheard; also that they are informed as to what alternative means of communication exist and where these are to be found.

To ensure the best results a closer liaison between the Brigade Section Officer and Battalion Staffs is necessary.

Attention is drawn to the following extracts from G.H.Q. letter Ia 13662 dated 4th July, 1916.

"It should be impressed on all ranks and particularly on officers that leakage of information of this nature, not only prior to an attack but also raids or in connection with reliefs, inevitably means sacrificing lives. The only sound rule with regard to telephone must be never to mention anything on the telephone that you would not mention in the presence of a hostile agent.

"Codes must be freely used where confidential information has to be transmitted. Officers should make it their personal duty to examine frequently the messages which are passing down the telephone wires, and severe disciplinary action must be taken in connection with any infringement of the existing regulations.

"This applied (sic) equally to the Signal Services, Regimental Signals and Artillery Forward Observing Officers."

WO 95/851

3
Memorandum cirulated by Captain R.H. Osborne for Brigadier-General, General Staff, First Anzac Corps, 19 March 1917

G.43/60

GENERAL STAFF CIRCULAR No. 60

Precautions to be taken to prevent information being given to the enemy by the transmission of messages.

1. Under instructions from G.H.Q. the following rules governing the use of STATION, POSITION and CODE CALLS, and the precautions to be observed in the use of signalling communications near the front, will in future be enforced.
(i) *Position calls* – Every signal and telephone office within a zone of 3,000 yards from any part of the front line (which zone is dangerous for the interception of messages by the enemy), or which has a direct circuit to a signal or telephone office within the above zone, will have allotted to it a call which will be termed its POSITION CALL. Position calls consist of two letters followed by a numeral, and are

issued by army through corps staff. The position call is a call allotted to an office in a particular position; it will never be changed and will never be used for a position other than that to which it has been allotted by the army. The allotted position call will be fixed up as a notice in the office, e.g., "Your call is "SZ.9", and this notice will not be removed when the office is handed over from one unit to another.

If a new office is established in the danger zone, or which has a direct circuit to an office in the danger zone, application will at once be made to corps through the usual channel for a position call to be allotted to it. The application will give the designation of the office, and the map square and co-ordinate.

Position calls will be used for the address "to" and "from"[11] in all messages passing within the danger zone whether sent by telegraph, buzzer or telephone.

The position call is sufficient to indicate the unit to which a signal office is allotted. Thus the "position call" for a signal office at battalion headquarters might be "SZ.6". No matter what battalion is there, the battalion to whom the office is allotted will be addressed simply as "SZ.6", and thus no indication will be given to the enemy when units change.

Similarly the artillery observing officer in an o.p. whose position call is "SW.3" will be addressed simply as "SW.3".

If the telegram is to go to a unit other than that to which the signal office is allotted, but which is also served by the office "SZ.6", say for instance to a trench mortar battery whose code name is "MARY", the telegram should be addressed "T.M.Battery SZ.6", or "MARY SZ.6". The address "from" must, as in address "to", be as far as possible a "position call" supplemented when necessary by code name.

The office of origin which is filled in on the top of the form by an operator sending the message must invariably be a "position call".

Position calls will be used for all signal messages transmitted by wireless or power buzzer.

The use of position calls also applies to telephone offices and exchanges in the danger zone. A telephone exchange in the danger zone must never be asked "Put me through to (name of unit in clear)". The request should be "Put me through to (position call)".

Similarly a telephone office or exchange within the danger zone, calling a telephone office, must never say "Is that" or "are you there (name of unit in clear)". The call must always be for the position call of the office required.

The position calls for all offices with which an office normally has to communicate must be known to the staffs, and it is only with these offices that communication should be allowed.

The term "office" includes all observation posts, also wireless, power buzzer, and amplifier stations.

N.B. – In the corps areas POSITION CALLS are temporarily in abeyance.

(ii) Every unit has allotted to it:–

    (a) Its STATION CALL, as laid down in Training Manual Signalling: Appendix I:

    (b) A TWO-LETTER CODE CALL, issued by corps staff.

    (c) A CODE NAME, issued by corps staff.

(iii) *Station calls* – The *station call* is for use as a signal call between signal offices both of which are outside the danger zone. This call will be used in such cases by the operator for filling in the "office of origin" on the top of the message form. The station call must never be allowed to go forward or to emanate from an office in the danger zone.

(iv) *Code calls* – The *two-letter code call* will be used –

    (a) for communicating with contact aeroplanes on all occasions;

    (b) in lieu of position calls when for any reason it is necessary to put the use of position calls into abeyance. Orders as to the latter will be issued by corps staff.

(v) *Code names* – Code names are for use in referring to units in the text of messages.

2. *Writing and censoring of messages.* It is necessary to distinguish between a message to be sent:–
(i) from or to offices both of which are outside the danger zone:
(ii) from or to offices both or one of which is in the danger zone.

Reference (i): the address "from" and "to" is to be in clear. Code names for units will as far as possible be used in the text, which will otherwise be in clear.

Reference (ii): it is not possible to lay down rules to cover all messages, as this must depend on what sort of instruments are being used on the circuit. The guiding principle is that in so far as is practicable the commander to whom a signal office in the danger zone, or working to an office in the danger zone, is allotted is responsible for having every message for transmission in the danger zone censored, and the necessary coding inserted in the message. The B.A.B. Code will be used for this purpose. Messages for transmission by buzzer or telephone will always be encoded, and signal offices in direct communication with other offices in the danger zone will not accept for transmission by these methods into the danger zone any messages which are not in code and signed by an officer who will be responsible for their contents. Fullerphones cannot be overheard by the enemy. Where installed they may be used for sending by key any message in clear. They are no protection in the case of spoken messages.

Arrangements must be made for the censoring of messages received by wire in clear from offices outside the danger zone addressed to offices inside the danger zone. It will probably be best to forward such messages by hand from the nearest office outside the danger zone.

Any messages which have to be forwarded by wire (except by Fullerphone on key) must be encoded before they enter the danger zone.

In the case of an office outside the danger zone (being) having to transmit a message originating from an office in the danger zone to another office outside the danger zone the necessary decoding will be done before the message is transmitted. The position calls (or code calls if used in lieu) in office of origin and address "to" and "from" will be decoded before transmission, the station call being substituted in the office of origin. This is particularly necessary in the case of messages addressed to offices on the lines of communication where the local codes and cyphers are not known, and where failure to have the messages decoded leads to delay and unnecessary correspondence.

Detailed instructions regarding the procedure to be adopted for encoding and decoding will be added locally to the card of instructions posted up in the signal office concerned: vide para 4 below.

3. *Instructions regarding the use of telephone and buzzer in the danger zone.*

(i) All circuits must be truly metallic.

(ii) Only urgent official matters will be dealt with through the telephone or by buzzer. Communications which are not urgent will be sent by hand. Operation orders should always be sent by hand if time permits.

(iii) Private conversations on the telephone are forbidden. It is mainly through such conversations that valuable information reaches the enemy.

(iv) Speech is always preferable to buzzing; the latter should only be used for special reasons.

(v) Conversations on the telephone, other than those necessary for the technical working of the telephone system, will be restricted to officers and to n.c.o's, to whom for the time being permission to use the telephone has been given.

(vi) All telephone conversations which may be of the slightest use to the enemy will be in code.

(vii) Any officer, n.c.o., or man who engages in conversation by means of the telephone or buzzer, and refers to matters which if overheard by the enemy would be to the latter's advantage, will be tried by court-martial.

4.   Cards embodying the above instructions are being issued, and one will be placed in every telephone and signal office in corps and division areas. A space is left at the foot of the card for the addition of any amendments or local instructions (vide para 2).

5.   In circumstances of urgency the above precautions may be disregarded on the personal responsibility of the officer commanding on the spot. He will, however, be required to justify his action.

6.   Commanders will be bald (sic) responsible that disciplinary action is immediately taken against any individual infringing these regulations.

WO 95/982

4

Excerpt from *Signal Notes* Number 6, 12 May 1917 issued by Director of Army Signals, G.H.Q.

Listening and Overhearing. (German)
The information given below concerning the procedure etc. adopted and *recent* steps taken by the Germans in connection with listening and overhearing has been obtained from captured German documents and by examination of German prisoners[12]:–

(1)   German Army Order No. 42373 of March, 1916, stipulated that –

(a)   All front line trench telephone stations were to be withdrawn at least as far as the second line, and all telephone wires farther forward than the second line were to be removed (accordingly, Company Commanders would remain in their dugouts without telephones, and would avail themselves of runners to the stations, or would remove to dugouts further back).

(b) The establishment of stations of Artillery Observers and Trench Mortars in advance of the second line was to be approved by the General Staff.

(c) Telephone lines to these stations were to be laid by the Reserve Telephone Detachment in the Communication trench with wire-cased Siemens lead cable buried at the depth of one metre, and if possible at right angles to the front – the shortest route being adopted.

(d) All lateral lines were to be taken back to the third line.

(e) The use of the telephone in forward areas was to be supervised most carefully – private conversations by officers and operators being forbidden.

(f) Code words and code figures were to be used.

(g) All concerned were to have explained to them the great risks incurred through misuse or thoughtless use of the telephone.

(h) The Telephone Detachment was to exercise more extensive supervision than hitherto of the lines and telephone service; its members were to have the right to tap lines for testing and supervision purposes.

(i) In order to train Reserve men for telephone work, the General Staff would hold courses of instruction in the Telephone Detachment.

(j) Men who had just come out as reinforcements would be attached to the Telephone Detachment for a few days.

(k) In future, greater importance was to be attached to the Messenger service.

(l) Shell-proof dugouts were to be built on a relay system so as to afford shelter to runners and give each runner a limited distance to traverse under enemy fire, and

(m) During an engagement, the maintenance of telephone connections is not to be counted on.

(2) A prisoner captured on 22nd April, 1917, stated that telephones in the German front line and within 3,000 yards of it

may only be used by officers, and during important operations the Company Commander must be present.

Linemen at work may only use calls and may not converse.

(3) A captured document shews that in January, 1917, a request was made to a German Artillery commander that in view of the importance of listening, shooting should not be carried out during listening hours, and that observers should not give *in clear* fire corrections and the names of their observation posts and of batteries and trench mortars engaged in firing. It was pointed out that German Listening Stations had heard corrections which could also be heard by the enemy who were thus able to take defensive measures.

Referring to the "English Telephone system" it was suggested that when the stations called up frequently it is safe to assume that some operation is projected. On 28th December the English stations in front of A.2 and A.3 (see para. 7 below) exchanged many morse messages and at 11.p.m. a mine was blown up. Further explosions were anticipated because mining operations had been heard in front of A.3 and A.4. When the gallery came closer it would be possible to avoid losses by issuing a warning from the listening set.

It was also stated that the English system is excellently arranged, and maintained and manned by experts so well acquainted with morse signals that almost all communication work is done by morse. The call and reply are perfectly clear and sharp, while the greatest care is taken to prevent overhearing. (This evidently refers to the Fullerphone).

Attention is then called to the unnecessary use of the German telephones during listening hours, the defective state of the lines in the German sector concerned and the telephoning of important messages without precautions. The German Artillery commander thereupon issued an order that (a) "silent hours" should be observed (b) shooting should not be carried on during these hours unless the circumstances were exceptional (c) code names and figures should be used, and (d) telephone conversations should be cut down.

(4)   A translated copy of a specimen form used on German Listening Sets, as drawn up by a prisoner, is furnished in Appendix I. It indicates that the Germans attach more importance to enemy Morse messages than to conversations.

Much success has been achieved in deciphering British messages.

At one station (A.13) six copies of every morse message or conversation were made and sent to the Ahrendt Gruppe which retained two copies and forwarded two to the General Staff 6th Reserve Army Corps and two to the General Staff 1st Bavarian Reserve Corps.

Reports are submitted every 24 hours, but important intercepted messages are communicated at once to the Officer Commanding the Battalion in the line. In the case of Station A.13, Battalion Headquarters was close at hand (i.e. in the same group of dugouts as the Listening Station). Individual units, Infantry, Artillery, Trench Mortars concerned, etc, are informed in code via the Battalion Exchange of intercepted messages which require urgent attention.

Excellent results had been obtained by the Listening Sets, but lately a falling off had been evident. The results at Stations 610 and 611 in Angres and Givenchy-en-Gohelle in May and June, 1916, were gratifying and it was claimed that the sets in this area kept the Germans well informed of the British order of battle.

(5)   According to a German prisoner, Listening Sets existed in January last at Gommecourt, Puisieux, Le Transloy, Miraumont (two sets), Sailly Saillisel (near) and Serre and several sets existed between Gommecourt and Arras. On the combined British and French fronts, there were probably over 200 sets.

Since additional precautions had been taken on the British front such good results, as previously, had not been obtained. Usually now there is one officer for every two German sets, and the personnel per set averaged 12.

Tests are continually being carried out to determine whether good results are obtainable by establishing listening stations at any point. It is not the practice to allot a fixed number of sets for each unit. Usually sets are situated in the support line next to the company Headquarters, and the telephone dugout.

Trouble due to leakage from power wires had been experienced, but so far no means for overcoming it had been devised.

Any telephone line that could be overheard by the Listening Set was closed down at once for repairs and not used until the repairs had been effected.

In this case, it was stated that messages were not written on special forms but on ordinary signal message forms and handed in to the Company Office. Important messages were telephoned.

Listening Sets were only used for communication purposes in an emergency.

In the event of an attack and of the lines being destroyed, warning to withdraw is sent to the set from the rear by power buzzer.

Very heavily insulated wire is used, and mine galleries are used as far as possible.

Lines which go over the surface are carried on insulators fastened to wooden stakes which are driven into the ground to keep the wire about 12 inches above the surface.

Earth pins are of cork screw shape (similar to those used for barbed wire) in hardened copper or bronze, a number being used for each earth.

Apparently three types of apparatus are in use. The prisoner had seen a new model (at Berlin) which was small and compact with 4 valves, the filament current of which was 4 or 6 volts. The valve was a more recent model than that captured on the Trench Set 2-valve Amplifier. The same box contained the instrument and a 100-volt dry battery.

(6) In a document issued by the *Bavarian* Listening Set Detachment No. 6 concerning correction of faults in Listening Sets it is stated that:–

(i) *The 90-volt Battery* is to be changed when the voltage has dropped to 70. Care is to be taken that the positive and negative poles of the 90-volt battery are connected properly. The voltage of the 90-volt battery is measured by means of the Galvanometer forming part of the Switchboard.

(ii) *The Connecting Leads* must not be damp, and

(iii) *If one amplifier is defective*, while the other is in good order, the fault may be detected in the following way:–

Fit all the detachable parts of the good instrument into the defective one (accumulator,[13] connecting leads, valves, Barreters, 90-volt Battery). If the apparatus is then still out of order, the fault lies in the internal workings (transformers, etc.) which are not to be interfered with *in any way* on the Station.

The same document contains the following outline of Precautionary Measures to be adopted in relation to German Listening Sets:–

There must be no superfluous equipment (such as maps, orders, and lists) on Stations.

All material and all papers, knowledge or possession of which could be of importance to the enemy, are to be kept in the dugout, where a sufficient number of hand grenades must be kept to destroy completely everything in case of extreme necessity. The N.C.O. in charge of the station is responsible for the safe disposal, accessibility and working order of hand grenades, and, on taking over a Station, must state in the daily report how many are available.

The taking of adequate measures in case of a hostile attack calls for, not only continual forethought, but also energetic action on the part of the N.C.O. temporarily in charge of the Station. He is responsible that the secret apparatus must, under no conditions, fall into the enemy's hands. If the enemy forces his way into our lines and pushes forward, then the most important instruments, the amplifier boxes, switchboards, power buzzers, papers, etc., are to be carried by men previously detailed for the purpose, under a previously detailed leader, to a place of safety in the rear, also previously specified by order.

The remaining personnel of the Station, under their N.C.O. will help in repelling the enemy. The carrying party must also be provided with hand grenades, in order to be able, at any moment, to destroy the apparatus in case they are surprised by the enemy.

If the enemy has forced his way in so unexpectedly that it is impossible to get the material away, and it is impossible to defend the dugout until relieved, only then are the costly instruments to be destroyed with hand grenades, by order of the N.C.O.

Entry to the dugout is permissible to members of the Listening Detachment in the execution of their duties, but to others only when accompanied by officers of the Detachment or when in possession of a stamped permit, signed by the Commander of the Detachment, granting permission on a specified date.

(7) The organisation of the German Listening Set Service appears to have been re-cast recently, but reliable information on the subject is scanty. It is clear, however, that before the change, the arrangements were as follows:–

All the stations (5) on the LOOS – ARRAS Sector were controlled by a central directing station in SALLAUMINES (later in AVION) known as KONTROLLZENTRALE, the staff of which consisted of 2 Lieutenants belonging to the Fernsprech Truppen (Telephone Troops) – one was a Technical Officer, and the other could speak English; a Sergeant Major, and two Interpreter Clerks. This staff worked under and was administered by a Captain of the Fernsprech Truppen. The KONTROLL-ZENTRALE was also directly under the Fernsprech Abteilung (Telephone Detachment) of the 12th Reserve Corps at DOUAI. The stations were 609 (Cite St Pierre); 610 (Angres); 611 (Givenchy-en-Gohelle); 612 (Vimy Ridge) and 613 (Augsburger Haus N.E. of Arras).

There seems to have been no fixed establishment laid down for the Listening Stations.

Reports from the stations were scrutinized, corrected, and collected at the Central Control Station and copies issued to all concerned.

The new organisation above referred to seems to be as follows:–

A series of Ahrendt Abteilungen (Detachments employed on work in connection with Ahrendt apparatus) have been formed. These are sub-divided into Ahrendt Gruppen (abbreviated to "Agru") the minimum number in an Abteilung being apparently 4. Station 609 became Asto 9 (or A.9); 610 became Asto 10 and so on. (The word Asto is derived from the underlined letters of Ahrendt Station). In the new scheme, the "Ahrendt Gruppe" took the place of the "Kontrollzentrale", and it carries out similar functions with apparently a similar staff, as described above. The Ahrendt Gruppe of the four stations quoted above is at Henin Lietard.

The personnel of the station now seems to be – 2 N.C.O's and 20 men (6 Interpreters, 6 Operators and 8 Linemen). One N.C.O. and 10 men are always at the Station but there is no regular roster of duties. The personnel are relieved every four days and have four days in rest billets.

Interpreters now receive a six weeks' course of instruction at Berlin on the "British Army", slang expressions used ("Whizz-bangs"; "Jack Johnsons" &c.) and in reading Morse telegrams and intercepting English conversations.

Hitherto, the Ahrendt apparatus manufactured by the "Allgemeine Elektricitats Gesellschaft" has been used at the stations quoted, but a new and superior listening set is expected to be issued shortly.

Specimen Report form used on German Listening Set as drawn up by a prisoner

"A" Station.....................

.......Army Corps......Res.Divn......Section.......Regt......Battn......

Time............1917   Morning

                                                      Circuit.............

                                        Afternoon

Receiving Clerk...................   Superintendent....................

Call   Method of communication

Service Instructions and Office of Origin.....   A.M.

Number of words.......................................   Time   P.M.

Address to..

Sender's Number....................................... Date............AAA

Contents (Text)

Translation

Any special formations recognised should be recorded.

RG–9/111/C–5/4443

5

Excerpt from the War Diary of the Canadian Corps Wireless Section compiled by Lieutenant J.C. Manson, Officer Commanding, December 1916

Ranchicart[14]   Original and Confidential

Place	Date	Hour	Summary of Events and Information
Ranchicart			
Jcm	1/12/16	–	Station at Rid. 5. sheet $N^o 36^B$ $SE2^{15}$ received 10 messages sent 8.
Jcm	2/12/16	–	Investiged (sic) front at M14cq.6. sheet $N^o 36^c$ SW1 big placing loops from our listening saps[16] to along front of enemy's wire for 200 yds keeping loop out overnight with patrol on watch & bringing same in next evening having overheard enemy's calls. This decided the positions for permanent loops in front lines & supports.
Jcm	3&4/12/16	–	All W/T stations working well.
Jcm	5/12/16	–	Put out new loops for IT set at 520 684 sheet $N^o 36^a$ SW3. Results fair all other W/T stations working o.k.
Jcm	6/12/16	–	Moved Z.G. W/T station to Advanced Bde HQs. The position they were in when taken over from 17th Corps not found suitable for our Bdes & Battlns. at this time.
Jcm	7/12/16	–	Put out loop in defensive gallery for $N^o 4$ I.T. set M14c9.6 sheet $N^o 36^g$ SW1. Good results obtained intercepted many enemy messages. Buzzed and spoken signals very loud.
Jcm	Sig.10/12/16	–	All wireless stations working OK $N^1 4$ post intercepting enemy calls.

Place	Date	Hour	Summary of Events and Information
Jcm	11/12/16	–	Loops at N°2 post continually going open with trench mortar fire unable to repair loops in front line in day time. Since no enemy's messages were intercepted here it was decided to move to the left a dugout was asked to be built & was (illegible word) on the morning of the 12th owing to run down condition of the men N°2 personnel was brought in to Corps to await completion of new dugout.
Jcm	12,13,14/ 12/16	–	Stations all working well N°5&6 posts not yet intercepting enemy's messages.
Jcm	15/12/16	–	Investigated location of N°5 post putting loops in disused trench in "no mans land" through mine craters & back in support line. This loop was carefully watched by patrols each night for one week & still no enemy messages were intercepted.
Jcm	16/12/16	–	Moved Z.Q. to advanced Bde HQrs. this being considered position where a wireless station would be necessary should the air line[17] between Bde & Bde advanced be broken.
Jcm	17/12/16	–	At N°6 Post A10cB.4. sheet N°51[B]N.W.1. Had loop laid through mine crater & defence gallery & support line. Immediately thereafter enemys messages intercepted station was then moved back out of trench Mortar fire range, personnel relieved by new personnel & set from G.H.Q.
Jcm	18,19/12/16–		All stations working well.

48

Place	Date	Hour	Summary of Events and Information
Jcm	20/12/16	–	Placed new loop at N^o5 Post at A8G5.7. sheet N^o51^G N.W.1. to left of loop installed on the 16th & owing to conditions of trenches this looked like a good place for permanent loop. Loop was then stapled up in Front Line supports & connected to set. The set, I had always considered to be much too far away from loop. A long lead to loop becoming slightly earthed picked up too many of our own messages so loud that enemys conversation would have been jammed out efforts are being made to have dugouts constructed in new support line.
Jcm	21,22,23, 24/12/16	–	No change all stns working well N^o5 not yet intercepting enemy's calls.
Jcm	25/12/16	–	Put out 600 yd earths base at N^o5 G7 putting out earths in listening saps 600 yrds apart.[18]
Jcm	26/12/16	–	Dugout at N^o2 post now completed N^o2 post installed in new dugout.
Jcm	27/12/16	–	Put out earths in 3 listening saps & owing to heavy trench mortar fire loops would have been useless. Linesmen were kept busy keeping the 3 earths out.
Jcm	28,29/12/16–		All W/T stns working well N°s 4&6 Posts intercepting enemy's messages N°s 2&5 controlling our own conversations by attention to extracts from intercepts & reports by intelligence corps.
Jcm	30/12/16	–	N^o2 post dugout flooding, evidently

Place	Date	Hour	Summary of Events and Information

			from stream water coming up through floor, set moved into higher part of dugout, & still operation no enemy's messages yet intercepted.
Jcm	31/12/16	–	All Stns working well.
	Dec./16		Remarks:– Each I.T. Post consumes the energy of 1 accumulator per day. These accumulators each weighing 50 lbs and owing to the long distance which these accumulators have to be taken to be recharged viz. 1st Army. This necessitates Box car being over-worked. We have had considerable trouble over the temporary loss of accumulators when left at Brigade to be forwarded by ration cart so it was decided about the beginning of Dec that accumulators could be taken to almost all stations after Sundown by our box car. Numerous accumulators boxes have been broken & some of the cells damaged in transport. If charging Lorry now authorised on our establishment could be had, a long rough trip both for accumulators & car could be eliminated. The Lorry Set placed at a very central point the life of the accumulators would then be lengthened & the service improved.

J.C. Manson Lt. C.E.
O.C. Canadian Corps Wireless Section

RG–9/111/D–3/5006

6

Report on Conversations Picked Up by Wireless

INTELLIGENCE IN 2ND. CANADIAN DIVISION SECTOR

The reports of the Wireless Intelligence show that even now, after repeated warnings, not enough precautions are being exercised by persons in using the telephone, to prevent the enemy from gaining valuable information through his Listening Apparatus. That he makes extensive use of Listening Sets is shown by the large number captured on every part of the front on which we have made an advance, and his using them extensively shows that he must obtain information through them, for a much smaller number would be sufficient to "police" his own lines. Their efficiency is proved by tests made with those captured.

The method used by the enemy is to lay out a "loop" of wire as near our lines as possible and this "loop" picks up by induction or through leakage the currents in our wires: the nearer his "loop" is to our wires, the better results he will obtain. It follows that when we are occupying territory captured from him he has a great opportunity to use prearranged "loops", pipe lines, old buried cables, etc., within our lines, and consequently, the necessity of additional precautions on our part.

The Fullerphone is the only apparatus in use by us at present which cannot be overheard by either induction or earth leakage. *SPEAKING* over the Fullerphone is overheard exactly the same as over an ordinary telephone.

Below are given a few examples of conversations picked up by our "police" sets. These show that the worst offenders are Battery Signallers and Signal linemen. The sets pick up daily a practically continuous stream of personal conversations between Battery Signallers at Battery Headquarters and O.P.'s.

Station called – 121. 10.50 a.m. 30th July.
"Hello! who is that? 121?"
"No, it's 121's O.P."
"Hello! this is 121" "How do you hear me?"

"Good" "Is this Mac" "When are you going on leave, thought we might click together again".

"Yes, that's right, well, if we don't we won't be far apart – only 24 hours".

"Yes, that's right, cheerio".

The above is typical of the innumerable unnecessary personal conversations carried on.

Conversation. 2.45 p.m. 30th July.

"Hello! "Yes" "Well we got down there and found that the 2nd Division and 1st Division Artillery were holding it, getting ready for the big push I suppose".

"Yes, Oh! all right".

An example of utter carelessness.

Station called – MC, 5.50 p.m. 30th July.

"Will you get an officer on the 'phone, please."

"This is O.P. speaking. The Colonel gave me instructions to follow up any wire or machine gun emplacements I could see. I could call up any Battery. I've located a machine gun strong point at H.31.d.55.28. I can register on it. I don't know how many rounds I'll use on it."

"How many have you got".

RG–9/111/C–5/4438

II
Traffic Analysis

These documents refer to the little examined practice of traffic analysis. They show the combination of meticulous observation and careful deduction, induction and extrapolation which marked the discipline and the precision and power of the material which it provided. Incidentally, these documents indicate that traffic analysts relied far less on arbitrary rules of thumb or intuition than did codebreakers or the personnel who assessed intelligence. Traffic analysis was more science than art. Documents One and Two are raw traffic analysis reports. They show the fundamental characteristic of the science: scrupulous attention to and analysis of a host of details in the procedure and structure of a communication system and especially to changes in these matters. Document One, which is among the first such reports in history, shows the tactical and Document Two the strategic intelligence derived from such work. Similar reports were probably produced daily or weekly by every WOG throughout 1914–18. Documents Three, Four and Five are examples of the weekly summaries of raw traffic analysis reports produced by every British Army in France during the last twenty months of the war. These, along with Appendix Two of Document Eight, Chapter Seven, show the remarkable quantity and quality of intelligence on the enemy's order of battle and operational dispositions, movements and intentions derived from this source. They also demonstrate that, despite the notable changes in the nature of British military operations during 1917–18, the value of traffic analysis as a source of intelligence remained constant, and significant. Document Six, a memorandum produced by the WOG in Iraq, discusses many of the technical and organisational aspects of interception, direction-finding and traffic analysis. Document Seven is a German report on traffic analysis against the British Army during the Great War, which reveals the techniques and triumphs of the enemy's service. Altogether, these documents demonstrate the great success and effect achieved by the traffic analysts of every army during the First World War.

I

Report by Captain H.P.T. Lefroy,[5] Royal Engineers, 16 May 1915

[Copy]

O.C.
W/T.
Since report of 28–4–15 re interception undertaken by us on short wave lengths, BAILLEUL station has been working continuously and daily receives a large number of remarks from German aircraft (these will be found on sheets marked W M A in daily abstract of intercepts sent in).

On evening of May 3rd a new short wave intercepting station was opened at BETHUNE, using as usual a single long wire hung from the top of the Church Tower there. Though this station receives daily a large number of calls from French and British aeroplanes, it had up to 10th instant, intercepted nothing from German aircraft, except very weak signals on 3 occasions (12.30 on 6th instant, 14 10 on 7th instant and 0600 on 8th instant) from a station calling FI on 150, whence it appears probable that there were no German aircraft fitted with wireless operating in the neighbourhood of BETHUNE; they were probably concentrated around YPRES, and perhaps somewhat to the south of that place also.

On 4–5–15 at about 11 p.m., BETHUNE station heard a German station working at 350; it was calling UI (?) and the strength of its signals varied rapidly to a marked degree; this may have been a German airship.

It was shewn in the previous report that a captive balloon to the East of YPRES was almost certainly using the call letters FI. Since then, on 6th instant and other occasions, other stations which were obviously (from the nature of their remarks) German aeroplanes, have used the same letters FI, whence it appears almost certain that the call letters signalled by German aircraft are indicative of the ground station to which they are working and not of the aircraft which is transmitting.

On 5–5–15 at 0934 the call letters DA were followed by the remark "Battery 98 fire". It is believed that the same call was used during latter half of April in connection with the same battery No. 98 (records were sent forward so not to hand for reference); if this is so it would seem that DA are the call letters of the W/T. station working with that battery, and the evidence that call letters refer to ground stations is strengthened. Careful analysis of the remarks made by German aeroplanes has shewn that at present they can be classified under 2 headings, which for convenience may be called:

(1) "Civil" (2) "Military". These terms refer to the type of Wireless procedure used by the operator transmitting from them.

(1) Uses IMI as signal for "Fire again", as in ordinary W/T. commercial procedure

(2) Uses SSS ″   ″   ″   ″

(1) Uses AR ″   ″   ″   "Message ended", as in ordinary W/T. commercial procedure.

(2) Uses UM ″   ″   ″   ″   ″   ″   ″ German W/T. Military procedure.

(1) Is used by stations calling FI, FG, ZU, which were heard in March.

(2) Is used by stations calling DA, DB, LQ, DC, which were heard first in April or later.

The operators in (1) may perhaps be Reservists (or suchlike).

The operators in (2) are probably officers.

German aircraft appear to use the same call letters from day to day (as also their field stations do) and the calls given in previous report have been frequently heard since; FI and DB are the commonest; DA, DC, ZU, ZX, ZY are fairly common; others heard once, or perhaps twice, are PD, FG, XU, FA, whence it will be seen that the number of different calls heard since previous report is considerable, and it grows daily.

From remarks intercepted there have been several indications that German aeroplanes are fitted with Wireless receiving as well as transmitting apparatus, e.g., on 7–5–15 (at   ) the aeroplane working to FI was heard to say "Antwort spaker",[1] and on 8–5–15 (at 0650) it was heard to say "KKK – Sprecht g p ticfer"[2] – This latter remark, together with others, rather suggests that they receive by wireless telephony, in which case the ground station working to them would be using a continuous wave system, possibly on a short wave length, but more probably on an ordinary one; further evidence however is required to establish the above suggestion.

From a remark made about 5 p.m. on 21–4–15 "Telephoniese gleich"[3] – it seems probable that German batteries are connected by telephone, with a central receiving wireless station serving several of them, e.g., FI would be such a central station.

On the whole it seems probable that a German wireless aeroplane works with only one such central receiving station.

The normal hours of working daily are at present about 4 a.m. to 9 a.m. and 5 p.m. to 7–30 pm.

They continue to use the same code mentioned in previous report, and the interpretations suggested appear to hold good on the whole.

Other signals noticed and not previously mentioned are:–
(0534 pm 8–5–15)

AS which probably means "Wait" (as in W/T procedure).
AZ   "   "   "   "Fire percussion shell".
BZ   "   "   "   "   "   time   "   ".
MMM   "   "   "   "Increase range by . . ." (mehr.)

The expression "Gebt rot" occurs frequently, and once or twice "Gebt Grun". On 28–4–15 (at 1853) a remark about "red-green" was made to DB.

One or two remarks (if taken down correctly) seem to suggest that their wireless aeroplanes have both pilot and observer, at any rate sometimes, but there is no definite evidence yet.

A remark to ZX on 1–5–15 (at 0743) suggests that they use the white X near our batteries to aim on. Remarks made to ZX on

1–5–15 (at 0652) and on 5–5–15 (at 0610) indicate that they use a X also, possibly as a landing mark for their aeroplane.

There is no evidence that they are using a large number of wireless aeroplanes; half a dozen or so could do all they are observed doing. They appear to give numbers to their batteries and to their targets, to refer to when directing fire from their aeroplanes, but on one occasion at least, viz., on 12–5–15 (at 1916) the targets appear to have been indicated by the letters A, B and C.

As regards the energy used by them, a remark was made on one occasion that they were using "1.7 on reduced power and 3.3 on full power", and on 12–5–15 (at 1753) remark to FA was "full power 2.7". The unit referred to was not mentioned, but it is probably their primary current and not that in their aerial, unless the latter is of a different design to ours, so as to have a less "equivalent resistance" than ours, in which case it would probably be less radiative than ours, which would explain results as well as the hypothesis that their numbers stated above refer to the alternating or direct current being taken from their generators when transmitting. Two stations MA and WA have once or twice used a 3 letter code in which F is always the first letter and the 2nd and 3rd letters are the same, e.g., FZZ, FDD, etc. It is not certain that they are working in connection with aircraft. On 11–5–15 our station at BETHUNE got rather more than on other occasions, viz., several clear intercepts from the station working to FI, between 0550 and 0710; also one call at 0602 from station working to DC (the only thime (sic) this call has been heard there). Later in the morning 2 more remarks apparently from German stations observing fire were intercepted there, and at 1539 a German station was heard to say "Ready to Observe" Its signals were strong, so it was probably only 5 or 6 miles from BETHUNE; but the day may have been an exceptionally good one for wireless from aircraft.

Rough translations of remarks intercepted[4] between 28–4–15 and 8–5–15 instant are attached; accuracy cannot be guaranteed. On 13–5–15 a very remarkable decrease in activity in German Wireless aeroplanes was observed; only 2 calls to DB being recorded (at about 0430) at our BAILLEUL station, instead of 60 to 70 as previously; this inactivity continues.

Remarks taken down as "Gehirund", "Geheich runt" etc., have occurred frequently. These are probably abbreviations of "Gehe ich rund" – "I am turning now", sent by the wireless aeroplanes as a warning to the batteries they are working with not to fire till observer is ready again. These remarks have not appeared lately, so have probably been replaced by some code signal (e.g., some letter repeated 3 times as usual) e.g., JJJ, perhaps.

AIR 1/754/204/4/71

2

Memorandum by the Wireless Intelligence Organisation, British Headquarters, Salonika, 15 February 1917

SECRET

Salonika 4
Feb 15th 1917

Section 2

Locations
I (a) *Military stations*
(1) MACEDONIA

DL   The calls of the main stations at least have again been
FF   changed, from the 10th inst. DL appears to have replaced
AU   SW at Uskub, AU the former VY, and FY the former KX.
FY   The routine practice by SW of FY exchanging calls with
FF, VY and KX at definite times every twelve hours is
continued by DL with FF, AU, and FY at the same hours.
The bearing of DL is that of SW, that of FY is that of KX;
but on AU the mean of 4 day bearings is 23 degrees while
that of VY was 20 degrees.
(i) *Eastern front*
VY   On the 9th one CHI and one ZIF[6] – otherwise no
PI   traffic in the area.
(ii) *Western front*
No calls have been heard.

(2) OLD GREECE

No calls have been heard.

(3) ROUMANIAN FRONT

WP   Slight traffic between WP with MV and GK, otherwise
MV   complete inactivity. The Austrian stations have seldom
GK   worked.

(4) RADIOGONOMETRIC stations and AIRCRAFT

WOQ were heard on the 10th sending + bearings timed 1344 to
WOR the call GER (previously heard on 24/11/16).
WOX
GER   On WOR one bearing of 316.5 degrees (G) was recorded.
     At 1610 WOX sent balloon soundings to a height of 4500
     metres, prefixed "CHIF HXWS"

(5) *Other Enemy Stations*

SM   These four stations, of whom the last three work with the
SP   Turkish naval group, appear now to form a small group
SY   working in a code unlike that of any other stations. (See
     intercepts herewith).[7]

SU   SM who had previously not been heard on a wave length
     of less than A' 300° has now been heard on A' 1200 calling
     SY.

AY   These stations are now heard daily, and day bearings
YPZ have been obtained.[8] AY has a mean day bearing of 30.5
     degrees (6 readings) while the night readings vary from
     30 to 65. YPZ gives a mean of 320 degrees by day (4
     readings) and is far more consistent at night.

     For AY one hearing from ZAB of 346° gives an intersec-
     tion at Bucharest, no location is yet indicated for YPZ.

     Tuning up signals and ZIF's have passed but no other
     communications: the communications of these two
     stations are peculiar to themselves, intercepts are
     attached. It is worth noticing that certain isolated words
     sent by them e.g. CASAR and BERTA are the names of
     ciphers used by Constantinople.

Doubtful station

PP   This station, reported last week, on the 13th sent to LO and
LC   LD "BEWDL EYWOR" from a bearing by day of 53, which
LD   gives a very good intersection at SERES with the mean
Mudros bearing. Its note is however now recorded as
musical: a number of English five letter groups such as
FAYCO MPTON and RAGPI OKERS have been recorded at
Mudros, though the call does not appear known to the
N.I.O. Mudros,[9] or the Army Wireless Officer at Salonika.

I (b)   NAVAL Calls
(1)   GERMAN
DG   At 0600 on the 14th the call DG again using F as a divide
BB   sign was heard on a wave length of 1600 calling BB and
BX   BX from 157 degrees, with a musical note.
Between August and December 1916 MB, with a musical
note from a mean bearing of 160°, was frequently heard
about 0600 calling BB and EO and on two occasions using
F as a divide sign.

(2)   AUSTRIAN
Greater activity than is usual has lately been noted in this
group; with a number of new calls,
BRU   were called on the 13th by PY: of these QR received a ZIF
DE   from PL on January 18th.
QR
OR
TS   called by PY on 9th.
DP   from a night bearing of 304 degrees worked with PY on
the 12th.
GF   were sent 10 letter code by PY on the 12th.
RE
ZK   was sent OBGEALPIST by PY on the 12th.
EC   sent "K" to PY on the 12th.
OL   was called by QA on the 12th.
PX   was called by QA on the 10th and was sent 10 letter code
by NC.

GW   from a night bearing of 310 sent 10 letter code to EN
EN   and was called by QA.
KR   was sent 10 letter code by NC on the 11th.
NK   "   "   "   "   "   "   "   "   " 13th.
ND   was called by NC on the 12th.
HS   "   "   " OB " " 10th.

(3)   TURKISH AREA

The normal traffic continues, including the CHIFS and INGO's without call signs from the bearings of PM and Constantinople.

On the 9th "1739 INGO" and "1741 CHIF" were intercepted at 0822 on 3000 from 136.5; at 0839 "1741 CHIF" was repeated on 1650 from 125 degrees (BM); at 0900 from 84° on 1650.

It is possible though not certain that the 0822 intercepts came from KBU whose average bearing is 135 (+180) though 3000 is not usual for KBU.

(4)   GREEK. No calls heard.

Section 3

GENERAL
The wireless inactivity seems in keeping with the general military inactivity in this area.

It will be noted that the enemy in changing the calls of the chief Macedonian stations, has not even changed the hours at which these stations have lately exchanged signals every twelve hours.

WO 157/753

3
Intelligence Summary by Lieutenant Colonel, General Staff "I", Third Army, 31 July 1917

SECRET.

THIRD ARMY WIRELESS INTELLIGENCE SUMMARY, No. 19.

Period 6 p.m. 22nd to 6 p.m. 29th July 1917.[10]

PART "A"

1. *Enemy Activity*

Enemy activity has been slight this week. The chief activity was in Sector B. All the work seems to be done by the same machines, i.e., NM, MD, FW. NM seems to be flying right along the Northern area.

Date	No. of flights	No. of batteries ranged	No. of targets engaged	No. of registering flights	Aggregate time of observation.		Weather
					Hrs.	Mins.	
23–7–17	8	8	12	8	7	54	Fair
24–7–17	7	6	6	6	5	56	Fair
25–7–17	5	3	3	3	2	34	Bad
26–7–17	nil	nil	nil	nil	nil		Very bad
27–7–17	12	7	10	7	8	29	Fair
28–7–17	8	5	8	6	5	16	Indifferent
29–7–17	4	1	1	1	0	49	Bad
Totals	44	30	40	31	30	52	

Average time of ranging per effective flight = 59 minutes.

2. *Activity of Calls*

Call	No. of flights	Time		Call	No. of flights	Time	
		Hrs.	Mins.			Hrs.	Mins.
AK	5	nil		LK	1	0	21
CK	6	5	47	LT	1	0	42
FW	8	5	15	NM	8	6	43
GA	6	5	08	RB	1	1	09
GK	1	nil		YU	1	2	01
HY	1	nil					

3. *Calls.*

No new calls have been heard. The total number of different calls heard opposite this Army front was 13, as against 23 last week, and 25 the week before. The following calls which were heard last week have not been heard this week:–
AQ, BD, BW, HD, KC, ML, RG, US, VL, ZO, IL, OQ, JS.
Calls not heard last week, which have reappeared are RB, LT, GK.

4. *Interference with enemy aircraft*

10 warnings were sent to R.F.C., 4 machines sent no going in signal, and 4 machines stopped working abruptly. One machine sent S.O.S., and was not heard after this signal.

5. *Wireless Reception*

Several shoots have been carried out, and one of them was successful. The following aeroplanes and ground stations have been concerned:–

KO aeroplane and FW ground station.
IF " " FW " "
PR " " FW " "
NI " " FW " "

It follows from this that the call emitted by the aeroplane on each occasion was FW. The directing aerodrome is located at ST. HILAIRE.

6. *Coordinate Targets*
On the 23rd YU sent PA 634 (51B.U14). VI Corps R.A.[11] were warned immediately. No subsequent shelling was reported.

Chart and graphs are attached.

PART "B"

General Activity
The number of messages intercepted this week shows an increase of message activity of 25% over last week, although last week the number was swelled by what was probably a test scheme, and this week there was 24 hours inactivity owing to atmospherics. A great increase in the number of messages sent between stations of group 505 is chiefly responsible for this larger total.

Group	Div'l area	Stations in Group	No. of messages	Most active stations	Probable directing station	Remarks
480	238 Div.	DB, FA, KV, RU.	32	FA, RC.	FA.	
505	26 Div.	C1, KY, LM, L5, RB, U8, V7.	26	V7, KJ.	V7.	
515	?39 Div.	HL, KB, VO, 77.	3	KB.	KB	
520	?26 R.Div.	AJ, KO, N2, Q6, RF, TO, 53.	18	RF	RF	
540	121 Div.	GN, HU, KW, MJ, OR, WV, YL.	14	MJ, KW.	? KW.	

Group	Div'l area	Stations in Group	No. of messages	Most active stations	Probable directing station	Remarks
545	18 Div.	BL, DH, FO, IO, VR.	7		FO	
560	3rd R.Div.	AK, DS, LN, TG, RV, RU.	6		RU or LN.	
?		FP, NI, PR.	nil			
		Total messages	106			

Calls

A certain amount of camouflage appears to be taking place in one or two Groups. In Group 505 the call LM which was in use before the change of call signs took place, disappeared for a time with that change, but re-appeared on the 24th. V7 has been heard to use its old call sign 84, but this may have been a mistake on the part of the operator.

TV of Group 560 has reappeared, and AK remains active. When TV ceased activity AK was thought to be the new call adopted by this station. U9 of Group 515 has not been heard since it was told by its directing station to dismantle on the 21st inst.

The exact composition and purpose of the new Group E. of CAMBRAI is not clear. Activity is very slight in this Group.

Lateral communication between Groups has been very slight.

Information from Messages

A message from 77 to KB in Group 515 gave the first indication that the 39th Division was in this area. A later message between the same stations confirmed this. It is probable that Group 515 now works for the 39th Division. The Northern boundary of this Division is not yet exactly known, but it is certainly further North than the Northern boundary of 220th Division was before it was relieved. KB is located near ETERPIGNY, and 77 in the region of VIS on ARTOIS.

The following identifications have been made:–

Persons indentified

Date	Stations	Name	Remarks
15–7–17	ĀT v 62	GETHOEFER.	Signature.
23–7–17	GN v OR	A.B.ANHOECK.	A.B. (= ? Artillerie) (Boobachtung.)[12]
25–7–17	V7 v KJ	Uffz KLAHOLT.	Address.
26–7–17	MJ v WV (o1	KOTHE.	Signature.
27–7–17	(KJ v V7 (Ū8	Leut. TRAUN.	(WO ist Lt. TRAUN).

Units identified.

Date	Stations	Unit	Remarks
26–7–17	KB v 77	172 I.R. 126 I.R.	} . . . 39th Division.
28–7–17	do	61st Bde.	
"	D3 v KV	Regt. Kumunster.	Address.

Chart showing location of Stations and communications is attached.[13]

PART "C"
LISTENING SETS

Set No. 21 (VII Corps) continues to get German Power Buzzer Signals. Loops are going to be put out with a view to picking up German conversation. Set No. 24 (VI Corps) has been over-hearing a large amount of German conversation. In some cases the German overheard proved to be of extreme value. The following is an extract from a VI Corps report dated 26–7–17:–

"Owing to the frequent calls for A.V.O. and the general nervousness displayed on pages 9, 10, 11, 12 etc July 25th the operator considered that something was on foot and warned the Brigade, who sent down the warning to batta-lions. These conversations were intercepted at 6.50 a.m. In the afternoon the enemy attempted a surprise raid on our post at U.21.d.95.15. and found our troops on the alert."

WO 157/154

4

Examples of Weekly Wireless Intelligence Summaries by Second Army, July 1917

No. 21 SECRET.

Second Army Wireless Intelligence
HOSTILE FIELD STATIONS
Week ending Noon 10th July, 1917

1. *General*
On July 4th., the enemy began a general change in his Field Station Calls, and to prevent us from identifying the new calls with the old ones, he introduced a considerable number of dummy calls.

Most of the latter were heard on one or two occasions only, and stations in different groupings were, and still are emitting them indiscriminately.

The number of reversed calls was noticeable.[14]

2. *Activity*
Activity was moderate along the whole front except on 4th July when it was slightly below normal.

294 messages were intercepted during the week, compared with 314 last week.

Owing to the shifting of calls it is impossible to say which group showed the greatest activity.

3. *Distribution of Stations*
There is no evidence yet of any material changes. 38 Field Stations were located during the week, against 35 last week. The number of unlocated stations in each group cannot be accurately stated yet.

Group 305 in the 10th Bav. Div. which was supposed to have disappeared, was found to be active after three days silence.

GROUP	AREA	No. of STATIONS LOCATED THIS WEEK	LAST WEEK'S LOCATED	STATIONS UNLOCATED
215	119th Division	5	7	4
220	195th Division	7	4	2
305	10th Bav. Div.	7	6	0
315	18th Res. Div.	2	5	0
320	207th Division	5	5	0
325	22nd Res. Div.	7	4	2
340	18th Bav. Div.	5	4	1

NOTE:– One Station "Y.3" has been located between YPRES-COMMINES Canal and the River LYS, for the first time since the Battle of Messines.

No. 25   SECRET.
Second Army Wireless Intelligence Summary
GERMAN FIELD STATIONS
Week ending Noon 24th July, 1917

1. *Enemy Activity*

The hostile activity has been normal with the exception of group 325 (WARNETON) which again shows the strongest activity, and group 305 (HOLLEBEKE) which again shows the least activity. A total of 319 messages were sent during the week (an increase of 89 on last week) the most active day being the 18th with 57 messages. (Average per day 45 messages).

2. *Hostile Signals*

The wireless traffic continues to be very badly regulated. At times it is utterly impossible to read anything owing to the fact that all stations are sending at the same time and consequently jamming each other. The same trouble seems to be experienced by the German operators to judge from the number of repetitions asked for and "Not understood" signals emitted. Our success in solving the enemy code enables us to understand part of most of the messages and it is noticeable that a good percentage of these are complaints about bad sending or encoding.

3. *Instruments employed*

A study has been made this week of the instruments used by the enemy distinguishable by their note. According to documents and prisoners' statements the G.Fuk instrument, which is used with motor or man power driven dynamo, is used by Division or Brigade H.Q. Stations. The M.Fuk used with accumulators, by Regimental or Battalion Stations. As there is a distinct difference in note between these two instruments it has been possible to classify several stations on the Army Front.

4. *Identifications*

By succeeding in decoding hostile messages we were able to obtain several identifications of units opposite the Army Front.
The following identifications were obtained:–

22nd July	PL & HI	(Group 215 BECELAERE)	12th Brigade.
23rd "	Group 215	Identified as	FUKLA 44
24th "	PV & C7	(Group 320 LINSELLES)	23rd Field Art. Regt.
24th "	QD & YN	(Group 320 LINSELLES)	29th Regt.

5. *Positions and Grouping of Stations*

GROUP 215 (BECELAERE). 119th Division

Call Sign	Location	Working to	No. of Messages	Remarks
HI.	28 L 8 a.	PL, UL, RK, NP, XA.	5	
PL.	28 K 7 c.	RX, ZS, S9, ZM, GD, JO, HI, RK, GF, UL, MJ.	37	Divisional Battle H.Q.
RK.	28 J 22 a.	PL.	2	Last heard on 17th

Call Sign	Location	Working to	No. of Messages	Remarks
UL.	28 J 17 a.	DO, K3, D9, CO, PL, JR, KV.	NIL	
9S.	Unlocated		NIL	Last heard on 12th
ZD.	29 G 8 d.	PL, HI.	NIL	
		Total	44	

WO 157/116

5

Wireless Intelligence Summary produced by Lieutenant-Colonel W.G. Charles for Major-General, General Staff, Third Army, August 1918

SECRET   *Not to be reproduced.*

THIRD ARMY WIRELESS INTELLIGENCE SUMMARY NO 14.
Period week ending midnight 8th/9th August 1918.

1.   ENEMY ARTILLERY AEROPLANE WIRELESS ACTIVITY

(a) *General.* Owing to unfavourable weather conditions activity has been very slight during this period. Only four ranging flights were located opposite this army front.

(b) *Number of Flights.* Four ranging flights were carried out by the enemy opposite the Third Army front, as compared with 13 last week. Four non-ranging flights were located by wireless and found to be opposite this Army front, and three others are presumed from their call signs to have been opposite this front. The average time of ranging flight was 49 minutes as compared with $51\frac{1}{2}$ minutes last week.

(c) *Co-ordinate Targets.* 2 co-ordinate Targets were sent down by enemy observers, and both were found to be behind the enemy's lines.

(No chart of Enemy Artillery Aeroplane Activity is issued with this summary)

2. GERMAN FIELD WIRELESS STATIONS

(a) *General.* During the past week the activity of German Field Wireless Stations was normal. Message traffic and calling activity was almost exclusively in the area COURCELETTE-ERVILLERS. Immediately north of this area calling activity was moderate and message traffic negligible.

The general distribution and arrangement of groups still appear unchanged. No stations have been heard in the 214th. Divisional area since July 18th., when the group serving this Division appears to have been withdrawn. The sectors occupied by the 2nd. Guards Reserve Division, and the 111th. Division appear to be served by one wireless group, while the remaining Divisions opposite the Army front appear to have one group each.

The Field Stations located respectively at GOMIECOURT and GREVILLERS have been exceptionally active. These stations appear to be hubs of Wireless traffic in the area COURCELETTE – ERVILLERS.

(b) *Lateral Communication.* Lateral communication was considerable throughout the week in the area FLERS – GOMIECOURT. On the 4th and 5th., communication took place across the Corps Boundary. The extensive use of lateral communication by the enemy appears to be adopted in order to conceal the exact arrangement of the Divfunkas.[15]

(c) *Artillery Stations.* 2 groups of two stations each were heard between BOUZINCOURT and BUCQUOY on the 7th, but they were not definitely located.

(d) *Sector BOUZINCOURT – BUCQUOY.* Throughout the week activity was normal, and it was very consistent in the area MIRAUMONT – GOMIECOURT. The group in the area ACHIET-le-PETIT – GOMIECOURT showed very regular activity.

Several Field Stations in this sector were heard using both short and medium wave lengths.

(e) *Sector BUCQUOY – SCARPE.* Activity was mainly in the area GOMIECOURT – ST LEGER. North of this very little activity was observed. A long wave station was heard in the region of ST LEGER.

(f) *Meteorological Stations.* 12 messages were intercepted from Z5 at MARQUION and 4 from Z6 at LE CATELET.

(g) *Power Buzzer and Wireless.* The close relation between the enemy's Power Buzzer Service and Field Wireless Service was again clearly shown this week. In the sector of the 111th division messages sent between the Field Stations at GOMIECOURT and PUISIEUX-au-MONT were intercepted by wireless. The same messages were found to have either originated from Power Buzzers or to have been retransmitted by Power Buzzers (according to the direction in which intended to be forwarded) and were also picked up by one of our Listening Sets. The Power Buzzer and Amplifier Set near PUISIEUX-au-MONT and the Wireless Station near PUISIEUX-au-MONT employed the same call signs in each case and were presumably together.

(h) *Messages.* 59 messages were intercepted during the week, as compared with 55 last week. 53 were in the sector BOU-ZINCOURT – BUCQUOY and 6 in the sector BUCQUOY – SCARPE.

SUMMARY

No change.

WO 157/165

6

Memorandum by Brigadier-General, Signal Officer in Chief, Mesopotamian Expeditionary Force, Baghdad, 15 February 1919

NOTES FOR MANUAL OF MILITARY INTELLIGENCE, CHAPTER VI.

SECTION (1)   FUNCTION OF WIRELESS IN WAR AND ITS VALUE AS A SOURCE OF INFORMATION

1. The function of Wireless Telegraphy in War from an Intelligence point of view cannot be discussed without first

referring to its primary employment, to supplement or replace the ordinary methods of line and visual telegraphy.

Wireless Stations with an Expeditionary Force may therefore be roughly divided into two groups:

(a) Field Stations.

(b) Observation Stations.

The former may be used for any of the following purposes:

Vide Signal Training Part VIII, 1913

(i)   For urgent traffic or to relieve pressure on the Land Line.

(ii) For communication between Higher formations and moving columns, such as Cavalry Brigades etc.

(iii) As an alternative Route in case of interruption of L/T or V/T.

2. This, of course, applies equally to the Enemy as to ourselves, and for this reason we have Observation Stations (b).

These are employed in collecting every possible scrap of information sent out by the enemy transmitting stations and are sub-divided into interception and direction finding stations.

3. This brings us to the question of the value of wireless telegraphy as a source of information, and will be considered under the two sub-headings of

(a) Interception Stations.

(b) Direction Findings Stations.

(a) INTERCEPTION STATIONS

(i)   These intercept all messages and conversations between enemy wireless stations, transmitting all matter so obtained *by the quickest and most secret route*, to the Intelligence Branch of the Formation under which the station is working. For this purpose it is highly desirable if not essential, that the Operators on these stations should be familiar with the languages used by the enemy operators. [See Section (iii)].

(ii) The importance of speed in transmission of intercepts

and strict secrecy as to their existence cannot be overrated.

(iii) Given intelligent and efficient operators it has been found possible to intercept messages from enemy headquarters, which, by reason of atmospheric disturbances and jamming, the enemy stations attached to their lower formations have been made unable to get without frequent repetition. It will be obvious that in this case speed in transmission to G.H.Q.[16] would enable "I" and "O" to deal with the intercept and thus, during operations, to anticipate the enemy's movements or intentions. It will also be obvious that unless strict secrecy is maintained, information gained in this way must lose much or all of its value.

In this connection it is suggested that Wireless Units employed for intelligence purposes should have no outward difference as to title from a Field Wireless Unit. The title of "Wireless Observation Group" make its purpose patent to anyone; thus adding to the difficulties of maintaining secrecy.

(iv) Another function of interception work is the scrutiny of logs with a view to ascertaining relative volume of traffic between individual enemy stations. By this means it is often possible to locate a formation headquarters.

(b) Closely allied to this last we have the work of *D.F. Stations*.

These are established on fixed base lines working in pairs or threes and by means of special apparatus (See Section 2) take compass bearings on enemy W/T signals. By cross bearing and intersection, stations can be located with a degree of accuracy depending on the delicacy of the instruments and the efficiency and intelligence of the personnel. This information, collated and compared with that obtained as noted in para 3a(iv) is often of assistance, not only in locating the position of enemy headquarters, but in determining its rank, i.e., whether Brigade, Division, Corps or Army.

SECTION (2) TECHNICAL APPARATUS FOR WIRELESS INTELLIGENCE

1. The most desirable features in a Wireless Receiver are sensitivity and selectivity and the ideal instrument would combine both qualities in the highest degree. As, however, general sensitivity over a wide range of wave lengths can only be obtained at the expense of selectivity one must concentrate on one or the other.[17] The latter quality is better for field station work and the former for intelligence work.

2. It will be seen therefore that the best instruments for observation work should combine maximum sensitivity with optimum selectivity.

3. The Signal Officer in Chief of a Force in the field is responsible for the supply and maintenance of all W/T as well as other Signal Service instruments and he will detail his Staff Officer for Wireless to ensure that the Observation Group are supplied with the latest suitable apparatus for their special purposes.

4. One of the duties of the Staff Officer for Wireless to the Signal Officer in Chief is to keep himself up to date in all the latest improvements in wireless telegraphy in order that the vitally important business of intercepting enemy W/T traffic shall be kept in a state of continually increasing efficiency; and it is the duty of Officers of Observation Groups to bring to his notice any suggestions regarding improvements to, or modifications of, the apparatus in use by their stations.

SECTION (3) TECHNICAL AND INTELLIGENCE PERSONNEL AND THEIR RELATIVE FUNCTIONS

1. The technical personnel for this work are drawn from Field Wireless Units. These are already highly trained as regards operating and technical knowledge, but officers and other ranks are selected for further instruction in observation work with regard to certain special qualifications or aptitudes.

2. OFFICERS. In addition to being experts in Wireless Theory and Practice, Officers for observation work must be first class operators and should know one or more foreign languages. On being selected for Observation Work they should be given some training in Cryptography.

3. OTHER RANKS. Those selected should have at least a colloquial knowledge of some foreign language, and should then be trained as Interpreter Operators in that language.

It is highly desirable that all operators should have a knowledge of the enemy language at least sufficient to translate any operators "Chat" that may pass between enemy stations. During the recent operations instances have occurred where enemy stations have stated in clear that they were going to work on an unusual wave length and send important messages. Owing to the fact that the Interception Station was some hundreds of miles distance (sic) from Headquarters, and that the N.C.O. in Charge did not know the language, the messages referred to were missed.

5. Officers with Wireless Observation Groups should work in the Intelligence Branch (see Section 5) as not only can the former frequently assist the latter in solving enemy ciphers etc., but information obtained from enemy intercepts will frequently be of assistance to the W.O.G. in identifying enemy stations. The more closely these two work together, the more mutual assistance they can give one another, and it would be well if selected intelligence officers were occasionally attached to W/T Units for instructions in the practical working of Wireless Telegraphy.

SECTION (5) THE DEDUCTION AND DISTRIBUTION OF INFORMATION

1. That obtained from W/T sources. Information obtained in this way may be divided under two headings:–
(a) That obtained from actual enemy messages intercepted which may be in clear requiring mere translation, if in a

foreign language, or they may be in code or cipher, requiring treatment by a cryptographic expert. All information under this heading must be passed to this officer, not only the actual messages, but all Operating signals and "chat" which may pass between enemy stations, as it may often happen that the key to a hitherto unsolvable cipher or code, or valuable information as to location or identification of enemy formations is obtained from any of the following:–

(i)   a carelessly written message.

(ii) incorrect procedure or coding by the operator.

(iii) local chat between stations.

(b) All other information which may (sic) collected by a W.O.G. i.e.:–

(i)   Location of enemy transmitting stations by means of Direction Finding Stations.

(ii) Allocation of Brigade, Division or other formation headquarters by means of combining (i) with statistical records as to volume of traffic passing between enemy stations. These records are compiled by the W.O.G. from study of the W/T Logs, not only of their own but those of Field Stations.[18]

(iii) Study of call signs, call changes, and systems, if any, by which calls are changed periodically. Types of stations employed, study and interpretation of enemy W/T procedure, distribution of wave lengths.

NAM 8312–69–10, Philip Leith-Ross Papers

7

Memorandum by General Staff (Intelligence), General Headquarters, 20 January 1919

Translation of a GERMAN document   SECRET

GERMAN WIRELESS INTELLIGENCE ORGANISATION REPORT ON BRITISH METH D (sic) OF CAMOUFLAGING SIGNAL TRAFFIC

In what way does the enemy try to hinder the exploitation of messages by camouflaging and improved traffic discipline, etc?[19]

Owing to the fact that the means of communication most commonly employed in the field, viz., telephone, wireless, and power buzzer, are liable to interception, it is necessary for us, as well as for the enemy, to take this circumstance into consideration and to reduce to a minimum the numbers and the bulk of messages which can be intercepted by the enemy and to hinder their exploitation. Although, as BRITISH prisoners have stated, no very great importance is attached to camouflage on quiet fronts,[20] the BRITISH are especially careful to prevent by various means an insight into their wireless, telephone and artillery system of communications when they are expecting an attack or are preparing one themselves.

1. *Traffic.* Every formation in line or in reserve requires a certain number of wireless, telephone and artillery stations, in order to transmit and receive messages within its own sector and to other formations. These stations are generally located near a headquarters, so that a close study of their traffic enables conclusions to be drawn regarding the strength and composition of the units concerned. This danger is primarily guarded against by the BRITISH by means of a signal traffic discipline (in certain cases, carried out in an exemplary manner), which imposes on the headquarters concerned, as well as on individuals, the utmost caution in the use of means of communication. This applies particularly to telephone and power buzzer communication. In the danger zone, i.e., within 3 kilometres of the front

line, where messages are liable to interception by the enemy, traffic is kept down to a minimum, and is controlled by minute traffic regulations. At every telephone station a notice is posted up which constantly reminds the personnel of the necessity for caution. Conversations are only allowed in the gravest emergencies and the most advanced power buzzer stations may only transmit in case of emergency, so that the amount of material intercepted is small, and this, in itself renders exploitation difficult.

In the case of wireless, the same object is achieved by the enemy by means of "silent days" frequently ordered on certain sectors, and on these silent days it is impossible for us to make any observations.

One of the commonest methods of camouflage is the change of station call signs. The more frequent such changes are, the more difficult it becomes to recognise the formations to which the stations belong. The call signs of telephone stations used formerly to show certain characteristic peculiarities, e.g., a typical series of call signs remained permanently in use for certain units, which naturally rendered the identification of units and call signs very much easier. At one time, call signs were arranged alphabetically from north to south along the BRITISH front.

It was not until September, 1917, that a reorganisation of the system of telephone call signs was introduced, which revealed a systematic attempt to place difficulties in our way. At present, station call signs are allotted to sectors, and are changed at irregular intervals. In addition, these are replaced during active operations by special station code calls which come into force when a special order is received.

In the case of wireless traffic, the measures of security of the BRITISH as regards call signs, showed no improvement until last year. Until the middle of 1917, changes of call signs were infrequent. Moreover, the BRITISH system of recognition letters (one letter for each Army) facilitated the recognition of the enemy's organisation. After the middle of June, 1917, *four* recognition letters were used instead of *one*, and changes of call signs took place about every three months. This change in the system itself rendered our exploitation considerably more difficult. If the BRITISH had not often been so careless in other respects, our knowledge of the enemy's order of battle would have been greatly reduced for, at any rate, a considerable time after the change of call signs.

It was not until July, 1918, that the BRITISH adopted the system of a daily change of call signs without any recognition letter, which has already been in use by ourselves and the FRENCH for a long time, and this accentuated in a very marked degree the difficulty of exploitation. For instance, if on any day, tactical formations are located with stations situated at definite places, it is in itself a difficult matter to confirm their presence on the following day, unless the stations (with changed call signs) are located at the same point as on the previous day.

Theoretically, every change of call signs can only fulfil its object entirely if, as has already been suggested, carelessness in other respects does not frustrate the purpose in view. If a change of call signs is to serve the purpose of camouflage, stations must not betray the fact day by day that they belong to one and the same tactical formation by means of the contents of their messages, even though they change their call signs every day.

Another method of camouflage which is frequently employed is an increase in the number of call signs, sometimes quite sudden, which prevents us for a time from knowing the number of stations active and consequently the number and strength of the corresponding formations. For instance, several call signs may be allotted to a station, to be used indiscriminately. This number varies; in general, each station has 3 or 4 call signs, while certain artillery stations have been known to use as many as six. As each of these call signs is equally valid, the impression produced is that of an increase in the enemy's strength. This deception must be regarded as successful unless accurate bearings are quickly obtained which enable the various call signs to be identified as belonging to a single station, or unless the enemy frustrates his own purpose by carelessness in the text of the messages. This general change of call signs in the middle of

June, 1917, caused difficulties in exploitation particularly in its early stages, as the principal call signs were not yet known. It was only by degrees that we were able to identify the enemy's organisation. This was partly due to the BRITISH themselves, as the use of the additional call signs was gradually dispensed with, for the sake of convenience, and each station once more worked mainly with a single call sign.

The possibility of counteracting or minimizing the effect of the change of call signs and of the use of multiple call signs in the case of a *single* station depends mainly on obtaining good bearings on the stations. Knowing this fact the enemy makes use of technical methods for his purpose. He frequently uses directional or mobile aerials. The electric waves which, in ordinary circumstances, would be propagated uniformly in all directions, are thus concentrated in a particular direction, which, as far as possible, is made parallel with the front, because this is the direction in which it is most difficult for us to intercept. The enemy thus succeeds in making our bearings very inaccurate, and this again makes the identification of call signs of the corresponding formations considerably more difficult.[21]

Pecularities in transmission, due partly to the apparatus and partly to the operating, which can also give some indication enabling the transmitting station to be recognised, are counteracted and rendered harmless by frequent changes in apparatus and reliefs of personnel.

The enemy obscures the boundaries between formations by very lively lateral communication. He makes Corps stations call up divisions which do not belong to them, or causes messages to be exchanged between formations of the same category not belonging to the same higher formation. This greatly obscures the picture of the enemy's order of battle which would be obtained if traffic were perfectly regular.

It has not yet been possible to ascertain whether the BRITISH attempt to maintain dummy traffic,[22] by making wireless stations work as though organised in tactical formations, although there are no troops present; this was a device which we used before our great ITALIAN offensive in the TYROL in October, 1917, and before the offensive in March, 1918, on the Western Front, when a whole GERMAN Army was impersonated successfully on the FRENCH front.

2.   Contents of messages. The best camouflage of all would be not to use wireless or telephone at all. As it is naturally impossible in practice to approach this ideal, ways and means must be devised to protect the text of the messages (which should be as scanty as possible) from exploitation. In the turmoil of battle, when urgency of transmission takes precedence of fear of interception, it is inevitable that the contents of wireless or power buzzer messages will contain indications which will afford the enemy valuable information regarding the tactical situation, the order of battle, or other important matters. But such faults occur even on quiet fronts, mainly owing to carelessness or to save trouble. This is well known to the enemy, and various counter-measures are adopted.

The necessity of enciphering the text of messages is an indispensable measure of security, which even the easy-going BRITISH only neglect in emergencies. Any method of enciphering, even though it has already been solved by the enemy, will at any rate delay the exploitation, owing to the necessity for deciphering. The enemy is, however, not content with this, but employs additional measures of precaution.

Tactical formations are not named in clear, but are indicated by means of code names. The nature of these code names has undergone many modifications in course of time. The abbreviated code names, now no longer used by the BRITISH, were comparatively simple and obvious. The BRITISH are fond of abbreviations for their own sake, particularly in telegrams, and more especially for the names of units, e.g., WF = WELSH Fusiliers, YLI = YORKSHIRE Light Infantry, ES = East SURREY, are abbreviated code names which frequently occurred (particularly in power buzzer traffic), and consist merely of the initials of the various words. This type of abbreviated code name has not been observed since about the autumn of 1917. It was replaced by an equally simple system in which the letter Y stood for a division and Z for a brigade, while the letters of the alphabet in their normal sequence represented the numbers of formations from 1 to 25 (e.g. 6th Div = YF; 20th Div = YT; 17th Brigade = ZQ). In the case of formations with numbers higher than 25, the 2 digits were each replaced by letters, (e.g. 48th Div = YDH), and in the case of numbers of three digits, the first two digits were taken together and the last separately, (e.g. 121st Brigade = ZIA). In the case of Colonial formations, (AUSTRALIANS and CANADIANS), the code name was preceded by the letter A(AUS-TRALIAN) or C(CANADIAN); only one characteristic form, NZ, has been observed in the case of the NEW ZEALANDERS (E.g. AZB = 2nd AUSTRALIAN Brigade, CYD = 4th CANADIAN Division, NZY = NEW ZEALAND Division. Formations in the line were distinguished from troops in back areas by the letter A(Advanced) and R(Rear) respectively. A modification of this system was in use for designating the AUSTRALIAN and CANA-DIAN Corps, the word Corps being replaced by the letter O (e.g. AUO = AUSTRALIAN Corps, CAO = CANADIAN Corps).

In addition to the code abbreviations, the BRITISH also used code names for formations. Until about the end of April, 1918, these were very varied. It was possible to observe complete series, some allotted permanently to sectors and others to formations, which were seldom changed. For instance, divisions designated all the headquarters of the formations and units under them by the names of animals, colours, flowers, natural phenomena, etc. In other formations, the code names for the various units all began with the same letter. The BRITISH obviously thought that this system of code names was difficult to recognise, as it was used for a considerable time. It was only replaced in May, 1918, by a new so-called 4 letter call system, which was first introduced in the BRITISH First Army, and is now in use on the whole BRITISH front. After two months of careful observation, we succeeded in analysing almost completely the structure and the highly systematic application of this system of code names, which changed twice monthly, as well as the allocation of code names to tactical formations; it is at present, therefore, possible to regard the purpose of these 4 letter calls as frustrated. (For details, compare the "Special Report on the 4 letter Calls" attached to the report on the "Exploitation of Wireless Messages").

No case has yet been observed of the BRITISH using wireless in order to give us a false impression of the tactical situation by means of the contents of messages. Prisoners have stated that there is no intelligent appreciation of wireless telegraphy on the BRITISH side, and that it is therefore neglected.[23]

WO 170/4268

III
Aircraft Intelligence

These documents deal with a complete branch of signals intelligence, which was closely allied to traffic analysis. Document One discusses how by late 1916 information on the redeployment of individual spotting aircraft could indicate the movement of the enemy's artillery formations – and hence the latter's intentions, perceptions and centres of strength. This source of intelligence retained such power until 1918 when, as Document Six demonstrates, that declined sharply. Documents One, Three and Five of Chapter Two illuminate the procedures by which such intelligence was collected and interpreted. Documents Two, Three and Four of this chapter trace the effective and highly coordinated fashion by which the aircraft wireless intelligence service collected and distributed information on enemy artillery bombardments. Along with the home air defence command in London which dealt with enemy bombing raids on the United Kingdom, this was the most sophisticated command, control, communication and intelligence system created by any armed force during the First World War. It could direct aircraft to strike with an extraordinary degree of precision and speed. It was strikingly similar to the procedures used for tactical and strategic air defence by both Britain and Germany during the Second World War. These reports and Document Five show how this material guided RFC attacks on enemy spotting flights, and thus disrupted the enemy's power in the struggle of attrition. Document Six compares German and British approaches to the security of the radio traffic of their air forces in 1918. While the report may exaggerate the superiority of German practices – the study rested largely on guesswork and was intended to frighten the Royal Air Force into improving its security – its deductions in this regard might well have been correct. In any case, its discussion of the state and techniques of signals security is illuminating.

I

Memoranda by J.F. Tuohy for Officer Commanding, Wireless, sent to Brigadier-General, General Staff, Royal Flying Corps, December 1916 to February 1917

Brigadier-General
General Staff
Royal Flying Corps.

In the past week, German artillery machines with the calls "LC" and "LH" have recommenced work in Area 6Z about opposite ARMENTIERES (straight over the line separating Areas 6Z and 2A should find them best). "LC" has been up on three occasions since the 27th ult. "L" calls previously worked in this area prior to the SOMME offensive, and their return may signify the first withdrawal of artillery machines from the battle zone.

Intelligence	J.F. Tuohy
Wireless HQ.	2nd Lieut. I.C.
5/12/16	

Brigadier-General	I/W.104.
General Staff	
R.F.C.	

1. There has been a very considerable increase in hostile artillery aeroplane work around YPRES. Prior to the 23rd inst., the following calls were being taken in Areas 1 and 6:–

LN   RA   MA
LA
LB
LC

During the past 48 hours, the following have been located in the areas in question:–

DA	RA	MA	LC
DB	RB		LE
DC	RC		LN
DK			LK
DM?			LP
			LR?
			LI
			LB
			LD

It is probable that the "D" series represents the Artillery Flight which recently fell out in the neighbourhood of BAPAUME. The new "D" planes at YPRES are using a particular code closing signal previously peculiar to the "D" series at BAPAUME.

2.   On the SOMME, about 10 calls less are being taken each day than at the period of maximum activity in Mid November.

3.   Interception of the enemy's wireless during the past two days suggests that the strength of at least 1 Artillery Flight have ceased to work on the SOMME, and that many of these machines are probably now in the YPRES salient.

Wireless (Iz),[1]   J.F. Tuohy

G.H.Q. 24/1/17.   Lieut., I.C.,

                                                  for O.C. Wireless.

                                  COPY

Brigadier-General   I/W.135.

General Staff

R.F.C.

    Reference this office I/W.104 of 24–1–17, para. 3, the following has been received from Intelligence A, G.H.Q.:–

    "The 227th and 257th Artillery Flights were transferred in December from the SOMME Area to LORRAINE".

During the opening three weeks of this year, there was practically no aeroplane registration done by the enemy, so that the withdrawal of these two flights became known through wireless interception almost on the first day.

It was, however, suggested that some of these machines has gone (sic) to YPRES, in view of the increased activity there.

Wireless (Iz),   (Signed) J.F. Tuohy,
G.H.Q. 7–2–17.   2nd Lieut. I.C.,
                                          for O.C. Wireless.

AIR 1/996

2
Memorandum from General Headquarters to British Armies in France and Flanders, March 1917

SECRET   O.B./1846.
First Army,
Second Army,
Third Army,
Fourth Army,
Fifth Army.

Revised instructions dealing with the methods of reporting the movements of hostile aircraft are issued herewith.

These instructions cancel those issued under G.H.Q. letter No. O.B./1846 of the 2nd November, 1916.

General Headquarters   K. Wigram, B.G. for
8th March, 1917.   Lieutenant-General,
                                          C.G.S.

Copies to:–
G.S.O.(a).,
     "I".,
A.G.,
Q.M.G.,
R.F.C.,
A.A.,
D.A.S.,
O.C.Wireless,
G.O.C., L.of C.Area.[2]

SECRET   O.B./1846.

WIRELESS INTELLIGENCE OF HOSTILE AIRCRAFT

1. *Compass Stations*

Compass stations for intercepting wireless from hostile aeroplanes are in existence at HONDSCHOOTE, ABEELE, CHOCQUES, TINQUES COURCELETTES ("and BEAUQUESNE", deleted), and MONS-EN-CHAUSSEE, ("at QUERRIEU. The last is moving shortly to WARFUSEE. It is proposed to place a sixth station in the Belgian Area" – deleted)

Trained observers are attached to each Station.

These Stations –

(a) Pick up calls from hostile aircraft using wireless.

(b) Watch for hostile aircraft which may have crossed the front line.

Compass Stations are in direct telegraphic communication with each other and are in direct telephonic communication with the Army Wing R.F.C. in their own Army Area.

2. *Forward ground stations*

Two forward ground stations are established in each Army Area.

These Stations –

(a) Receive by telephone from the compass stations reports of hostile machines using wireless.

(b) Indicate by ground signals to any of our fighting machines passing over them the area in which a hostile machine is reported.

The ground stations are in telephonic communication with their compass station over the Anti-Aircraft telephonic system.

The ground signal consists of a circle of 16 yards inside and 17 yards outside diameter displayed permanently, alongside which the number of the area in which the machine is working is put out when a hostile aeroplane is reported by the compass station (see para. 3).

3. *Method of working in case of hostile machines using wireless*

Hostile flights normally use two-letter calls. The first letter, which is constant, is believed to correspond to an Artillery Area on the enemy's side of the line, usually served by one flight: the second denotes the particular wireless ground station in that area.

A chart showing the areas in which hostile flights using any particular "flight call" normally work is kept at compass stations. This chart is amended from time to time as flights change their location or alter their calls.

In addition, maps are provided on which the front has been divided into certain sectors and areas. The sectors on the enemy's side of the line are indicated by Roman numerals, the areas on our side of the line being indicated by letters of the alphabet. Each sector on the enemy's side of the line is divided into two halves, the northern one lettered A and the southern Z: thus sector I includes IA and IZ. In addition, certain areas on the L. of C. have been allotted letters.

Procedure

(i)   A *Compass station* overhearing a hostile machine using wireless will telephone direct to the Army Wing and to the Anti-Aircraft Exchange concerned, giving the number of the sector in which the hostile machine is working. Forward Ground Stations are warned by the Anti-Aircraft Exchange. If more than one machine is working in the sector, the number of machines will be added.

(ii) *Army Wings* will inform Squadrons by telephone.

(iii) On receipt of the information mentioned in (i) above, forward ground stations will put out the number of the sector in Roman numerals alongside their circular signal (see para. 2 above).

N.B. – Compass stations will not send warning messages on the report of hostile aircraft by forward ground stations, as this would usually result in fruitless attempts to engage machines crossing the lines for a short time only. Hostile machines working for any time will be located by the compass stations.

4.   *Method of working in case of machines crossing our lines.*

(a)   For the purpose of the location of hostile aircraft on our side of the line, the area between the compass stations and the trenches and certain areas on the L. and C. have been assigned letters as shown on the map issued.

The trained observers at the compass station will keep a constant look-out for hostile aircraft crossing our lines to any considerable distance.

On a hostile machine or machines being seen, compass stations will at once inform the Army Wing or Wings concerned by telephone. The message will be in the following form:–

(i)   Number of machines seen.

(ii) Area in which seen: A, B, C, etc.

(iii) Direction in which flying: N, S, E, W, NE, SE, NW, SW.

(iv) Time seen.

Should six or more hostile machines be reported H.Q., R.F.C. and 9th Wing, R.F.C. will also be informed.

(b) On a hostile machine being sighted by the L. of C. Anti-Aircraft Defences, a telephone or telegraph report will be despatched to the compass station at BEAUQUESNE giving –

(i)   Number of machines seen.

(ii) Area in which seen.

(iii) Direction in which flying.

(iv) Time seen.

If this message emanated from any of the L. of C. areas marked on the map, BEAUQUESNE compass station will inform the Army Wing or Wings concerned through their compass station as in (a) above, repeating the message to H.Q. R.F.C. and 9th Wing, R.F.C. if six or more hostile machines are reported.

If the message emanated from a place not in any lettered area, such as ROUXMESNIL, ROUEN, HAVRE, or DUNKIRK, the BEAUQUESNE compass station will not inform other compass stations or Army Wings, but will telephone at once to H.Q. R.F.C. who will be responsible for all further action both as regards transmitting information and issuing any necessary orders to R.F.C. units.

AIR 1/996

3

Memorandum by Brigadier-General, General Staff for Lieutenant-General, Chief of the General Staff from Advanced G.H.Q., 22 June 1917

X CO-OPERATION OF WIRELESS INTELLIGENCE, A.A., R.F.C.

1. *Locations*

The compass stations working on 2nd Army front are located as under:–

(i) ABEELE   – Northern Compass Station – P.A.B.
(ii) VIEUX BERQUIN – Southern   "   "   – P.A.Y.

The intercepting station is located at ABEELE and with the compass station constitutes the control station.

These stations are so located that a good bisection can be obtained on any machine on the Army front.

2. *Communications*

The main communications concerned are:–

(i) The 2nd Army R.F.C. system. This system is for the exclusive use of the R.F.C.

(ii) The 2nd Army A.A. trunk. This system is used by A.A., Balloons, Field Survey Company.

(iii) Wireless Intelligence system.

     A. *Inter-communication between Compass Stations.*
     Southern Compass Station is connected to control station by a sounder line for exclusive use of Compass stations through Central (LOCRE) A.A. trunk Exchange.

     B. *Communication between Control Station, R.F.C., A.A.*
     Control station is connected with XI Wing through Central (ST. SYLVESTRE CAPELLE) R.F.C. Exchange.

     Priority calls are used and the maximum time taken between control station and XI Wing up to the present is 2 minutes.

Control station is connected to A.A. batteries through Central (LOCRE) A.A. Exchange.

A system of preference calls has been arranged and the average time taken for control station to get through to A.A. batteries is 1–2 minutes.

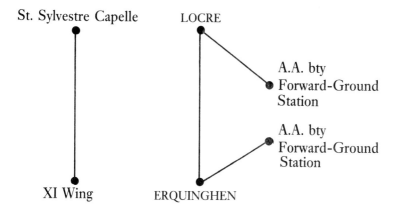

St. Sylvestre Capelle   LOCRE

A.A. bty Forward-Ground Station

A.A. bty Forward-Ground Station

XI Wing   ERQUINGHEN

III. PROCEDURE

A. *Compass Station*

A "Black List" of hostile Artillery calls is published by Aeroplane Wireless Intelligence nightly, which includes:–

(i) All machines that carried out successful shoots during previous day.

(ii) All machines that habitually carry out successful shoots. Intersections on hostile machines are termed X, Y, Z, according to their accuracy – Z being the most accurate.

Warning is sent to the 11th Wing of all black listed calls on which a Y or Z bearing is obtained, and on all other calls which settle down to shoot and on which a Z bearing is obtained.

When a hostile machine is located the Compass Stations determine the limits of its flight and the Control station informs the A.A. battery concerned. If A.A. battery can see the machine they inform the control station (i) the height at which it is working (ii) whether any hostile fighting machines are in the immediate vicinity.

The control station then gives 11th Wing complete information of the machine.

B. *Anti-Aircraft*

Two forward ground stations are located with A.A. batteries at 28 N 14 b and 28 T 21 b respectively, and are manned and maintained by them.

When an A.A. battery sees a hostile artillery machine working – whether warning has been sent by control station or not – they put out ground signals as under. If warning is received from control station but A.A. are unable to see the machine no signals are put out.

The signals used consist of the following:–
(i)   A white circle 17 yards in diameter.
(ii) A white arrow 17 yds long and 3 ft.6″ wide.
(iii) A series of white strips 10 yds long and 3 ft.6″ wide.

The arrow is laid across the circle and gives direction of hostile machine.

The white strips indicate height – each strip signifying 2000 feet.

In all cases an overestimate rather than an underestimate of height is given. Thus if a machine if flying at 9000 feet 5 white strips are put out.

The strips are put 5 yards apart from each other and at least 10 yards from the outside of the circle.

These signals are left out only as long as A.A. can see the machine.

C. *R.F.C.*

A number of machines are kept on the ground standing by for compass station warnings, on receipt of which sufficient to deal with the situation go up. If they fail to see the hostile machine they patrol the locality for 20 minutes to half an hour and then return.

VIII.   SPEED OF WARNING

The average time that elapses between a hostile machine starting work and our machines leaving the ground is 30–40 minutes. This is made up as follows:–

Machine starts work Y or Z bearing obtained	} 20–30 minutes.
Bearing obtained Information received from A.A.	} 5 minutes.
Information received from AA. XI Wing warned	} 1–2 minutes.
XI Wing warned Machines leave ground	} 5 minutes.

First Army (Intelligence).   Ie/1632.
Second "   "
Third   "   "
Fourth "   "
Fifth   "   "
XV Corps.
H.Q., R.F.C.

1.   In view of the results already being obtained, and the immediate prospect of better, it is necessary to impress on all concerned that secrecy is absolutely essential in connection with the Wireless Intelligence system.

2.   It may be pointed out that the enemy, should he become further suspicious, has it in his power, by taking technical measures only, considerably to impair our results.

3.   No document, map, or anything bearing on the subject will be taken beyond Divisional Headquarters, whilst only such officers as are directly involved should be kept acquainted with developments. It is particularly desirable to warn wireless operators, etc., who may be proceeding on leave.

AIR 1/996

4

Memorandum by General Staff (Intelligence), General Headquarters, 18 May 1917

SECRET   Ia/22963.
INTELLIGENCE SYSTEM FOR THE INTERCEPTION AND COL-
LATION OF THE ENEMY'S AEROPLANE WIRELESS MESSAGES

1. **Intelligence Stations.** One "aeroplane intercepting station" and two "aeroplane compass stations" (see O.B. 1846 dated May 1917) are allotted to each Army. The necessary communications between these stations are notified in O.B. 1846. The location of these stations will be for Armies to decide, but the aeroplane intercepting station should be with one of the compasses, this forming the "Control Post" of the Army. The above stations will be employed exclusively on interception and compass work relating to hostile aeroplanes.

2. **Duties of Intelligence Officers**
(a) The Intelligence Officer attached to Army H.Q. for aeroplane wireless purposes will be responsible to the General Staff, Intelligence, of the Army for the proper working of the system, as briefly outlined below, and in O.B. 1816 of /5/17, and for the collation and circulation of all information derived from the study of the enemy's methods.
(b) Intelligence Officers, Corps Heavy Artillery, will make "shelling connections" between the local call signals and the actual shelling. They will be issued with all known particulars of the hostile call signals in their area. They will continue to prepare a weekly report on the form shown in Appendix C. of Ia/22963 of 3/12/16.

3. **Objects.** The principal objects in view are:–
(a) The collection of intelligence regarding the movements and groupings of the enemy's heavy artillery and of his artillery flights;
(b) The rapid dissemination of information available, so as to assist the R.F.C. and the artillery in taking counter-

measures to prevent the enemy registering by means of aeroplanes;

(c) The warning of batteries and other localities when they are about to be shelled.

It will be found of practical value to maintain a "black list" of the most active calls. The Aeroplane Wireless Intelligence Officer will keep up this list, which should be constantly revised and should comprise all the most active groups on the Army front.

4. **Method of Work.** The whole of the system will be centralized at Army Headquarters. The two Army compass stations will work together and independently of all other compasses in the neighbouring Armies. Compass areas will be confined to the Army front, the object being to obtain immediate intersections on any hostile artillery machines as they commence registration on the Army front. It should be possible for the compass stations to obtain simultaneous cross bearings on the same aeroplane. These intersections should be plotted at the control post in each Army throughout the whole day, so that they will represent the situation on that Army front at any time at which information is required.

5. **Procedure at the compass station.** As soon as a hostile aeroplane is located, the intercepting station should be referred to in order to ascertain whether it is ranging or not. If it is not ranging, no further action is necessary. If it is ranging and is on the "black list," the R.F.C. and the Corps Heavy Artillery on whose front the hostile machine is flying should be warned at once.

The Corps Heavy Artillery require warnings of aeroplanes duly located on their front, but not on the "black list." The R.F.C. will only need information of duly "black-listed" calls.

The Corps Heavy Artillery will give all necessary warning to observation posts, balloons and sound rangers.

Warnings to batteries and other positions about to be shelled should be arranged by the Army.

All wireless signals intercepted during the day will be entered as hitherto, on the special form shown in Appendix B of Ia/22963 of 3/12/16. Fair copies of these forms will be made out by the operator, each call signal being allotted a separate sheet, on which will be entered all the signals intercepted in connection with that call signal. One of these fair copies will be forwarded each evening to the Intelligence Officer attached to each Corps Heavy Artillery Headquarters in the Army; one copy each will also be sent to the Army Aeroplane Wireless Intelligence Officer and G.H.Q., Intelligence (E).

The following returns will be submitted by all Armies:–

(a) *Weekly.* To G.H.Q. and to such officers within the Army as the General Staff, Intelligence, of the Army may decide. Intelligence summary of general activity, Diagram and graph showing activity of wireless aeroplanes.

(b) *Daily.* A daily telegraphic report made up to noon and to 9 p.m. will be sent to G.H.Q., Intelligence (E).

Experience has shown that the following officers within the Army require wireless information:–

> General Staff, Intelligence,
> M.G.R.A.,[3]
> R.F.C. (Brigade and Army Wing),
> Corps Heavy Artillery,
> Anti-Aircraft H.Q.,
> G.S. Intelligence of Corps.

6. **Change of site.** – Recent events have demonstrated that an aeroplane wireless intelligence system is of most value during an advance. Armies should make the necessary arrangements for changing the positions of the compass stations when necessary.

AIR 1/996

5

Memorandum by Colonel W.F.E. Newbigging, D.D. Signals, Third Army, 26 May 1918

D. Signals.   N.4/487.

Reference D.Sigs./4418/1 dated 22/5/16.

1.   The system of dealing with enemy aircraft which attempt to range by means of wireless is as follows:–

Two aeroplane compasses are employed connected by a sounder circuit.

The office of the wireless and Aeroplane Wireless Intelligence Officers, one of the compasses, and the aeroplane intercept station are grouped together.

Immediately an enemy ranging machine is located the 3rd Squadron R.A.F. is warned. A direct telephone circuit is provided to the Squadron for this purpose.

The 3rd Squadron has six machines continually standing by for these warnings. 2, 3 or 6 machines are employed for one patrol, the number being dependent on whether the A.A. report protecting scouts with the enemy ranging machine or not.

The patrols average three minutes in leaving the ground after the warning has been received.

After the 3rd Squadron R.A.F. has been warned the Corps A.A. concerned is asked for the height of the enemy machine. This information is passed immediately to the 3rd Squadron R.A.F.

If the patrol has already left the ground but is still gaining height over the aerodrome the height is given them by means of a code of coloured Very lights. If the patrol has left the vicinity of the aerodrome they obtain the information in the same manner from the Observation Group. All patrols fly over the Observation Group on their way to the line for this purpose. A spotter is kept at the Observation Group whose duty it is to recognise the patrol, and prevent inconvenience being caused by signals being given to other patrols.

2.   A sketch of the communications is attached. The Sounder

circuit between two compasses is super-imposed on the telephone circuit.

3. The following results have been obtained during the last fortnight:–

Enemy machines driven down in flames	3
″ ″ ″ ″ out of control	3
″ ″ ″ ″ under control	1
Enemy machines crashed	1
Enemy machines driven east	28

All the above can be definitely verified by wireless evidence as having been ranging machines, and do not include other machines which have been met by the patrol and engaged by them.

Specimen daily reports are attached.

4. The success may be chiefly ascribed to:–
(i) The fact that one Squadron R.A.F. is detailed purposely specially for this work, and the keenness of the C.O. and the officers of this particular Squadron.
(ii) The close co-operation between the Squadron and the Observation Group. The pilots have the greatest confidence in the locations and have even gone out on a single bearing with successful results. The pilots and the officers of the Intelligence Group visit each other and discuss the work. The patrols always return over the Group after a successful patrol, and show that they have been successful by dipping as they pass. This all helps to keep up the enthusiasm of both sides.
(iii) The excellent communications which have been provided. Without these it would be quite impossible to locate the enemy machines, warn the Squadron, and obtain the heights from the Corps A.A. with the requisite speed. Two very valuable features are the direct line to the Squadron and the sounder circuit between the Compass Stations. The latter compels businesslike methods in obtaining locations by the prevention of useless talk over the telephone, and enables a record of the day's work to be kept.

(iv) The fact that the Wireless Intelligence Officer and the Aeroplane Wireless Intelligence Officer both live on the spot, and one or the other is always on duty to control the working of the compass and intercept stations.

They have local telephones for this purpose.

AIR 1/966

6

Memorandum sent by B.W. Bowdler to   Goldsmith, 18 October 1918

GENERAL HEADQUARTERS
BRITISH ARMIES IN FRANCE.

My dear Goldsmith,

The attached is a screed on aeroplane wireless intelligence and security, which your B.G.G.S.[4] said he would like to have, when I saw him at Fosseux the other day, so will you please give it to him with this explanation.

It does not pretend to be exhaustive, but gives some idea of the necessity for and the employment of a security officer, which was the question under consideration.

Please let me know if this is what was wanted or whether we can make any points clearer.

Yours ever
B.W. Bowdler

Ie/6045

SUMMARY OF INFORMATION REGARDING
THE CONTROL OF THE GERMAN AEROPLANE WIRELESS SER-
VICE AND ITS APPLICATION TO OUR OWN METHODS

1. *General*

Arguments for the formation of an R.A.F. Security Section can be based on:–

(a) Knowledge of the information *obtained by us* from the German aviation service.

(b) Knowledge of the extent of the German organization for *obtaining* information *from us*.

(c) Captured documents showing what information is *obtained from us*, by the enemy.

(d) Measures taken by the enemy to *prevent* information being *obtained by us*.

Such evidence as we possess is given under these headings in paras. 2 to 5. All information, which does not appear to be definite, is excluded.

Indefinite evidence is, however, the most valuable of all. For instance, it is clear that any changes in the German aeroplane wireless system, if it is in the direction of further complications, must be dictated by a desire to make the system more difficult for *us* to work out. In other words, any complication which is introduced must be a hindrance to German operations, and the introduction of these complications must, therefore, be due solely to a desire to defeat our Intelligence Service. Further, a change in the direction of greater complication (for instance, by the introduction of a system of changing call signs at frequent intervals), means that the enemy is alive to the dangers of the old system and that, almost certainly, his realization of the dangers of the old system is due to information obtained from a study of the Allied systems.

2. *Information obtained by us from a study of the German Aviation Service.*

The information obtainable by us from the German Aeroplane Wireless System, may be classified under the following headings:–

(a) *Activity*

(Amount of registration, contact patrol and artillery aeroplane work, in various sectors.)

Admittedly, a study of the German wireless activity and its distribution does not, at present, give us direct information as to the enemy's intentions.[5] It does, however, give us information regarding the German general camouflage scheme. If, either by comparison with other sources of information, or by comparison with the enemy's wireless procedure in other directions, discrepancies appear, an opportunity is afforded of penetrating his general camouflage system. This camouflage, being carefully controlled and co-ordinated from German General Headquarters, results of far-reaching consequence can be expected, if it can be thus penetrated. The information obtained by us is, however, decreasing, in spite of the more extensive use of wireless by the enemy, on account of the improvements in the German methods of wireless working during the last 9 months.

(b) *Distribution of flights using wireless.*

Information may be obtained by observation of observers' peculiarities in signalling, combined with the call signs used by observers and ground stations.

Information is only obtained from this source after great labour. The amount of information obtainable depends on:–

(i) The degree of uniformity of training of observers.

(ii) The frequency of change of the ground station and aerodrome call signs.

(iii) Other points which may assist in grouping the observers in their proper squadrons, e.g., use of wireless over the aerodrome, use of wireless from ground stations to the aeroplane, allotment of wavelengths, etc.

It is desirable to point out that, though information is only obtained after great labour, *it cannot be entirely hidden*, except by attention to the points (i) to (iii) above.

(c) *Distribution of flights using distinctive methods of wireless working*

Under this heading may be classed aeroplanes with receiving apparatus, for use with super-heavy artillery, with wireless telephone, with C.W.,[6] etc.

The movements of flights equipped in a distinctive

manner are more easily followed than those of the majority of flights, because it is easy to concentrate attention on these flights. As the distinctive equipment is designed for use in a distinctive manner, presumably the squadrons so equipped are more suitable for their purpose than others not so equipped. They are therefore likely to be employed in major operations.

(Before the German attack on the 21st March, the flights using wireless receiving apparatus (for use with super-heavy guns) were chiefly concentrated in the LILLE and CAMBRAI – ST. QUENTIN areas).[7]

(d) The use of wireless for reporting the presence of hostile aircraft, in certain sectors *only*, is again a source of danger.

(e) Of peculiar importance is the control of all practice in co-operation between infantry and contact patrol, or artillery aeroplanes. These practice messages can be intercepted at a great distance and the stations roughly located. These locations, unless great care is exercised, may indicate the sector of attack.

Similarly, practice by a flight new to a sector, particularly practice in the neighbourhood of a new aerodrome, may indicate the arrival of the new flight in that sector, before its appearance in the front line. Similar information may also be given away by the use of a faulty call sign system, or a bad system of allotment of wave lengths, or mention of officers' names and nicknames.

(f) *Information from messages.*
(Map squares and targets about to be shelled.)
The information contained in short wireless messages sent by the aeroplane are of value, both for warning areas about to be shelled, and occasionally, for information of general value regarding the attitude of the enemy, i.e., whether this attitude is defensive, or offensive, in given sectors.

From our experience of the German aeroplane wireless system, it is perfectly clear that the intentions of the Higher Command have been expressed in the various ways enumerated above; it is therefore possible for the Germans to determine the intentions of our Higher Command by a proper study and correct interpretation of our aeroplane wireless activity, especially if the activity is not camouflaged or hidden in any manner.

3. *The German Organization for obtaining information from our aeroplane wireless activity.**
* See S.S.713, "The German Wireless System", para. 58.
Our knowledge of the German Ie organization is necessarily very incomplete, but it is probable that particular intercepting and compass stations are not allotted definitely for aeroplane or for field station work, as are our stations.

(a) *Compass stations.* Of these, there are two for each Army and one for each Corps. (See Appendix 11 to S.S. 626, "The Signal Service", Part 9 of the Manual of Position Warfare for all Arms.) These compass stations "take bearings on small wireless stations *and aircraft*".

Captured instructions, issued by the Sixth German Army on 27.7.16, give the following details regarding the aeroplane wireless intelligence system in use at that date:–

"There are two aeroplane intercepting stations in the Army, each furnished with transmitting apparatus for purposes of jamming. A senior artillery officer, especially nominated, decides for each jamming station whether it is more important to jam the hostile machine, and thereby interfere with German work as well, or whether jamming shall be disallowed."

"The results of all important observations of hostile squadrons (zones of activity, changes of position, disappearances and reappearances, systematic aeroplane registration of certain parts of the front) will be reported to Army Headquarters."

"The Staff Officer for Aviation, Sixth Army, will supply Wireless Headquarters with the necessary material for taking advantage of aeroplane wireless messages ("warning" maps, codes, etc.) . . . As several minutes elapse between the indication of the target and the commencement of registration, the warnings can be given in good time – as has been proved by experience."

"Warning of impending hostile bombardments will be sent by the jamming station, direct by wire, to the Artillery Commander of the Corps in whose area the target lies."

The organization in Nov., 1917, was controlled by Corps, the Corps wireless station ("Gruppen-Funkenstation") being used for the interception of our aeroplane messages. When this station intercepted an aeroplane message mentioning a known target, the artillery commander and the observation section of the sector concerned were warned by "priority" telephone.

The Artillery Commander of the sector and the unit mentioned above rendered reports to the Corps daily, before 11 p.m., stating:–

(i)   If the warning had been followed by shelling within an hour, and the exact time at which the target was engaged.

(ii) In case the fire had not been directed on the target indicated, the exact position of the target which was engaged.

(iii) The compass bearing of the hostile battery, its calibre, and the number of rounds fired.

Units which had been engaged with aeroplane observation, and had not received warning of the bombardment by telephone, notified the Corps immediately.

(For further information, see Appendix I.)

(b) *Intercepting stations.* In addition to the Army intercepting stations, each Corps has at least one intercepting station (probably more), and in addition, some of the divisional stations are used for the interception of British wireless traffic.

The following extract is from a schedule headed "Duties of an O.C. *Divisional* Wireless Detachment", issued by the War Ministry as far back as March, 1917:–

"(b) Observation of the enemy's aeroplane wireless and warnings".

In particular, there is definite evidence that the results obtained by the Group Wireless Detachment (c.f., the old "Flieger-Storer") are passed to a Corps Exploitation Centre ("Auswertungsstelle"), where information is also collected from listening sets, sound rangers and flash spotters.

4. *Information obtained by the enemy from the wireless system of our Air Force.*

(a) Our knowledge of this information is derived chiefly from captured documents. Below are given a few extracts from recent German Intelligence Summaries. (In this connection, S.S.582 (Weekly Intelligence Summary of the Fourth German Army) should be consulted):–

1. Genl.Kdo. XI A.K. Abtg. IId. Gruppen-bildstelle III. No. 1462. 5.6.18.

"Aeroplane wireless activity was again lively. *In addition to English,* 3 French aeroplane observers were heard registering".

2. Genl.Kdo. XI A.K. Abtg. IId. Gruppen-bildstelle III. No. 1469. 7.6.18.

"The presence of the 37th French and 3rd Australian Divisions can be regarded as confirmed. The wireless activity of enemy aeroplane observers was great. *In addition to* several English observers, 11 different French observers were heard sending down targets between 7.35 a.m. and 9.45 p.m."

3. Genl.Kdo. XI A.K. Abtg. IId. Gruppen-bildstelle III. No. 147A. 8.6.18.

"*Reliable information:–*
Aeroplane Wireless Traffic. The following French artillery observers have been active in front of the Corps area. (Recognized by means of known call signs.)"

4. Genl.Kdo. XI A.K. Abtg. IId. Gruppen-bildstelle III. No. 1446. 30.5.18.

"*Reliable Information:–*
No aeroplane wireless heard ("Gru-konach 611")."

5. Genl.Kdo. XI A.K. Abtg. IId. Gruppen-bildstelle III. No. 1441. 29.5.18.

"*Reliable Information:–*
"From 12.30 to 1.30 p.m. French aeroplane observers, using call letters X, K, L and J, were heard."

"Registration with target corrections was attempted by an aeroplane observer of the J group, from 1.31 to 1.34 p.m. An observer of X group requested his battery to fire. Registration by aeroplane observation could not, however, be carried out. ("Grukonach 611")".

6. Weekly report on the activity of the French aeroplane wireless in the PROSNES sector, 16th to 22nd Jan., 1918.

"All the aeroplanes located have been reported to the Fighting Squadron (AVANCON), who succeeded in some cases in putting the aeroplane to flight.

"It is interesting to note that the old aeroplanes in this sector, with calls beginning with A, D, E, M, etc., are hardly ever heard. Lately, the aeroplanes which have been heard have had calls beginning with B or C."

The following prisoner's statement of 27.2.18, showed that warnings were issued, when the target called for by wireless could be recognized:–

"About midday on the 18th or 19th Feb., 7 field guns belonging to the 31st Div. Arty. were knocked out by British shell fire. No casualties occurred among the gun crews who received timely warning from the wireless interception station that the guns were going to open fire on them".

(b) It will be seen from the above that:–
  (i) Allied aeroplane wireless activity is watched by the enemy with the object of obtaining information from this source.
  (ii) Warnings are issued as a result of intercepted messages referring to targets which are to be engaged.
  (iii) An attempt is made to drive away Allied machines engaged in registration.

(c) The following extracts from Part 13 of the "Manual of Position Warfare for All Arms" (25.10.17) also show that the Germans turn to account the results of their intercepting service in the employment of pursuit flights:–

II. ALLOTMENT OF DUTIES TO PURSUIT FLIGHTS

5. The dislocation of the enemy's aeroplane and balloon observation is of decisive importance for the artillery battle. The principal task of pursuit flights is, therefore, to destroy the enemy's artillery machines which are observing for registration from behind the lines, by continuous and repeated attacks; the enemy's artillery will thus be deprived of its "eyes".

In order to determine when and where our machines are to carry out these attacks, the results of our *wireless interception stations* will be turned to account. Rapid transmission of such information to the pursuit flights must be ensured.

V. THE COMMANDER OF A PURSUIT FLIGHT

19. He will be able clearly to appreciate the enemy's aerial activity by personal observation from the high, advanced observation posts of the "air protection officers". From here, it will also be possible for him to watch the activity of his own pursuit flights. The reports of the air protection officers, anti-aircraft observation posts and balloons, will prove a valuable addition to his own impressions, but cannot replace them. He will obtain further information from the reports of pursuit flights and *from intercepted enemy wireless traffic.*

5. *The German Security Organization.*

Our knowledge of the German Security Organization for preserving secrecy, in spite of the use of wireless by his aeroplanes, is practically nil.

The measures, however, lately taken by the enemy (e.g., more frequent change of call signs) show that such an organization is in being. Our knowledge of its activities is derived chiefly from the operations of his camouflage activity, which show that there is some co-ordination with the general camouflage scheme.

The following extract from an order issued by a Long-Range Artillery Group, dated 2.6.18, throws some light on this subject:–

"During registration from the positions intended for the reinforcing batteries, an aviator will occasionally send observations by wireless for camouflage purposes. Connection with the wireless ground station is not therefore required, because the observations themselves are not as important as that there should be no discrepancy in time between the wireless message and the actual shooting.

If possible, orders in this connection will be communicated in writing. If, however, their communication by telephone is necessary, the orders will be abbreviated as much as possible.

The order will be recognizable by the word "Markus". This will be followed by the time at which the shoot will begin, which must be noted with the utmost precision; then follows the interval (in seconds) between rounds, and finally the number of rounds.

Example:– Markus 116 1415 120 12.

This means:– At 2.15 p.m., there will be a camouflage shoot of 12 rounds, with intervals of two minutes, from reinforcing battery 116. (The time will always be given on the 24 hours system)."

Captured documents dealing with the disguise of signal traffic are particularly instructive. In this connection, should be read:–

S.S. 643, para. 45.

S.S. 643A, particularly Section I, 2, (c) and Section VI.

S.S. 748, paras. 83, 86, 87 and 93.

S.S. 749, para. 4(c).

6. It will be seen that:–

(i) The German Aviation Service has an organization for dealing with the security and camouflage of its aeroplane wireless traffic, and that this organization has, at least in part, achieved its purpose.

(ii) That the German Aeroplane Service has an organization for obtaining information from *our* aeroplane wireless traffic, and that it does obtain information from this source.

It therefore seems clear that the formation of an R.A.F. Signal Security Section would reduce the value of the information obtained by the enemy.

It should also be pointed out that some organization for controlling measures of a deceptive character is essential. Unless these deceptive measures agree with those carried out under the general camouflage scheme, it will be easy for the enemy, by a process of comparison, to separate the real from the false and thus to penetrate our whole camouflage system.

7. In view of the foregoing and our general knowledge (which however is necessarily more or less indefinite) obtained by a study of the German wireless system and of the information which the enemy is probably obtaining from us, the appointment of an officer by the R.A.F. to deal with the following matters is considered to be more than justified:–

(a) Control of all wireless traffic (including that of contact patrol aeroplanes and practice working) of R.A.F., with a view to increasing the efficiency of any camouflage measures and preventing information being obtained by the enemy.

(b) The use of clear language by aeroplane observers and the decision whether "clear" is justified by circumstances, or not. Misuse of the wireless telephone, etc.

(c) Examination and modification, if necessary, of the syetem (sic) of calls used by aeroplane observers, with a view to confusing the enemy as much as possible.

(d) Measures to prevent the enemy obtaining immediate information as to targets, which enables him to give warning to localities about to be shelled.

(e) Concealment of the distribution of flights, etc., by noting and abolishing any distictive (sic) methods of wireless working. (Uniformity of training is essential).

(f) Careful examination of special codes used in special circumstances, from the point of view of security, and the modification, if necessary, of such codes.

(g) Maintenance of close touch with G.S.Ie., G.H.Q. in order to keep touch with the enemy's methods of security as regards his aeroplane wireless.

(h) Liaison with Security Branch of G.S. in connection with concealment of *real* information and the promulgation of *false* information (camouflage).

(i) Liaison with the R.A. in connection with shoots, camouflage and otherwise.

(j) Liaison with the French or Americans on a flank, so as to prevent the enemy from obtaining a clue to our camouflage methods from the wireless activity of the French or American air forces.

General Staff (Intelligence),
  General Headquarters,
    18th October, 1918.

APPENDIX I   Ie/1720.
(Translation of a German document.)
Flanders Group.   Corps H.Q.
10th Res. Corps H.Q.   25.7.1918.
Ic/Art./Group Signal Commander No. I/3231, secret.

AEROPLANE WIRELESS WARNING SERVICE

The observation of the enemy's aeroplane wireless traffic on the front of the Group (Corps), its exploitation and the transmission of warnings to divisions, are effected by the work carried out under Group Signal Commander 710 in conjunction with Group Wireless Detachment 518.

The following method of work is laid down:–

(a) The enemy's artillery aeroplane signals a target in code (floeting (sic) target, battery in action, column, etc.). The position of the target so signalled has to be transposed into German map co-ordinates and communicated as quickly as possible to the troops forming the target in question. The Group Wireless Detachment telephones the Signalling officer attached to the artillery Commander of the division in line, who is personally responsible for rapidly transmitting the warning. The telephone lines from Group H.Q. to the Artillery Commander are at the disposal of the Group Wireless Detachment for this purpose.

In order to verify the results and to utilize each particular instance, in case the signals are repeated, an early report from the troops is required. This report will be obtained from the troops concerned, by the signalling officer attached to the Artillery Commander. He will obtain answers to the following questions, and will forward them as quickly as possible to the Group Wireless Detachment:–

(i) Is there a battery at the location given (which?), or some other target?
(ii) Was the battery firing at the time of the warning, or had it fired just previously? (Time?)
(iii) Was the position engaged after the warning was received? (Time?)
(iv) From which direction? Type of gun or howitzer? Calibre? Number of rounds?
(v) Was the warning received in time?
(vi) Was an enemy aeroplane observed, and in which direction?

(b) If the hostile aeroplane has arranged with his battery, before leaving the ground, which target was to be engaged, he only sends the call of the firing battery, not the co-ordinates of the target. In this case, it is important to locate the enemy's battery and the target engaged. The Group Wireless Detachment communicates with Sound Ranging Section 73 and remains in communication for the duration of the registration. The Group Signal commander arranges for good telephonic communication between the Group Wireless Detachment and Sound Ranging Section 73. The Sound Ranging Section endeavours to ascertain what battery is firing at the exact time and what target is being engaged. The information gained thereby enables a timely warning to be sent if the shoot is repeated.

General Staff (Intelligence),
  General Headquarters,
    14th October, 1918.

AIR 1/1155

IV
Signals Security and Cryptography

These documents discuss the signals and cryptographic security of the British Army in the field during 1917–18. Its earlier practices had been primitive. Since the German Army did not establish a codebreaking bureau on the Western Front until October 1916 (roughly when Britain did so) these technical failures were of minor consequence. Those of 1917–18 proved more costly. Document One shows Britain's discovery of the vulnerability of its standard field cipher of that time, the 'Playfair' system – precisely during the opening stages of the great British offensive of 1917. This weakness may have compromised the secrecy of British preparations; the need to develop new cryptographic systems while a major battle was being fought presumably created problems of communication. Nor were the British Army's efforts in this area successful. The failure of British cryptography during 1917 and 1918 occurred in large part because of the low degree of cooperation between codemakers and codebreakers – who knew best the main lines of vulnerability in cryptographic systems. Document Two outlines the systems used in the field during 1918 while Document Three shows how difficult it was to maintain even rudimentary cryptographic security.

Documents Four and Five show the first British attempt of 1918 to monitor the security of its radio traffic, the astonishing weaknesses in its earlier practices – and, by implication, the extraordinary opportunities open to German traffic analysts throughout 1917–18. Documents Six to Eleven, written by British military cryptanalysts, discuss the technical problems involved in the maintenance of cryptographic security. Documents Twelve and Thirteen (and Documents Two to Four of Chapter Five) discuss Britain's systematic attempt to heighten signals security from the middle of 1918, including the establishment of specialist monitoring personnel. Altogether, these efforts achieved a respectable degree of success, but were far from perfect. Document Fourteen is an excerpt from the standard German orders on signals security and cryptography for 1918, which were more sophisticated and systematic than those of the British Army. Ultimately, however, they were little more effective. These procedures could work only if the German Army maintained a constant and superlative level of signals and cryptographic security. It failed to do so, as Documents Fifteen and Sixteen show. Similarly, German personnel compromised a central element of these procedures, the three number code system, quite literally in its first day of use. Within two weeks this system was little more secure than the British BAB code, which was far more primitive. Altogether, these documents demonstrate why no army of the Great War established effective systems of signals and cryptographic security, and why their signals intelligence services achieved such notable successes.

I

Memorandum by Brigadier-General K. Wigram for Lieutenant-General, Chief of the General Staff, 30 April 1917

SECRET   *Third Army No. G.7/37*
Third Army.
O.B./2032.

1.   Information has been received that wireless messages sent in Playfair Cipher have been deciphered by the enemy.

2.   Field Cipher will therefore be used for wireless communications as soon as wireless operators of the Army Wireless Companies can be trained in its use, the actual date being selected by Armies. The training will be carried out under Army arrangements.[1]

3.   Cipher code words for the use of the wireless trench sets should be chosen by each Army, and should be changed daily. Enciphering and deciphering may be done by the Wireless personnel.

4   For wireless communication between G.H.Q., Armies and Cavalry Corps the code words provided for Playfair Cipher will be used, but in conjunction with *Field* Cipher, from May 15th inclusive.

5.   Twenty copies of "Instructions for the use of the Field Cipher" have been sent under separate cover.
Copies to:– D. Signals
            O.C. Wireless, G.H.Q.

WO 95/363

2

Memorandum by Brigadier-General, General Staff, Australian Corps, 6 January 1918

SECRET.
Australian Corps.
6th January 1918.
GENERAL STAFF CIRCULAR No. 2.
SUBJECT – Uses of Ciphers and Codes.

1. CIPHERS

The *Cipher* systems in use are *"Playfair Cipher"* and *"Field Cipher"*.

(i) The *Playfair* system is for universal use within the Army, except for the transmission of messages by Wireless or Power Buzzer. The enciphering and deciphering of messages in *Playfair* is done entirely by the Staff of formations and units to whom the code word is issued. The method of enciphering and deciphering *Playfair* is laid down in officers field service pocket book.

  The code word for *Playfair* is issued from time to time by Army headquarters through the Intelligence sections of the General Staff.

(ii) The *"Field Cipher"* is used by wireless operators for the transmission by wireless of all messages handed in in clear except such messages as are endorsed "by wireless in clear" and signed by the commander to whom the wireless station is allotted. The enciphering and deciphering in the case of Field Cipher is done by the wireless operators, acting as clerks and trained for the purpose. The *Field Cipher* may also be used by operators in charge of power buzzer stations for sending messages handed in in clear, if they have been trained in the use of this cipher.

  The code word for Field Cipher is issued daily by D.D. Signals, Army, through A.D. Signals, Corps, and Os.C. Divisional Signal Companies.

2. CODES.

(i) B.A.B. Code is used for the transmission of all messages sent over circuits any portions of which are within the 3,000 yards zone of the front line, except artillery messages giving ranges from gun to target, and such messages as are ordered to be sent in clear on the personal responsibility of the Commander on the spot. B.A.B. Code is used for the transmission of all messages sent by power buzzer, except when field cipher is used as in paragraph 1, and such messages as are endorsed "by power buzzer as written" and signed by the commander on the spot.

Encoding and decoding by B.A.B. code is done by Staff of formations and units. It cannot be done by signallers.

The correction to B.A.B. code is issued from time to time by Army Headquarters through the General Staff to units.[2]

Attention is drawn to the instructions on this subject contained in S/3500/5 of 30th October 1917.

(ii) The "F.U.P." (Formation, Unit, Place) code is only used by the Staffs of certain specified formations to whom this code is issued.[3]

3. Instructions as to use of "Position Calls", "Station Code Calls" and "Code Names" are given in General Staff Circular No. 106 of 19th November 1917.

Brigadier-General,
General Staff,
Australian Corps.

DISTRIBUTION

Copy No.	To.		
1–2	Fourth Army.	75	13th A.L.H. Regt.
3	XV Corps.	76	Cyclist Bn.
4	IX Corps.	77	69th Sqn R.F.C.
5–14	1st Aust. Div.	78	6th Balloon Ccy.
15–24	2nd Aust. Div.	79	'K' Corps Sig Coy.
25–34	3rd Aust. Div.	80	Aust Corps School.
35–44	4th Aust. Div.	81	G.O.C.
45–54	5th Aust. Div.	82	AQ.
55–64	B.G.H.A.	83	A.
65–74	A.D. Signals	84	QM

85		89	12th Army Bde R.A.
86	G.O.C.R.A.	90	O.O.File
87	3rd Army Bde AFA thro'	91	Corres. File.
88	6th " " G.O.C.	92–94	War Diary.

WO 95/985

3
Memorandum by Colonel W.E. Newbigging, D.D. Signals, Third Army, 30 April 1918

A.D. Signals,   N.14/84
VI Corps,

Twice recently the cipher key-word for the day has been compromised by repetitions of cipher groups being sent in clear.

Please issue orders to all Signal Units in possession of wireless sets that the operator who is transmitting a message is never to have both the clear and enciphered copy in front of him whilst so doing.

The very serious consequences which may result from the enemy obtaining possession of the keyword for the day will be impressed on all wireless operators.

RG–9/111/C–5/4443

4
An Example of a Weekly Summary of Wireless Traffic, July 1918

SUMMARY OF WIRELESS TRAFFIC OF STATIONS IN THIRD ARMY AREA FOR WEEK ENDING JULY 15th, 1918.

1. The attached map shows the Message Traffic between Stations (Wilson Sets and Trench Sets) for week ending July 15th, 1918.

2.   The following is the wireless record of the week as it might appear to the enemy.

(a)   The Message Traffic in IV Corps area has shown a marked decrease throughout the week. The general activity of Back Area Stations was below normal and fewer stations appeared to be active during the period 11th July–15th July.

(b)   The Message Traffic in V Corps Area has shown a marked decrease throughout the week.

   The Message Traffic of the stations in the Right Divisional Sector, was considerably below normal from 11th July to the 15th July. Previous records showed these stations generally above normal in activity. It is possible that a Divisional relief may have taken place in that sector during this week.

(c)   The Message Traffic in the VI Corps area has been generally normal throughout the week.

   An increase in Message Traffic was noticed in the Right Divisional sector during the week, probably in connection with operations S. of AYETTE on the 14/15th July.

3.   It will be seen from the Diagram that Divisional Boundaries are still clearly marked by the Wireless Traffic.[4]

   The chief point which appears from the above is the advisability of maintaining the normal volume of traffic when Divisions are withdrawn or when Divisional reliefs are carried out.

WO 95/371

5
Another Example of a Weekly Summary of Wireless Traffic, 9 August 1918

SUMMARY OF WIRELESS TRAFFIC OF STATIONS IN THIRD ARMY AREA. WEEK ENDING AUGUST 4th, 1918.

1.   The attached map[5] shows the Message Traffic between Stations (Wilson Sets and Trench Sets) for week ending August 4th, 1918.

2.   The following is the Wireless record of the week as it might appear to the enemy.

(a)   Except for a slight decrease on 29th July, the traffic of Trench Sets in the IV Corps area is normal throughout the week. Wireless calls and Power Buzzer activity have been very irregular. There is a large decrease apparent between July 29th and 30th, on which dates the 57th Divn. was moved from the Corps and the 63rd Divn. to it. On August 3rd there is again a decrease in Wireless calls but an increase in Power Buzzer. This may be accounted for by the enemy raid on that date against the 42nd Divn.

(b)   In V Corps area Message Traffic shows a slight decrease on July 29th. This is the date of the move of 63rd Divn. The increase apparent on August 2nd is accounted for by the raid of 17th Divn. which took place on that date. Trench Set traffic is normal throughout, and Power Buzzer activity is on the whole below normal.

(c)   In VI Corps area Wireless activity is normal all through, but a marked increase in Power Buzzer activity on August 1st is noticeable.

3.   The diagram shows no clear demarkation of Divisional boundaries, but the boundary between IV Corps and V Corps is rather clearly marked.

4.   Wireless Traffic is now normal in all three Corps.

WO 95/372

6

Report by Captain Officer in Command, Intelligence E. (c), G.H.Q. 2nd Echelon, 17 September 1918

Intelligence E.
General Staff.   Int. E.(c) 3100/1

In the course of the last few weeks we have had occasion to interview all the Army Security Officers. They have one and all emphasised the difficulty they will experience in lecturing officers on the necessity for care in enciphering or encoding messages without disclosing the fact that we are in a position to solve German Codes.

The danger of leaving such a delicate matter in their technically inexperienced hands is very apparent.

We suggest that it would be advisable for us to draw up a series of draft lectures for these officers on all technical matters. By this means the staff of our security section will be usefully employed until such a time as a steady supply of messages from the various Army fronts is available.

It is suggested that the best form in which the reason for these various instructions could be placed before the officers to be lectured is in extracts from captured German documents on security.

We understand, from conversation with Captain Stevenson, that a great number of documents of this nature have been recently captured, and are at present being translated. Could you supply us as soon as possible with as many of these documents as possible in order to commence this task which we consider most urgent.

ADM 137/4700

7
Memorandum by G.S.I., G.H.Q., 5 October 1918

Ie(C)3030/1

HINTS ON CODES AND CIPHERS.

1. GENERAL

Experience shows that no cipher or code can be completely "Fool-proof". This is especially true of Field ciphers and codes, owing to the very large number of people to whom the enciphering and encoding are entrusted, very few of whom have had any previous experience of the work. Regulations and instructions, however detailed they may be, and however carefully worded, are bound to fail somewhat in actual practice.

Experience with German ciphers and codes shows that mistakes are generally made in far larger numbers on the introduction of a new system than later on, when it becomes more familiar to users. Thus, when the enemy introduced their Tri-numeral code, accompanied by very definite instructions regarding the enciphering of all messages with the aid of secret grids ("Geheimklappe") of the various formations, the majority of the messages were sent un-enciphered. The system was thus very soon betrayed.[6]

Mistakes have never been completely eliminated. Whether they can be so eliminated by means of an efficient system of control, remains to be proved.

Numerous as the mistakes are, they can generally be traced to lack of discipline and care on the part of the encoder.

Our short experience of English messages shows that this lack of encoding-discipline is very marked on our side of the line. On the whole, the faults shown in enciphering our messages are very similar to those committed by the enemy. In the list of errors which are likely to occur (given below), we are quoting more from our experience in German code and ciphers than from any knowledge of our own. It is therefore possible that several of the mistakes quoted may not have occurred in English, while, on the other hand, several mistakes which will occur on our side are omitted.

CIPHER

2. *Mistakes in enciphering.*

It frequently occurs that, especially when a new system is introduced, a message is carelessly enciphered in such a manner that it cannot be translated at the other end. On the meaning being queried by the receiving station, the sending station repeats the message in the correct form. Variations of this mistake are many. It may arise after the introduction of a new keyword. The sending station, for instance, enciphers a message on a new keyword, which has not yet been received by the receiving station, so that the deciphering of the message is impossible; a repeat is, therefore, called for, which is sent on the old keyword.

With the introduction of the new method of making up the Field Cipher Key Square,[7] the following mistake will very likely occur:– The encipherer will construct his Key Square on the old method. He will encipher a message which cannot be read and which has to be repeated with the Key Square constructed in the new method. This, of course, will give away the new system to the enemy solvers.

It should be a point of duty for everybody enciphering a message to check his encipher by deciphering the message himself, *before* he hands it in to the Signal Office for transmission. Should mistakes nevertheless creep in, which render the message unreadable at the other end, the repeat must *on no account* be sent in the same words, but must be completely paraphrased.

(2)

3. *Enciphering of "Address to" and "Address from".*
Enciphering of addresses has been observed once or twice in the few messages which we have already dealt with. Addresses must be in code *whenever possible*; if enciphered, they must be embodied in the text. (Compare S.S.209, amendment to Section 15)

4. *Signatures to Messages.*
One of the greatest aids to the solution of German ciphers was the frequent enciphering of officers' names at the end of messages. This applies of course equally to the names of recipients of messages, such as, "All Companies", "All stations", etc. It will generally be found that the inclusion of these names is unnecessary. If unavoidable, the officers in question should vary their signature as much as possible, e.g., "Captain Smith", one day; "O.C., D. Coy.", next day; etc.

5. *Replies to Procedure Groups in Cipher.*
In the first days of German code solution, we were frequently aided by German operators sending the *procedure groups* for "What is the time?", and receiving the reply *in code.* Several of

our wireless procedure groups lend themselves very easily to this purpose, and steps are being taken to have them altered. In the meantime, careful control should be exercised. Procedure groups have been in use for such a long time that their meaning is certain to be known to the enemy.

6. *Replies to Cipher Messages in Clear.*
Cipher messages requiring an affirmative or negative reply have frequently been answered after a few minutes by "Yes" or "No". From the point of view of the solver, a question and reply constitute the same message, and the rule that cipher and clear shall not be mixed therefore applies in this case. No reply, however short, should be sent in clear to any code or cipher message.

Similarly, if by any chance a request has been made in clear, it should not be answered in code.

7. *The Use of Dummy Letters.*
It is found that the average encipherer has a very hazy conception of the correct use of dummy letters.

Dummy letters and, in code, dummy groups are introduced to hinder the enemy, and not to provide a padding to the message. Unless they are correctly used, they will not attain their purpose.

In cipher, it is found that infrequent letters of the alphabet are almost invariably used as dummies. This practice does not hinder; on the contrary, it helps solution.

We have also found that dummy letters which are added to messages to complete the requisite multiple of 5 are being replaced by final words, e.g., "stop", "end", "ends", "AAA", "finish", etc. This practice has been prohibited.

8. *Enciphering AAA.*
The enciphering of AAA is very common and has been prohibited.[8]

9. *Abbreviations.*
The use of abbreviations is advisable:–
(a) In order to cut down the length of the message.

(b) To avoid repetition of letters in frequently used words, e.g. such a word as 'visibility'. The letter 'i', occurring as it does four times, may produce peculiarities which would at once suggest this word to an enemy cryptographer.

On the other hand, an excessive use of abbreviations may make the message unintelligible to the addressee. It would be fatal if a message containing many abbreviations had to be repeated in full.

CODE

10. The replacement of cipher by code will no doubt cause a certain amount of confusion to those who have now been accustomed for 4 years to encipher their messages. A specially careful control should therefore be exercised during the period following the introduction of code. The following mistakes are likely to occur:–

11. *Spelling.*

To the person who has been accustomed to encipher his messages, the search for code groups representing words may seem tedious. He will therefore prefer to spell out his message. This should be most rigorously discouraged. We are trying to work against this tendency by introducing the spelling groups in the alphabetical order of the words of the code.

Should the encoders nevertheless spell out words which are included in the index, their attention should be drawn to it at once. They should be made to realise that there is a system of control, checking irregularities.

12. *Use of Alternative Groups.*

All the most frequent words and spelling groups will be given several alternative code equivalents. These should be used indiscriminately. Experience of the German code shows that encoders have a tendency:–

(a) To give preference to those code groups which are pronounceable, and therefore more easily memorised, e.g., the encoder will prefer to use the code group B.A.G. from memory, than look for the alternative (say) V.J.Q.

(b) In some sectors it is found that the encoders give preference to the first or the second alternatives.

The misuse of alternatives is most marked and also most
dangerous in spelling. If the letter is repeated inside a word or
even twice in the same message, the use of the same code
equivalent would reduce this to a case of simple substitution
cipher.[9] Several repetitions of the mistake will lead to the speedy
solution of spelling groups.

Not only must this be discouraged, but the operator must be
made to use, wherever possible, the syllables in places of single
letters.

13. *Dummy groups.*

The correct use of dummy groups in code is extremely important. If used intelligently, they will form an enormous hindrance
to the solution; wrongly used, they will assist the solver. It is a
mistake to think that an excessive use of dummy groups will
hinder solution. It is here that the Germans made a very great
mistake. They instructed their operators to pad up their messages with dummy groups. In most cases, the result is that the
operator, no doubt for convenience sake, uses his dummy
groups absolutely regularly, e.g., he places 5 at the beginning
and 5 at the end, or alternates dummy with code groups. But
even if there is no regularity in their position in the message,
their excessive use betrays their presence and does not hinder
solution. They should be used carefully, rather than liberally.
Introduced with judgement in the middle of spelling, they form
a decided obstacle to the cryptographer.

14. *Stereotyped messages.*

The sending of stereotyped messages is fatal if, after the change
of a code, a message continues to be sent in the same form.
During the life of a code, the sending of stereotyped messages
will prove a hindrance to the solver. I suggest that, unless one
can be certain of being able to ensure a change of the form of
message simultaneously with the code, the use of stereotyped
messages should be strongly discouraged.

15. *Tabulated messages.*

There is no greater aid to the correct solution of numbers than tabulation. We are going to counteract this danger, by introducing in future codes a special list of numbers to be used for tabulation only. In any case, the form of tabulation should be changed simultaneously with every code. If, for example, during the life of one code, the number of casualties were reported under para. 7, the meaning of this heading could be altered to, say, "Great artillery activity" the next code. Its continued use as "casualties" would provide a help to the solver in detecting many useful words.

16. *Punctuation.*

Punctuation should only be used where it is absolutely necessary to the correct meaning of the message. This applies particularly to "point of interrogation". German operators have absolutely revelled in an abundant use of punctuation, and we have been very glad of the fact.

17. *Nonsense messages.*

It *may at some time* be necessary to create a fictitious activity in a certain sector. For this purpose large numbers of nonsense messages may possibly be sent. These will fail in their purpose, however, *if they can be solved.*

During solution of German codes we have come across 3 kinds of dummy messages:–

(a) Messages which make sense, but consist of quotations from poems or popular songs, proverbs, etc. These can be easily solved, as their encoding naturally necessitates excessive spelling, and, of course, the detection of one or two words immediately yields the complete message. The sending of such messages as "Got you, Steve?", or "Estaminet beor no bon" is very dangerous.

(b) Whole columns of code groups are copied out of the book. These hindered us for some time, but, as soon as we found out what was the matter, we derived great benefit from this practice.

(c) *Real* dummy messages, i.e. messages consisting of code groups chosen haphazard in the book, the first and last groups being ones which generally form the initial and final components of straightforward messages. Such messages are real hindrances. It is generally claimed as an argument in favour of the use of codes that, whereas in cipher the "clear" of one message will provide the key to others, the clear of a message in code will provide the meaning of the code equivalents for the words in that message only, and will therefore not endanger the remainder of the book.

Though there is no doubt that code is by far the safer of the two, the above argument will not hold water. It is astounding to anybody who has not actually worked on solution how the discovery of one code group will lead to that of numerous others. One apparently insignificant word discovered in a practice message, and applied to other messages from different parts of the front, may yield between 10 and 25 code groups.

ADM 137/4701

8

Memorandum by General Staff (Intelligence), G.H.Q., 12 October 1918

Ie(e)3030/4

CODES AND CIPHERS.

1. Numerous instances may be quoted in the history of war, where the interception of despatches and orders has resulted in defeat and disaster for the force, its intentions thus becoming known to the enemy. For this reason, codes and ciphers have been introduced, which render the contents of such communications unintelligible to those whom they do not concern.

(a) During the campaign of Louis XII in Italy, it is recorded that the great reverse sustained by the French was entirely the result of the capture of a letter in clear. The General

Officer Commanding, on being informed of its contents, immediately ordered an attack, as a result of which the French were severely defeated and driven out of Italy.

(b) The absence of a sufficient number of trained officers in Napoleon's army often prevented the effective exchange of secret correspondence, and indeed at times necessitated important despatches being sent "in clear". For instance, in 1807, when the Russian Army in Eastern Prussia was about to be drawn into a dangerous position by the strategy of Napoleon, the Duc de Fezensac, who was bearer of despatches to Bernadotte, was captured by some Cossacks. Despatches, which were not in cipher, contained a detailed description of the positions of the French Corps, and the manner of their intended employment by the Emperor. They were at once sent to the Russian Commander, who, warned of the danger he ran, retired to Eylau.

(c) The Franco-German War furnishes similar instances. Thus, when the third German Army reached the banks of the Meurthe, its Headquarters Staff at Luneville did not know the exact position of the V French Corps, and it was thought that the French troops were continuing to retire on Chalons in order to concentrate. A day later, a party of German cavalry captured a French orderly in Commercy, and the despatch he was carrying, which was not in cipher contained information on the following points:– The presence at the camp at Chalons of the cavalry of the VI Corps; the calling out of all men between the ages of 25 and 35; the formation of the XII and XIII Corps under Generals Trochu and Vinoy respectively; and the retreat of the I and V French Corps.

2.   Under present war conditions, it is impossible to avoid the interception of messages by the enemy. Wireless especially, but also telephone, telegraph and lamp signals can be intercepted, while even the best pigeons and messenger dogs are liable to go astray. We are therefore faced with the problem of having to devise some form of military cipher or code which, while being

practical in use, affords sufficient security to keep the contents of messages secret until the news contained is obsolete. The enemy's Intelligence Service is doing its utmost to intercept our messages. For this purpose, it employs special wireless stations, listening sets and observation posts stationed along the front. As soon as they are intercepted, these messages are sent to a staff of solvers, who have unfortunately, up to the present, been working with considerable success. For instance:

(a) We have good reason to believe that our projected attack on the Belgian Coast in July, 1917, was betrayed to the enemy by information obtained from wireless sources.

(b) A captured German Intelligence Summary, dated the 21st May, 1918, contains the following paragraphs:

"The VI. English Corps (south of ARRAS) sent the following 2 wireless messages to its divisions:

"The captured officer, under special examination, says that a big offensive will begin north of the SOMME on 21st May"

"30 black square objects are moving slowly between CAMBRAI and MARQUION. No infantry or transport."

(c) In July of this year, a captured document proved that the Germans had obtained definite information from wireless sources of the presence of a certain American Division on the British front.

(d) Captured documents prove that as recently as the 18th September, 1918, the enemy was obtaining invaluable information from wireless sources about the movements of our Allies' and our own troops. This must have been from solution of one of the cipher or code messages sent by our stations.

It is therefore imperative that we should do our utmost to deprive the enemy of this source of valuable information. For this purpose, it would be necessary that all of us, realising the dangers incurred by successful interception, should constantly co-operate in baffling the Boche.

I therefore intend in this short lecture to enumerate the various forms of codes and ciphers used by us, and to warn you against the most frequent pitfalls of enciphering and encoding.

3. It is essential from the very start that you should distinguish between codes and ciphers.

A code is a *list* of arbitrary equivalents for phrases, words, or parts of words, contained in the message.

A cipher is a *system* by which the letters composing the message are altered or re-arranged, so as to become unintelligible to one unacquainted with the Key.

Whereas with code the whole message may be expressed by one arbitrary sign, it would be necessary in cipher to express each letter separately. It may as well be stated here that no practicable military cipher is mathematically indecipherable, if it is intercepted the most that can be expected is to delay for a longer or a shorter time the deciphering of the message by the intercepter.

It has been stated that a military cipher should fulfil the following requirements:

(1) The system should be materially, if not mathematically, indecipherable.
(2) It should cause no inconvenience if the apparatus and methods fall into the hands of the enemy.
(3) The key should be such that it could be communicated and remembered without the necessity of written notes, and should be changeable at the will of the correspondents.
(4) The system should be applicable to telegraphic correspondence.
(5) The apparatus should be easily carried and a single person should be able to operate it.
(6) Finally, in view of the circumstances under which it must be used, the system should be an easy one to operate, demanding neither mental strain nor knowledge of a long series of rules.[10]

A brief consideration of these six conditions must lead to the conclusion that there is no perfect military cipher.

4. The military cipher used by the British was for a long time the Playfair System. It was replaced some time ago by the Field Cipher

which, owing to the discovery of the fact that it also is soluble without too great difficulty, has now to be further complicated. Ideally, this system fulfils all 6 conditions necessary for a good military cipher. In practice, it is found that, owing to carelessness on the part of those using it, solution may be considerably aided. This has been inevitable up to the present, owing to the fact that enciphering has been entrusted to the wireless operator. A review of the more frequent mistakes will indicate what can now be avoided by officers carrying out the enciphering themselves.

(a) *Misuse of Dummy letters.*

Dummy letters are introduced into the Field Cipher for 3 reasons:

To break up letter doublets; e.g., MM.
To complete the necessary multiple[11] of 10 letters;
To confuse the enemy.

The examination of a large number of messages shows that –

(i) X, Y and Z are nearly always used as dummy letters. This is wrong. It is quite clear that, if the enemy solver finds the letter X in the lower row of letters, he will immediately try the next letter in the row as being equal to the one above X in the upper line. The encipherer should make it a rule to avoid the use of infrequent letters as dummies. The dummy may be introduced 2 or 3 places to the left in the lower row, or even in the upper row.

(ii) Letters employed in completing the necessary multiple of 10 are added in the form of words, e.g., end, stop, finish, etc. This is particularly bad. The letters used to complete the message should be chosen haphazard, and *not placed at the end of the message, but introduced at irregular intervals throughout the* 'clear'. For example, the message "Please use three-letter calls" should not be written out as follows:

P L E A S E U S E T
H R X E E L E T T E
R C A L L S S T O P

but P L E A S E U S E T

G H R E E D̲ L E T B̲ (Dummy letters are underlined)

T E R N̲ C A L Q̲ L S

(b) *Enciphering of things not necessary to the context.*
Certain signals are necessary in the sending of clear messages by morse, in order to indicate to the operator receiving them how the message is to be written. Wireless operators enciphering messages were in the habit of enciphering these procedure signals as well. For example, ZZ, meaning "Write in block capitals", may be quoted. This mistake is not likely to occur when enciphering is done by Officers.

There are however, some signals, which are not necessary to the context of the message, but which officers may be tempted to encipher. AAA may be taken as an example, for the use of which German cryptologists must be rendering heart-felt thanks daily. If punctuation is absolutely necessary to the sense of the message, introduce dummy letters.

5.   When compiling a message for enciphering, thought should be given to the following points:
(a) *Be as concise as possible.* The shorter the message, the less material the enemy will have to work upon. Abbreviate all long words, especially those which show peculiar repetitions of letters, e.g., "visibility" may well be written "visib.", in order to avoid the peculiar repetition of the four 'i's. Be very careful in abbreviating though, as it would be fatal if a message had to be repeated in full owing to excessive abbreviation.
(b) *Avoid, as much as possible, frequent beginnings and frequent endings of messages.* By frequent beginnings, I mean such expressions as "Reference your ? ? of even date", or "Please", or "Situation report", etc. etc. By frequent endings, I mean such expressions as "addressed so and so, repeated so and so", or "addressed all concerned", or "urgent".

(c) *Avoid mention of units by numbers.* Every unit has its code name and these code names should invariably be used. This is what the Germans say on this subject:

Orders issued by the Third German Army.

"The mention of the number of a small unit is sufficient in most cases to recognise the presence of larger formations".

(d) *Avoid mention of Officers' names.* Here is what the Germans say on this point, in a document dated the 14th April, 1918, after stating the fact that Officers' names are often mentioned:

"By the continuous mention of Officers' names, which are frequently repeated, the enemy will be able easily to establish the presence of certain divisions in the line. Systematically compiled lists of names will enable the enemy to identify a division which has newly moved to a different sector".

The enemy would not issue orders to this effect, if he were not getting benefit from it himself, so we are not surprised to find in a document dated the 17th May, 1918, a definite statement to this effect:

"The use of names enables the enemy to secure information respecting reliefs and reinforcements. *We ourselves have been able by this means to obtain the first indication of the enemy's reliefs.* For this reason the use of names must be avoided as much as possible and, instead, the names "battery commander", "fire control officer", "observer", should be used."

(e) *Avoid stereotyped forms of messages.* It was noticed the other day that a certain division is in the habit of sending, half an hour after the change of the Key-word, a message which never varied its form from day to day, and consisted of a statement of the number of messages received and sent by its various brigades.

It is hard to conceive anything which is more likely to play into the hands of the enemy cryptographer than a periodically repeated and stereo-typed message. That the enemy has benefited by this and realises the danger is apparent from an order dated the 17th March, in which the following words occur:

"The context of daily reports must be continuously varied, *especially those which have to be transmitted by wireless or power buzzer.* Stereotyped reports give the enemy a lead into the solution of our secret code".

Always remember that no cipher can ever be considered mathematically insoluble although, (sic) no doubt, the enemy will find the Field Cipher, if properly used, a very tough proposition, he may find it worth his while to continue working at it until he solves it. This may be two or three days after the message is sent. Most of the information contained in the message would therefore be stale and useless, but a good deal of it would still be of very great value. Everybody should therefore keep this danger in mind and avoid, if possible, the mention in communications, which have to be transmitted by wireless, of anything which may be of such use to the enemy.

After enciphering a message, make certain that your cryptogram is correct by deciphering the message, before handing it in for transmission. This is most important. If the message received at the other end cannot be understood owing to some (perhaps a trivial) error in the construction of the Key-square, or in enciphering, and a repeat has to be sent in a corrected form, it will mean that the key-word for the day is given away to the enemy.

Should a repetition of the message be unavoidable, it should never be given in the same wording as the original. If, for example, the original message was "We shot down 13 E.A.[12] yesterday on Army front", the repeat might read "13 E.A. were shot down by us on Army front yesterday".

CODES

Codes have, for many reasons, not been used by us to any great extent in the forward battle zone. In fact, the only code used has been the well-known BAB. Numerous copies of the latest edition (No. 4) have been captured during our retreat. The system of corrections in use is transparent and, as used, is not likely to cause the enemy more than temporary delay in solving. Once a code is captured, no correction, however skilfully applied, is likely to prevent the solution of messages encoded by its means. For this reason, BAB is considered to be extraordinarily unsafe.

In addition to this, it is not convenient, owing to the difficulty many people seem to find in dealing with numerals, map co-ordinates, etc. We intend to replace it shortly by a Chart Code which will be far simpler and safer in use.

In future, codes are to be more extensively used. They will eventually replace cipher entirely.

Field cipher for wireless will be replaced by a code. Two different types of code book are being issued. The first, which is reserved entirely for staff and tactical communications will always remain in the hands of officers. The second will be used by the wireless personnel for signal service communications. To ensure security, each already encoded message will be enciphered by the wireless personnel before transmission.

7. When encoding messages, great care is necessary. The mistakes made are not so apparent as those committed in cipher. Whereas a mistake in cipher will generally make the message unreadable at the receiving end, a mistake in encoding will not necessarily materially influence the sense.

Some pitfalls which have to be guarded against are the following:

(a) *Spelling*. To all those who have been accustomed up to the present to encipher their messages, letter by letter, the search for words in a vocabulary will be tedious and the temptation to spell out the message will be great. It is apparent that, if spelling is excessively indulged in, the whole nature and character of the code will be lost. Cryptograms will then be reduced to the level of simple and easily soluble cipher. The spelling section of code books is provided for emergency cases only. It should only be used if the required word or expression or a suitable synonym cannot be found in the vocabulary. If it is absolutely necessary to spell, do so by using the groups of letters (i.e. syllables) provided to as large an extent as possible.

(b) *Alternative code groups.* You will find that as you get familiar with the book, several of the most frequent code groups will stick to your memory; the reason being that the words expressed are very frequently used, and that, perhaps, the code group itself is pronounceable. All the most frequent words and expressions have been given several alternative code equivalents and full use must be made of them. To encode a message from memory may be quicker, but it endangers the code to a very marked degree. Remember that you are not the only person using this code on the front and, if only 10 people persist in consistently using the same alternative group, the meaning of that group is bound to be discovered. Its discovery may well lead to that of other groups.

It is particularly important that alternative code groups should be fully used in spelling and in encoding all messages containing repetitions of numbers. If a word is spelt out which contains several repetitions of the same single letter and the same code group is used each time, the solution of that particular word must be very easy. The same applies to numbers. If, for example, the 44th Division is mentioned and the same code equivalent for 4 used, the detection of that number will become childishly easy.

(c) *The use of Dummy Groups.* Dummy groups are introduced into code for the solo (sic) purpose of deceiving the enemy. Used properly, they will make a code absolutely insoluble. The following mistakes are generally made in the use of dummy groups:
(i) They are used instead of punctuation.
(ii) They are used periodically throughout the message, e.g. after every third or fifth code group.
(iii) They are used too much.
A dummy group here and there in the middle of a

sentence, or spelling, or numerals, will cause great
annoyance to the enemy solver.

(d) *Stereotyped messages.* The sending of stereotyped messages is
very dangerous, if messages are sent in the same form in two
successive codes. It is realised that situation reports and
periodical returns are bound to be worded approximately the
same way every day. It should be borne in mind that as long as
one code is in use messages may be sent in stereotyped form,
but very great care must be taken to completely alter the
phraseology as soon as a new book is introduced.

This applies especially to tabulated messages. If, for
examples, a tabulation, during the life of one code, has been:

    (i)   Enemy activity
    (ii) Our operations
    (iii) Aerial activity
    (iv) Casualties
    (v) Weather
    (vi) Miscellaneous

as soon as a new code is introduced the order of these
paragraphs can be altered to:

    (i)   Aerial activity
    (ii) Miscellaneous
    (iii) Weather
    (iv) Enemy activity
    (v) Our operations
    (vi) Casualties

Everything must be done to make it impossible for the
enemy to draw an analogy between messages sent on the
old code and those sent on a new one.

8. Both in dealing with ciphers and with codes a few general
rules must be remembered:–

(a) Every endeavour must be made to avoid unauthorised
persons having access to the book. A code book must only
be handled by a responsible officer and, when possible,
kept under lock and key. A careful check of it must at all
times be kept.

N.B. Remember that anyone trying to obtain access to a code book would, if he knew his business, endeavour to do so without anybody being the wiser. He would try to obtain access to the code book for a short period, and to photograph the pages.

(b) To obtain the clear language of the message is a great assistance to anyone trying to solve a code. For this reason, always remember that the text of a code message has a secret character of its own, apart from the nature of its contents. Therefore, in every possible case, the message must be carefully paraphased before it is circulated. If it is necessary to retain the original text of the encoded or decoded message, it should be kept for as short a time as possible and then carefully burnt.

(c) The code version must never be written on the same piece of paper as the message itself, and all rough workings must be carefully destroyed by fire.

(d) A telephone conversation must not be made which has any bearing on a message sent in code. The enemy can overhear your telephone conversation, and you are therefore presenting him with excellent information as to the contents of the coded message.

(e) It is extremely important that liberal use should be made of the alternative groups allotted to the interpretations, and that careful use should be made of the dummy groups.

(f) Remember that unless efficient steps are taken to safeguard the secrecy of your code book, it will become known to the enemy, with the result that all information sent by this means no longer remains hidden from him.

(g) Remember that everything sent on wireless can be overheard by the enemy. An "erase" will therefore not conceal what you have sent but only attract the enemy's attention. Be very careful, therefore, in encoding. Make it a point that you decode every message, to check its accuracy, *before* it is handed in for transmission. Mistakes are usually made at the encoding end. Avoid them.

(h) Whenever a book allotted to one formation is transferred to another, information to the effect must at once be sent to G.H.Q., the receipt being sent to the proper authorities without delay. It is very important that this rule should be observed, because, without this procedure, it is impossible to keep trace of a book which may eventually become lost and fall into the enemy's hands, without anyone being aware of the fact.

ADM 137/4701

9
Memorandum by Lieutenant C.H. Henderson, Lieutenant I.C., Intelligence E(c), 14 September 1918

Int. E. (c) 3010/2

Critique of "Alpha" Code[13]

I. General.

The security of a code is dependent on the number a) of the words it contains, b) of the alternatives for those which will be most frequently used, c) of messages transmitted and encoded by means of the code.

In attempting solution the cryptologist's first consideration will be to try to ascertain by the position and nature of the stations transmitting and receiving the messages, what nature of traffic the code is likely to conceal.

We have no knowledge as to what extent this code is being used, but should say that there will be no doubt in the enemy's mind as to the nature of the traffic.[14] It is obvious therefore, that the selection of words and phrases must in a case like this be very carefully carried out. First analysis will tell the enemy cryptologist that there can only be a maximum of 676 (that is presuming that no word has alternate code groups) different words in the code.[15] Even allowing for this maximum the vocabulary will not be sufficient to cover the military and technical phraseology without extensive spelling. In other words the code does not contain a sufficient number of words. This is especially marked in the absence of those words which are essentially connected with the flying service. Their non-inclusion will necessitate spelling which will be the first thing that the enemy cryptologist will attempt to discover.

It may be argued that one of the chief features of the code, namely the double and sometimes treble meaning applied to the code groups, will baffle him. We maintain, with the experience of several months spent in solution of most intricate German codes, that this will not be the case.

Careful analysis of frequently recurring code-groups will soon tell the experienced cryptologist in which messages these are being used as words, and in which as spelling groups, and furthermore the stationary, frequently recurring auxiliary groups for "Spell" and "Cease Spell" will not be able to conceal themselves for very long. After that the system, owing to the employment of the initial syllables, will provide a distinct help towards the detection of words.[16] But the detection of spelling is not essential for the solution of a code. In many a German code we have known with absolute certainty the value of words long before we were able to give a value to spelling groups. The only efficient precaution against this is the provision of several alternatives for all words which most frequently occur.

It cannot be claimed that this precaution has been taken in the compiling of the "Alpha" code. Indeed, it may be said that the alternatives of the most common words are conspicuous by their absence. These words will therefore be very easily detected.

Such is the double edge of the "Spell" and "Cease Spell" system that this will provide the enemy with a "short cut" towards the solution of spelling.

II. Words

The code contains 580 words for which not a single one has more than one code-equivalent.

Quite apart from the fact that such words as A, AN, AERO-PLANE, ALL, AM, AND, ANY, AS, BE, CAN, CANNOT, DO, FROM, HAVE, HOW, IN, -ING, -LY, MUST, MY, NO, NOT, OUR, OUT,

OVER, SEE, SEND, THEN, THERE, UNDER, UNTIL, UP, USE, WAS, WERE, WHAT, WHEN, WHERE, WHY, WHICH, WHOSE, WHO, WITH, YES &c., should have at the very least two equivalents (A, AND, AS, CAN, FROM, HAVE, IN, YES, NO and all words frequently used in questions should have at least three).

We recommend (a) that about double the number of words be introduced. These should include all words for parts of the aeroplane, types of aeroplanes, &c., and such words as HANGAR, AIR MECHANIC, OBSERVER, PILOT, in short all technical terms closely connected with the Flying Service. (b) that alternatives be introduced for all most frequently used words. (c) that code groups be allotted for names of places, officers, and formations. A count of words actually sent in messages will indicate what is necessary.

III.   Spelling

As we have already pointed out the use of duplicate meanings to code-groups, as applied in the "Alpha" code is considered most dangerous to the security of the code. In our opinion the plea of simplicity of manipulation is not sufficient to counter balance the danger. Indeed, a separate list of spelling groups placed in alphabetical order with the vocabulary of words would in actual practice prove just as simple.

The whole security of this code depends on the non-detection by the enemy of this system. A mere count of possible alternatives, together with a scientific analysis of a code-group frequently recurring in cryptograms, would soon reveal the secret to him. From this point onwards the system will aid rather than hinder the solution. Quite apart from this the selection of syllables leaves much to be desired. Such combinations as ABO, APPR, APP, BATT, CAS, DAN, DAR, EFF, GRO, HAST, NOTI, QUA to mention a few, would never be required. The words most likely to be spelt out are the names of French and Flemish places, for which such combinations of letters as "ville" "court" "bois" "beke" "au" "ui" "ieu" "eau" "gne" "la" &c.&c. are necessary. The Germans realized this long ago and introduced them into their codes.

We recommend (a) the provision of entirely separate code-equivalents for spelling groups. (b) The introduction of these groups in alphabetical order with the rest of the vocabulary. This is intended to counteract the tendency of the average encoder to spell rather than look up a word. (c) The provision of code-equivalents for a good selection of those syllables which are most frequently used in the spelling of French place names.

IV. Numerals

In the preliminary analysis of code cryptograms the most striking characteristics are always shewn by numbers. The system adopted in the "Alpha" code by means of which every code-group denoting a number may stand for two other entirely separate meanings would conceivably counter balance these characteristics, *IF* the selection of the other two meanings were carried out carefully. No attempt has been made to do this in the construction of the "Alpha" code. Indeed, figure equivalents are given for words which, with the exception of two alternatives for ZERO, all begin with the same letter as the figure would if spelt out; in most cases similarly sounding words are chosen; in all cases the alternatives are words immediately following each other in the alphabetical sequence, and, what is perhaps the most glaring fault of all *the same words are used in every succeeding edition*.

It would be folly to assume that in the course of the five editions which have already been used the enemy has not been able to detect numbers and their corresponding words accurately. The continued use of the same words therefore provides the enemy with (1) such useful words as ON, ONLY, THEN, THERE, SITUATION, SEND, NIGHT, NO, YOU and YOUR. (2) with the corresponding spelling groups. (3) with an easy check on the accuracy of their deductions. For Example:– If a series of code-groups are recognised as numbers, and the word alternative for one of them is found to occur frequently in a definite position in a message the figure value for the code-group can be immediately cut down to two or three posibilities (sic) by a mere glance at the list of word equivalents; it would be confirmed by, say the mention of a unit combined with the study of the position of its accompanying code groups when used as words. Then words will check figures, figures will check words, and this will in a very short time give the enemy a complete list of all figure alternatives, not to speak of words and spelling groups. In this manner what might have been the strongest point of the "Alpha" code is actually its most fatal weakness.[17]

Quite apart from these faults in the system, not nearly sufficient provision is made for numbers, the "OPEN SESAME" to all codes. We should say that, considering the nature of messages likely to be sent, frequent reference will be made to British system of Map Squaring, to heights in thousands of feet, to distances in thousands of yards. Yet no provision is made for numbers between ten and thirtysix, for hundreds or for thousands. Instead of providing only two alternatives for three, four, five, six, seven, eight, nine, and ten; and three for zero, one and two, there should be at least three for all numbers between zero and thirty six, two each for all fives from forty to a hundred, three each for a hundred and a thousand and two each for thousands up to twelve thousand, besides two each for ordinals up to thirty first.

To employ less is positively dangerous.

V. Miscellaneous

(a) Phrases

Experience has shewn that the accurate detection of phrases is practically impossible in code solution. From the point of view of security the inclusion of phrases is therefore most desirable. On the other hand it is found that the average encoder is very reluctant to use phrases. Phrases should therefore be carefully selected and attractively placed in the book.

Owing to our lack of knowledge of the nature of the messages sent in this code it is difficult to criticise the selection of phrases as thoroughly as one might wish to. We notice the absence of "Air Force Phrases" of which there should surely be a good selection, on the other handthe (sic) inclusion of "Map Co-ordinates Begin" and "Map Co-ordinates End" is dangerous.

In the present form of code they are admittedly necessary, but will not be so when the use of separate spelling groups and numbers come into use. We note from the nature of some phrases that the code is probably used in the forward area, say from contact patrol to the ground. If correct this emphasises the necessity for a safe code owing to liability to capture.

(b)   Punctuation

The use of punctuation in a code should be discouraged as, even with several alternatives it can be easily detected and may provide assistance in solution.

However, code groups for punctuation should be provided in case their inclusion in a message is imperative to make sense. We note the absence of "Note of Interrogation" and think this most excellent. It should either not be included at all or be given numerous alternatives as its detection is easy and most useful.

(c)   Auxiliary Groups

All auxiliary groups should have at least two alternatives, except PLURAL which should have five in order to avoid the use of S.

(d)   Dummy Groups

The "Alpha" code provides for no dummy groups. These if properly used are an enormous hindrance to the solver and should form a feature of every code, a selection to be placed at the foot of every page.

These alterations will necessitate a large number of new code groups which cannot be allotted with the code in its present form. As a first stage in the improvement we therefore suggest the adoption of three letter code-groups. According to the number of initial letters selected so the vocabulary will be able to be increased. We suggest the adoption of three initial letters. These will provide 2028 different code groups,[18] which might be distributed roughly as follows:–

(a)   About 1000 words to be represented by 1500 code-groups.

(b)   Separate Spelling groups to be represented by 150 code-groups.

(c)   Separate numbers to be represented by about 150 code-groups.

147

(d) Phrases to be extended and represented by about 50 code-groups.

(e) Place names and Formations 100 code-groups.

(f) The remainder would provide dummys, punctuation and auxiliary groups.

This will not tend to make the code more complicated and will certainly shorten the length of the cryptograms sent. It is shorter to send messages consisting of a few three letter code-groups, each of which stands for a word or a phrase, than to spell out the same message with two letter code-groups.

ADM 137/4701

10

Memorandum by Captain H. Wright, General Staff, G.S.I.(e), G.H.Q., 17 October 1918

Ie/6035.
Ref. 3010/18.

M.I.1.d.
War Office.

1.   With reference to your K.1731 M.I.1.D., of 11/10/18, I do not think that the suggestion of giving each interpretation two or more code equivalents is either inherently necessary or advisable in practice.

2.   The whole essence of code manufacture lies in the construction of a well-chosen and well-arranged vocabulary, accompanied by a judicious allotment of code equivalents on a scientific basis. A badly-arranged vocabulary will spoil any code book, and no number of additional code equivalents will then counterbalance its defects in this respect.

In order to secure a good vocabulary, it is necessary to study not only the general principles of language, but also the language used in military telegraph messages. This vocabulary should be based on an exhaustive consideration of the actual words used in military phraseology, and of their sequences and inter-relation, as well as of their relative frequency in actual use.

(The experience gained from the systems and methods employed by the enemy, and the points which enable these systems to be solved by our own cryptographers, should provide many a short cut).

A vocabulary so constructed would contain, not only all the necessary words and arbitrary phrases, but also such frequent combinations of words as "tomorrow morning", "and with", "enemy artillery", "men wounded", etc.

Unless the vocabulary meets all these "desiderata", the mere overloading of the code book by multiplication of code equivalents will not prevent solution. Moreover, it is not by the possibility of solving uncommon words that a code is compromised, but rather by the peculiarities shown by common words and expressions.

3. Having obtained the vocabulary of the code, it should be still further analysed by studying the code characteristics of various classes of words, viz:–
(a) Initial and final words.
(b) Sequences of frequent words.
(c) Words which consistently attract others.
Code groups should then be allotted in accordance with the result of this final analysis.

For example, one of the most profitable avenues leading to the solution of a code is a study of the characteristics of numerals and their tendency to attract:–
(a) each other.
(b) certain prepositions such as "from", "to", "until", "after", "near", "at", etc.,
(c) words such as "guns", "men", "material", etc.

It is only by allotting code groups on the above lines that security is obtained.

4. Taking all these points into consideration, we consider that the suggested multiplication of code equivalents (presupposing a

sound vocabulary and a good system of allotment) is unnecessary, and, from the point of view of practicability and size of the code books, undesirable.

ADM 137/4700

11

Excerpt from 'Amendment to F.C.I.' prepared by General Staff (Intelligence), General Headquarters, 10 October 1918

9. We think that the whole arrangement of words, phrases, etc., has been rather unpractical up to the present, both in German and other code books. The capture of so many German books has enabled us to decode many messages in their entirety, and it is noticeable how little use is made of the phrases.

This is due, we think, to the arrangement of phrases in a separate section of the book. The average encoder is not going to waste time, (in his opinion), by looking through the phrase section of the book, when encoding his messages. He naturally finds it far less trouble to encode his messages word by word by means of the vocabulary.

It is therefore necessary to arrange phrases in an attractive manner so that the encoder will find it worth his while to alter messages to suit the phraseology of the book. We therefore suggest that in future, each page of the encode book should consist of two columns – the one on the left containing words of the vocabulary, the one on the right containing phrases and remarks. If a word of the vocabulary is an important unit of any phrase, this phrase should be repeated in the right-hand column opposite the word. This will necessitate the repetition of the same phrase two or three times in the book. Possibly the phrases would have to be repeated in the "Phrase and Miscellaneous" section, in addition.

This re-arrangement will have the following advantages:–
(a) It will simplify the encoding. The encoder does not need to

worry about phrases at all. He simply proceeds to encode his messages word by word, and it will become perfectly natural to him, when he reaches some important word and finds the complete phrase, or a similar phrase, directly opposite that word, to use the code group for the phrase.

(b) The book need only consist of 4 main sections: Vocabulary, Numbers, Phrases Miscellaneous, *Unit and Places Names*.

(c) The number of phrases can be increased without making the book unwieldy.

(d) Remarks can be printed opposite certain words and letters. For example, "S" – "Do not use this for plural".

We have arranged one page from F.C.1 in this manner, to show the working of the idea (Appendix III).

10. All most common words should be repeated in their most frequent combinations with other words. It is by the aid of frequent combinations of words and numbers that German codes are solved. In the list of words to be added to the code, we have included a great number of these combinations. This certainly does not exhaust the list, but will suffice for the time being.

11. A section should be provided for names of units and places. This section should consist of blank pages in the book which are filled up according to their requirements by lower formations. A sufficient number of code groups (say 300) should be left blank in the decode for this purpose. A further communication, with examples, will be sent on this subject.

12. As the group "Code compromised" is only likely to be used once during the life of the code, one code equivalent only is necessary. This should be a code group consisting of consonant – vowel – consonant, so as to make it easy for the holder of the book to memorize it. It should be prominently printed on the title page in the following manner:–

Important

Memorize this group:–

Code compromised = GIG.

13. We think it is important to have a thumb index, both for the encode and the decode portions, that words and code groups can be found more quickly. M.I.1.b. (or e) have a copy of a captured giant aeroplane code which illustrates what is meant. For this to work effectively, it will no doubt be necessary to keep the encode and decode sections separate, i.e., to arrange so that the book is not turned upside down when changing from encode to decode, and vice versa.

14. We would like future editions to bear the following inscription on the cover:–
"This code book must not fall into the enemy's hands. If there is any danger of its capture, burn the book and immediately report that this has been done." For reporting the destruction of the book the code group (say) BAT may be used.

ADM 137/4700

12

Memorandum by Lieutenant for Captain, Officer in Command, Intelligence E(c), G.H.Q., 2nd Echelon, 11 October 1918

Int. E. (c) 3100/20

G.S.Ie.,
G.H.Q.

Notwithstanding our letters Int. E (c) 3040/2 of the 26th September and Int. E (c) 3100/11 of the 2nd instant, the latest messages we have examined show that the First Corps still continues to send a very large percentage (69%) of nonsense practice messages. I enclose the batch of messages complained of. May steps please to be taken to have this evil eradicated?

Messages from the Australian Corps show an abundant mention of Units, locations of Headquarters, and movements of

Headquarters both in cipher *and in clear.* Over 70% of the messages examined from this Corps front had been sent in clear. A good many of these clear messages are quite admissible, but many, of which I enclose a selection, are particularly dangerous.

I consider it very urgent that representations be made to this Corps to have the practice stopped.

Messages from the Second American Corps show a distinct tendency to mention Officers' names at the beginning and end of messages. The same Officer appears to sign most messages emanating from one Station. Not only is this sure to give solvers great assistance, but it is bound to indicate reliefs the moment they take place.

The 30th Division of this Corps is in the habit of sending very lengthy stereotyped messages. One of these messages is always tabulated. The encipherers do not seem to realise the purpose of tabulation, and persist in repeating the heading of each section together with the paragraph number, for example, "No. 3 Enemy Aircraft".

I enclose copies of these messages for two successive days to illustrate the point.

Our revised form of Field Cipher is obliging the enemy solvers to attack the messages letter by letter from the cryptogram.

Any message which, if even in part only, is worded the same every day, will enormously facilitate the process of solution. The Americans themselves have solved several keys of the German tri-numeral code merely by the habit of one Lieutenant Jaeger signing his name at the end of each message.

May representations be made to the Corps in question?

ADM 137/4700

13
Memorandum from General Headquarters, 1918

[COPY] SECRET

G.H.Q., I.E. 2 I S 2

The following points have been especially noted in the inspection of Intercept Messages in this Army.

1. Messages are of unnecessary length.
2. Dummy groups are not used properly, being nearly always at the end of the message.
   Too frequent use of "Ends" "AAA" & "XYZ" at end of Message.
3. Text very frequently begins with the word "To" (especially in 2nd American Corps).
4. The number of Clear Messages is still too high and many are decidedly dangerous.
5. 4-letter station code calls are used too frequently in the address.

A certain amount of difficulty is experienced in eradicating the above faults, chiefly owing to the present advance that is taking place, any very drastic reforms at a time like the present would probably do more harm than good, as Officers would become afraid of using the Wireless, and a good means of communication would thereby be lost.

A Security Officer appointed to each Corps would assist matters materially.

Great difficulty is also experienced in visiting the various Corps and Wireless Stations owing to the fact that no car has been allotted to the Security Officer, the distances one has to travel at the present time being very great, and cars very difficult to borrow.

A clerk at Army Headquarters would be of great assistance, as it is difficult to obtain the services of a clerk from the Intelligence department owing to their being already fully employed.

ADM 137/4700

14

Memorandum by General Staff (Intelligence), General Headquarters, 13 April 1918

Translation of Enemy Document, dated 22.1.18 (with amendments to 27.2.18). Issued by the Chief of the General Staff of the Field Army

NOTE BY GENERAL STAFF

1. It is of particular interest to note that the German General Staff has become fully alive to the value of the information obtainable by a close study of the German Signal Service traffic, and has considered it necessary to issue this document, not only to the Signal Service, but also to the troops, as far down as companies.

2. The measures proposed for limiting the amount of information obtainable by us from German messages comprise:–

(a) A new form of code, to be used in the front line for *all* means of communication, supplemented by the usual special code for wireless stations behind regimental headquarters.

(b) A new, specially secure, code for use by wireless stations attached to formations higher than divisions.

(c) Restriction of all signal traffic to what is absolutely essential.

(d) The introduction of the *"Utel"* instrument,[19] the signals from which are specially difficult to intercept.

(e) Within 3,000 yards of the front line, the use of the telephone is limited to officers (or others acting under their special orders), and all telephone traffic in this zone must be carried on in code. (Special listening sets have long been allotted in each German division for keeping a watch on the signal traffic.)

(f) Call signs of wireless and power buzzer stations to be assigned to *areas* and not to be changed on account of reliefs. Changes of call signs to be made from time to time, but call signs must never be taken with a unit from one part of the front to another. In open warfare, call signs must be changed with every change in the position of the station. A general call, to which all wireless stations belonging to a tactical formation reply, is forbidden.[20]

(g) Units and places must be designated by code names which are assigned to *areas* and must be changed from time to time.

3. The measures proposed for disguising the volume of the Signal Service traffic, including aeroplane registration, are as follows:–

(a) Every striking change in the distribution and working of signal offices and wireless stations must be avoided. New wireless and power buzzer stations must not commence work until this is essential.

(b) Deceptive measures may be used. During the removal of units, the volume of power buzzer and wireless traffic should be maintained, and prior to offensive operations, dummy traffic should be carried on in sectors other than that selected for the attack.

4. It is obvious that the enemy has become seriously alarmed as to the necessity for preserving secrecy, particularly as regards wireless communications which may be taken by our intercepting stations far in rear, where special facilities can be arranged for dealing with the messages. It is practically certain that the issue of these new and more stringent regulations was prompted by his experience in dealing with *our* Signal Service traffic.

5. The methods used by the German wireless service *prior* to the opening of the present offensive followed, almost exactly, the principles laid down in the new regulations; it appears as if the same principles were still being followed during the battle.

A. GENERAL[21]

1. It must be expected that the enemy will systematically watch our Signal Service traffic (telephone, wireless, power buzzer,

etc., traffic). By carefully piecing together the most trifling items of information, which may, at first sight, appear unimportant, he obtains results from which he is able to make valuable deductions regarding our order of battle, the distribution of our forces and our intentions.

2.   Our counter-measures must aim at limiting the amount of information obtainable by the enemy by these observations:–
(a)   By reducing to a minimum all traffic which the enemy can intercept, and
(b)   By employing secret signals, the meaning of which it is impossible (or at any rate difficult) for the enemy to understand.

3.   The messages sent by all means of communication are liable to be intercepted by the enemy. Wireless and power buzzer messages are as easily intercepted by an enemy receiving station as by one of our own. Telephone and telegraph messages can be intercepted from a considerable distance. Lamp signals can be read a long way off. Messenger dogs and carrier pigeons sometimes stray into the enemy's territory. So far, the "Utel" is the only means of communication which is fairly immune from interception.

These circumstances must be allowed for in selecting the form in which messages are to be sent. "The enemy is listening" is the golden rule to be borne in mind in the case of the most trivial message, or the most harmless conversation.

The danger of interception varies according to the means of communication employed. The risk is greatest in the case of wireless telegraphy. Wireless messages, even from stations far behind the front line, can be intercepted with ease by the enemy. The interception is carried out not only by the enemy's stations on the field of battle, where the fighting conditions render it difficult to turn the information to account, but also by wireless receiving stations far behind the line, where there is good accommodation and every technical and scientific facility for the immediate deciphering of the messages and their speedy transmission direct to the point where the information can be turned to account.

The danger is almost equally great in the case of the power buzzer. The interception is, however, limited to shorter distances, and the enemy is obliged to intercept the messages in his foremost battle zone, which is less convenient and less fruitful in results.

With regard to the telephone and telegraph, the risk of interception diminishes as the distance from the enemy increases.

The risk of messages, sent by messenger dogs, falling into the hands of the enemy depends on the degree of training and on the proper employment of the dogs. The method of employment is also the most important factor in the case of carrier pigeons.

4. The counter-measures employed will accordingly be more or less elaborate, in proportion to the risk of interception. Wireless and power buzzer messages must never contain any portion in "clear". They must always be in code, and, moreover, the codes used in wireless telegraphy (particularly for stations a considerable distance from the front) must be such as to offer a very high degree of security (for exceptions, see para. 5a).

As regards telephone traffic, a danger zone must be laid down extending at least 3,300 yards behind own front line. The code words given in the code-book must be employed in *all* conversations taking place in this zone, and only coded telephone messages may be sent (for exceptions, see para. 5a). Even as far back as divisional headquarters, the strictest telephone discipline (limitation of conversations to what is necessary for the service, the avoidance of conversations and telephone messages relating to especially secret plans, etc.) and the most careful maintenance of the lines, with frequent tests for leakage, are absolutely essential.

Messages sent by means of dogs and pigeons, particularly when the contents of the message holds good for a considerable time, must also be coded.

5. In the front line positions the coding of messages is rendered more difficult by the battle conditions (hostile fire, exposure to weather and moral influences). Experience shows

that the troops are inclined to use "clear" without considering that this may often have serious tactical consequences. This must be avoided in all circumstances.

Tactical reports or orders of purely local significance have generally lost their value for the enemy, in consequence of the rapidly changing situation, by the time the contents reach the local headquarters which are competent to take counter-measures.

Nevertheless, as proved by experience, these reports contain, in addition, so much general information that, by patient collation, the enemy is able to obtain an abundance of valuable intelligence.

Therefore, the coding of messages must be insisted on, even in the front line positions.

The "code-book" (*Schlüsselheft*), issued for use in the whole divisional area, and intended for all means of communication, also meets the requirements of the battle zone by its great simplicity, and has the advantage of brevity over messages sent in "clear". In cases where special secrecy is not essential, it gives an abbreviated form for the messages, which the enemy cannot understand at the first glance. In other cases, where there is sufficient time or when the messages are of some importance, it provides in addition, a simple, and at the same time sufficiently safe code.

5a. For traffic between artillery and the trench mortar observers (ground observers, computing stations of artillery survey sections, aeroplanes, balloons) and the firing batteries, and also often between the latter and the particular sub-groups (groups), and especially for inter-communication between the survey posts themselves and the computing stations of artillery survey sections, special facilities must be given, as otherwise the reconnaissance and fire activity of the artillery would be seriously impeded and delayed.

It is the duty of artillery commanders of all ranks to see that the use of such facilities is limited to what is absolutely essential.

6. Wireless messages, for the reasons mentioned in para. 3, require special protection against deciphering by the enemy. In

addition, therefore, to the book common to all means of communication, a "special code-book" (*Satzbuch*) is provided for the use of the wireless stations situated behind the infantry regimental headquarters, offering greater security against decoding.

7. Even this "special code-book" is not sufficiently safe for the use of the wireless stations situated behind divisional headquarters, whose duty it is to transmit the messages of the higher commanders. In this case, absolute security against decoding must be attained, and it is not so essential that the method adopted be a simple one. A special code, called the "Secret Wireless Code" (*Geheimschrift der Funker*, abbreviated to *Gedefu*), has, therefore, been prepared for this traffic.[22]

8. Apart from the above mentioned methods, staffs are in possession of the War Ministry code, which is intended to prevent the contents of telegrams and telephone messages being read by unauthorized persons.

B. THE USE OF CODE IN THE DIVISIONAL AREA

9. The use of the "code-book" is obligatory in the entire divisional area and for all means of communication (telephone, wireless, power buzzer, lamp signalling, carrier pigeons and messenger dogs).
Exceptions:– (a) On the telephone, conversations may take place in "clear" when the distance of both sender and receiver is more than 3,000 yards from the enemy and it is not necessary to keep the messages secret from unauthorized persons. Exceptions are permissible for the artillery, *Minenwerfer* and artillery survey sections (see para. 5a).[23]
(b) For communications passing behind infantry regimental headquarters, between wireless stations only, the "special code-book" will be employed.

10. When drafting code messages, words and phrases contained in the vocabulary of the "code-book" and "special

code-book" should be employed. Coding and decoding will thus be considerably simplified and accelerated.

11.   Messages should, as a rule, be encoded and decoded by the staffs which send or receive them.

In the case of wireless stations, however, this work is best done by the station personnel, as the inaccuracies inevitable in the transmission of wireless signals oblige the receiving station to decode the message as soon as it is received, in order to see whether it makes sense, and, in case of need, to make the necessary further enquiries.

12.   The "code-book" and the "special code-book" are secret, and must not fall into the hands of the enemy. They must be promptly destroyed if the need arises.

13.   For use in aeroplanes, an "abridged code," which contains in a handy form the signals most generally employed, will suffice. Special regulations exist for giant aeroplanes.

14.   It is permissible to use clear abbreviated signals of the "code-book" in combination with words in clear. On the other hand, the *code* signals of the "code-book" must not be used in conjunction with the clear abbreviated signals or with words in clear.

Messages containing the clear abbreviated signals of the "code-book" may only be retransmitted by intermediate (including wireless) stations in exactly the same form as they are received. Similarly, messages encoded by means of the "code-book" must not, when retransmitted, be reencoded by means of the "special code-book," as this would help the enemy in the solution of the latter.

The "special code-book" signals must not be used in conjunction with words in clear.

15.   In order that additional phrases or words may be employed besides those already provided for, several figure signals in the "code-book" and a number of spaces in the "special code-book" have been left blank. The Group Staff arranges for the uniform insertion of the required words or sentences. These must be communicated to the neighbouring staffs.

16. The Army Staff will arrange that the "special code-book" signals for requesting barrage and annihilating fire, and for reporting the enemy's tanks, are uniformly inserted.

17. Instead of the real nomenclature of the troops, only code-names may be entered in the "code-book" and "special code-book". For particulars, see paras. 39–43. *Lists* of code-names must not be taken beyond regimental or artillery sub-group headquarters. They must contain only those code-names which are obsolutely necessary for the station in question.

18. The "code-book" and "special code-book" are issued by the Director of Signals, and distributed by each division in its own area. Wireless units will receive their "special code-books" from the Signal Commanders. The "special code-books" are changed every four weeks, and must also be changed immediately in any area whenever a code-book used in that area is lost.

19. The secret grid (*Geheimklappe*) at the end of the "code-book" is issued by the staff (as a rule, the divisional staff), and changed about every week, and must also be changed immediately whenever a grid is lost.

C. MEASURES FOR ENSURING THE SECRECY OF SIGNAL SERVICE TRAFFIC

20. The safeguarding of the secrecy of our own intentions and measures is essential to the success of all operations. In an offensive, it is of vital importance to take the enemy by surprise.

21. Breaches or a perfunctory application of the regulations issued for protection against interception, seriously jeopardize our military strength in the field, and offenders will be tried by court-martial, according to Paragraph 62 of the Military Penal Code.

22. It is the duty of all Commanders to watch over the Signal Service traffic in their particular areas, to deal severely with irregularities, and to explain systematically to the troops, and

especially the administrative authorities, the great dangers attending faulty telephone and traffic discipline.

23. In order to impress on the troops the absolute necessity for ensuring the secrecy of our Signal Service traffic, it is not sufficient to issue written orders and verbal instructions at roll calls. Special measures, suited to the intelligence of an ordinary man, are necessary. Among these measures are, for example, popular lectures by commanders of regimental signalling detachments, lantern lectures, instructive descriptions in newspapers appearing at the front, and the decoration of billets, soldiers' homes and railway stations with suitable pictures.

24. *Every man in the unit must be firmly convinced that, by irregularities in conversation and traffic discipline, he not only harms himself, but also seriously jeopardizes the success of the whole.*

Telephone

25. In the case of telephone communications, only the strictest conversation discipline can prevent the enemy from deriving any advantage from the interception of messages.

26. Within 3,300 yards of the enemy, the use of the telephone will be limited to officers. N.C.O.'s and men will only make use of it on the special order of an officer. In this zone all telephone traffic must be carried on by means of the signals in the "code-book." Ordinary conversation is absolutely prohibited in this area. Exceptions are permissible for the artillery, *Minenwerfer* and artillery survey sections (see para. 5a). Farther back, ordinary conversation is allowed, but even here the use of the "code-book" is necessary when transmitting information which must be kept secret from unauthorized persons.

27. Especially important messages, such as arrangements for attack or orders to evacuate portions of positions, must not be transmitted by telephone even in back areas, but must be sent in writing.

28. Within 3,300 yards of the enemy, all telephone lines must consist of metallic return circuits, as single lines facilitate the

interception of conversations. Cross connections, which make interception especially easy, are not permitted in front of the headquarters of the commanders of front line troops (*K.T.K.*). All lines should run as nearly perpendicular to the front as possible.

29. Disused lines must be dismantled, as they facilitate interception by the enemy.[24]

30. Frequent and systematic searches of "No Man's Land" for the earth leads of the enemy's listening sets are indispensable.

31. The number of telephone connections in the forward danger zone must be limited to what is actually essential. In front of the headquarters of commanders of the fighting troops (*K.T.K.*), there should as a rule be no telephone connections except for observation posts.

32. All telephones in the danger zone should bear a conspicuous notice, with the words:–
"NOTICE! THE ENEMY IS LISTENING"

Lamp Signals
33. Whenever there is any possibility of the enemy reading them, all lamp signals will be encoded, irrespective of the distance of the lamp signalling stations from the enemy. Exceptions are permissible for the artillery, *Minenwerfer*, and artillery survey sections (see para. 5a).

Wireless and Power Buzzer
34. Call signs must be assigned to areas, and must not be changed on account of reliefs. On the other hand, a change of call signs, independently of reliefs, is from time to time essential in the case of all stations, in order to accustom the enemy to an occasional appearance of new call signs, which is inevitable whenever additional units are put into line.

In no circumstances must call signs be taken with a unit from one part of the front to another.

35. In open warfare, the enemy must not be allowed to trace the movements of the attacking troops by changes in the positions of the wireless and power buzzer stations attached to these troops. It is, therefore, essential that, in such cases, stations should change their call sign at every move.

Thorough preparations for these measures must be made by the Signal Commanders, in order to avoid confusion and uncertainty in the Signal Service traffic.

36. Call signs are allotted as follows:–
(a) In the case of fixed wireless stations and those under the direct control of General Headquarters by the Director of Signals on behalf of General Headquarters.
(b) In the case of wireless stations, down to the divisional station, inclusive, by the competent General Officer in charge of Signals on behalf of General Headquarters or of the C-in-C in that theatre of war.
(c) All wireless stations in the divisional area on the ground and in the air (except the divisional station) and power buzzer stations, by the Army Staff in consultation with the Army Signal Commander.

Armies and Groups of Armies will first of all make arrangements to avoid confusion on the borders of their areas. Neighbouring Armies will consult together for this purpose.

Changes of call signs are only permissible with the consent of the competent staff or of the General Officer in charge of Signals.

37. Call signs must not reappear periodically and must not be arranged in groups. Otherwise, an observant enemy is able to make deductions regarding the location of the staffs to which the wireless stations belong. Call signs must not afford any indication of the tactical formations to which they are allotted.

38. General calls of stations belonging to a tactical formation are not allowed, as this renders it easier for the enemy to ascertain the number and grouping of the units belonging to a higher formation.

Code-Names

39. Units and important topographical features must be designated by code-names. This renders it more difficult for the enemy to identify the order of battle. He is prevented from completely decoding the messages he intercepts. The code-names are allotted by Group or Army Headquarters.

40. The words selected as code-names must not give any clues to the enemy, and must not be liable to be confused.

Groups of code-names must not be used to denote similar formations or staffs (for example, names of federal states for Group Headquarters, names of provinces for divisions, names of towns for brigades, etc.).

41. Code-names are assigned to areas. They must be changed from time to time. This, however, must never take place in conjunction with reliefs or with rearrangements of the order of battle in an area.

42. Lists of code-names must not be taken beyond infantry regimental or artillery sub-groups headquarters. The lists must only contain those code-names which are necessary for the station in question.

43. Code-names must always be used in telephone traffic, and also in cases when it is necessary to use clear for urgent messages at critical moments within the danger zone.

D. MEASURES FOR DISGUISING SIGNAL SERVICE TRAFFIC

44. It is not only from the contents of intercepted messages that it is possible to make valuable deductions. Systematic observation of the enemy's Signal Service traffic may give important indications as to the distribution of the enemy's forces and of his intentions, even when it is not possible to decode his messages.

45. An increase in the enemy's Signal Service traffic points to approaching operations, for instance, rearrangement of forces, reliefs and attacks. The appearance of new wireless and power buzzer stations indicates the arrival of new formations. An

increased activity in aeroplane wireless suggests an approaching offensive. A decrease in Signal Service traffic may indicate that reliefs or rearrangements of troops are completed, that offensive operations are not intended or that the enemy does not mean to continue an offensive already begun. A decrease in the enemy's wireless and power buzzer stations is associated with the withdrawal of units. A reduction in the enemy's aeroplane wireless suggests a decrease in the hostile artillery.

46.   In order to prevent the enemy from obtaining information from our Signal Service traffic in spite of strict telephone and traffic discipline, every striking alteration in the distribution and working of our Signal Service must be avoided. Fresh wireless and power buzzer stations are not to begin work until this is essential for the fighting troops and for purposes of command.

47.   In addition, deceptive measures are useful. For instance, when units are being moved elsewhere, a wireless and power buzzer traffic equal to that previously carried on must be maintained for purposes of deception. The enemy must be misled in his estimate of the extent of the area in which we are preparing an attack, or from which we are moving troops, by the maintenance of dummy traffic in adjoining areas.[25]

ADM 137/4739

15
Example of a Captured Order issued to British Units, 13 August 1918

The following order issued by Ludendorff emphasises the importance attached by the enemy to strict signal discipline:–

C.g.S. of the Field Army.   G.H.Q.
Ia/Ic Nr. 5798 op.   19–12–17.

From a map issued by the British Intelligence Service, captured at CAMBRAI, it appears that the enemy was completely informed regarding the distribution of our forces in the line and the divisions which had been withdrawn. On the other hand, he was almost completely in the dark regarding the divisions newly brought in to back areas of the Army.

Judging by the military situation at that time, it is to be supposed that the enemy obtained part of his information from prisoners' statements. The larger part, however, he undoubtedly obtained from his Intercepting Service.

The opinion has been repeatedly expressed by the troops that the enemy during major operations, would not be able to make use of his intercepting service. This opinion must be vigorously combated.

The enemy and particularly the Nritish (sic), instals his mobile intercepting stations even under the most difficult conditions.

The fact that our signal discipline frequently is completely wanting, particularly on battle fronts, plays directly into the hands of the enemy's Intelligence. The fighting troops must understand ("that" – deleted) the necessity for this discipline, otherwise there is grave danger that the enemy, will prematurely learn our intentions, which are calculated on surprise, and will be able to take counter-measures accordingly.

(Sd) LUDENDORFF.

ADM 137/4700

16

Extract from letter from Divisional Signal Commander to Group d°, 1918

Ie/1730.

The reports from the supervising posts about German messages, have up to the present been kept from the Div. Sig. Com. He comes to the painful conclusion that on the one hand breeches (sic) of speech discipline are being hidden from him by the Commanders of troops, and on the other hand all power of checking irregularities is being withheld.

If therefore the Arendt. Station in addition to the work of listening to the enemy's intercourse, are to support the Div. Sig. Com. in the unpleasant and thankless task of regulating the troops, the supervising reports must be rendered to the Div. Sig. Com. daily. Then it becomes the duty of the Div. Sig. Com. to follow up breaches of of (sic) speech discipline and bring the transgressors to answer for them. And it will be possible to explain to the troops the conclusions which the enemy could draw from such messages, – the importance of speech discipline. This would be the best means to ensure the broken orders being understood and would provide welcome material to the troop signal officer for the instruction of his personnel.

ADM 137/4700

V
Signals and Operational Deception

These documents discuss operational deception on the Western Front during 1918. This was one of the two major campaigns of that sort conducted by the British Army during the Great War, the lesser known and, arguably, the more important of the two. Document One shows the views of GHQ France on the value, role and techniques of a systematic campaign of operational deception; it also reveals the centrality of signals deception to this effort. Documents Two and Three discuss the technical aspects of signals deception, and the degree to which it hinged on the maintenance of a consistent and high level of signals and cryptographic security. Without the latter, the former was impossible. These documents also illuminate the nature of operational deception itself. The best known campaign of military deception of this century, that conducted by Britain at a strategic level between 1942–45, is unusual in three ways. First, it is not easy to control entirely the enemy's intelligence services. When this is impossible, the security – as against the control – of information becomes the central element of deception. If the enemy cannot be fed only on the information which one wishes it to receive, one must prevent it from acquiring the material which one absolutely does not want it to know – certain and definite information on one's intentions and capabilities. Second, operational deception rarely centres on the use of controlled agents. Instead it rests on signals deception, the provision of misleading information to one's own troops and physical camouflage, the best means to confuse the primary sources of field intelligence, signals interception, prisoners of war and reconnaissance by camera and by eye. Third, of the two main forms of deception – misleading the enemy in a precise fashion as against engendering confusion in its mind – the former is the higher and more difficult form of the art. In operational deception, however, even the lower form can prove rather effective.

Documents Four and Five show how deception was used to support two major British operations during 1918. One must, however, be cautious in assessing the effect of this practice. The surviving evidence indicates that the enemy was badly confused about Allied intentions and dispositions during the last months of the war, and in some cases perhaps because of deception as against security. The precise degree of the success and effect of Allied deception during the last four months of the war, however, has not been clearly established. Given the destruction of so many of the operational and intelligence records of the German Army, it may never be so. Deception might have coincided with rather than caused much of the German confusion of this period. Document Six outlines the organisation and *modus operandi* of the system of operational deception which was intended to assist the proposed British campaign of 1919. Had this approach been married to Colonel J.F.C. Fuller's 'Plan 1919', the resulting campaign would not have been out of place in 1944. This memorandum was written by the leading practitioner of deception during the First World War, Colonel Meinertzhagen. While it lacks much of the permanent interest of the Hesketh Report, that classic of deception from the Second World War, the Meinertzhagen memorandum is the most mature statement of the principles and techniques of the art to survive from the Great War. Again, it shows the centrality of signals security and deception to the discipline as a whole during 1918. Documents Three and Six also show the range of philosophies about operational deception to be found among British practitioners during the Great War.

I

Memorandum by Lieutenant-General Herbert Lawrence, Chief of the General Staff, G.H.Q., 5 August 1918

First Army.
Second Army.
Third Army.
Fourth Army.
Fifth Army.
Cavalry Corps.
R.A.F.
Tank Corps.

O.A. 219.

1. In order to ensure that the element of surprise shall be present in our operations next year, it is essential that our resources for misleading the enemy should be developed now, and that the sources from which the enemy obtains his information should be controlled to the greatest extent possible.

Briefly, all leakage of true information must be cut down to the minimum, and the required amount of misleading information conveyed to the enemy.

2. Our principal resources for misleading the enemy consist of "Camouflage", judicious handling of our wireless, and the dissemination of false information to our own troops and enemy agents.

These resources will be controlled and directed by G.S., G.H.Q., in pursuance of a definite policy.

3. Leakage of true information can be traced to three main sources:–
(i). A too local use of camouflage and a tendency to employ it to

disguise preparations only, instead of also to simulate preparations.

(ii). Lack of control of our wireless.

(iii). Reliance on secrecy only to prevent leakage through our own troops and enemy agents, instead of secrecy combined with misrepresentation.

4. It is proposed, therefore, that when instructions are issued as to preparations for offensive operations in 1919, Army Commanders shall also be informed what impression it is wished to convey to the enemy as to the progress of these preparations.

Meanwhile, it is necessary to consider to what extent the Camouflage Park R.E., and wireless organization can be employed on the lines set out in para. 5.

5. It is not altogether possible to conceal offensive preparations on a large scale, but it is possible to mislead the enemy as to the comparative progress and extent of the preparations being made in different sectors:

(i). As regards preparations of the area:

Those can be partially concealed or simulated by "camouflage"; we ourselves followed the German preparations this year by plotting the progress made on dumps, sidings, railways, roads, artillery positions, hospitals, aerodromes and hutments; and we must prepare to conceal or simulate these indications in certain sectors of our own front next year.

(ii). As regards information conveyed through wireless activity:

At present our wireless system is so organized that the enemy can follow the movement of our reserve divisions, of the tanks, and of the cavalry, and can plot on a map the density of our troops in line. In addition there is a considerable leakage of information caused by the unnecessary sending of wireless messages; these can be intercepted by the enemy, who is thus given additional opportunities of locating units and formations and of learning our codes and ciphers.

Arrangements are being made to form a pool of wireless sets and operators, which will enable the movements of reserves to be effected without materially altering the comparative wireless activity in various sectors, and vice versa.

A reallotment of wavelengths will be made shortly to do away with the possible recognition of units and formations by the wavelengths they employ.

The question of limiting the number of messages sent by wireless is being studied.

As a result of these measures it will be possible to convey the impression of strength or weakness of troops in certain sectors by means of the judicious use of wireless, without interfering with the normal work carried out by units; and, by the installation of intercepting stations, to keep touch with the information conveyed to the enemy.

6. Information regarding the means adopted by the Germans to mislead us as to the extent and progress of their offensive preparations this year is accumulating, and will be issued.
Copies:–

G.S.,O (b).	(1).
G.S., I.	(2).
A.G.	(1).
Q.M.G.	(1).
M.G.,R.A.	(1).
E.-in-C.	(1).
D.Sigs.	(2).
Camouflage	
Park R.E.	(1).

IWM, Guy Dawnay Papers

2

Memorandum by Lieutenant-Colonel M.E. Festung, for Brigadier-General, General Staff, Canadian Corps, 23 August 1918

First Army No. G.S.1376/21.   S E C R E T

CANADIAN CORPS.

G. 302/2525–4

1st Cdn. Division.
2nd Cdn. Division.
3rd Cdn. Division.
4th Cdn. Division.
D.A. & Q.M.G.
G.O.C.R.A.
A. D. Signals

1. In order to prevent our troop movements being followed by means of our wireless activities, Corps will ensure that the wireless activity on their front remains, as far as possible, as at present, in spite of any moves of Corps, Divisions, Artillery R.A.F. and Tanks, which may take place.

2. Relieving formations will invariably take over and man for at least 24 hours after completion of relief, all the wireless and power buzzer stations maintained by the outgoing formation. Number of stations manned will not be diminished or increased without reference to Army Headquarters.

3. The number of messages to be sent daily by each Corps and Divisional Wireless (including C.W.), and Power Buzzer Station should be kept at the present average; the normal number should be two Signal Service messages and four other messages.

This normal average should only be increased in the case of a tactical emergency.

4. Corps and Divisional Wireless Spark and C.W. sets will exchange signals once only in every hour, apart from the

message traffic as given in para 3. Power Buzzer Stations will exchange signals once in every two hours.

5. Formations in reserve areas will not use Spark or C.W. Wireless sets, except loop sets which have too small a range to be intercepted by the enemy. Power buzzers may be used in reserve areas and any further training in wireless must be carried out at the recognized Army and Corps Signal schools.

RG–9/111C–11/3918

3

Memorandum by Brigadier-General K. Wigram for Lieutenant-General, Chief of the General Staff, G.H.Q., 28 August 1918

SECRET

First Army No.2234 (G)
T/1284

First Army.

1. In the past the enemy has been able to identify the position and movements of formations and units by means of our wireless traffic and activity.

Such identifications have been made by intercepting and noting the following:–

(a) Wireless calls (spark, C.W., Power Buzzer Amplifier and Loop Set Stations).

(b) Senders' numbers of wireless messages.

(c) Peculiarities in the procedure adopted by particular formations or units.

(d) The large amount of wireless traffic, which helps the enemy to solve our codes and ciphers.

(e) Abnormal amount of traffic whether greater or less than the normal and than that in formations on the flank.

(f) The group system of wireless working.[1]

2. It is of vital importance that such information should be

denied to the enemy, and to this end the procedure shown in the following paragraphs will be adopted.

(a) For Spark Stations the Basic Call System has been introduced.[2] This system will shortly be applied to all C.W. sets, thus providing a daily change of call.

(b) For Power Buzzer Amplifiers and for Loop Set Stations two letter calls will be introduced.

Each division will have at its disposal the total number of 2 letter calls, and will allot these calls to stations of that Division. To prevent the delineation of boundaries of formations, these calls will for the present be changed every fifth day throughout the British Armies in France, the changes being made at midnight on the nights 5th/6th, 10th/11th, 15th/16th, 20th/21st, 26th/27th, and 30th or 31st/1st of the month. Later these changes will be made more frequently. Divisions will arrange mutually with flanking Divisions that there shall be no duplication of calls.

On relief, a Division will notify the incoming Division of the calls in use. The incoming Division will use these calls until the next normal date of change.

The above procedure will come into force from 12 midnight 30th September – 1st October.

4. *With regard to para. 1 (b)*

In all messages sent by wireless, the senders' number will consist of figures only and no index letters will be used.

5. *With regard to para. 1 (c), (d) and (e)*

(a) The procedure as laid down in S.S.209 and amendments thereto will be rigidly adhered to.

The use of special symbols will be suppressed.

Standardization of procedure and of the training of wireless operators is essential.

(b) Spark Control Stations have been established in Armies, Corps, and Divisions. These stations will exercise a strict control on all spark wireless traffic and will at once report any irregularities in procedure.

It is also intended to establish C.W. Control Stations. When established, these stations will act in regard to all C.W. traffic in a similar manner to the existing spark control stations.

(c) Armies will check and control the amount of wireless traffic within Army areas, preventing the boundaries of any formation being defined by an abnormal amount of traffic.

(d) G.H.Q. will from time to time issue instructions regulating the amount of traffic within Armies.

6. *With regard to para. 1 (f)*
It is proposed to provide additional personnel and apparatus so that special stations may be installed to disguise:–

(a) The actual number of stations in any 'group' and

(b) The actual grouping of stations.

Until such time as this additional personnel and apparatus is provided, every care will be taken to avoid the grouping of stations being betrayed, e.g. the directing station of a group is forbidden to call up *in succession* the other stations of that group except when the tactical situation demands.

Lateral communication between Brigades and Divisions should be encouraged.

RG–9/111B–1/921

4
Memorandum by C.N.N. for Captain, Officer in Command, Intelligence E (c), G.H.Q., 2nd Echelon, 2 October 1918

Intelligence E.,   SECRET.
G. H. Q.   *Int. E (c) 3100/11.*

The whole purpose of my letter Int. E (c) 3040/2, of the 26th September, 1918, seems to have been misunderstood.

Messages of this nature can only serve three purposes:

(i)   To create an artificial wireless activity in an otherwise inactive sector;

(ii) To break up the grouping of stations by continued inter-communication between neighbouring groups;

(iii) As practice in encoding and decoding.

If they are intended for headings (i) and (ii) the context of the messages obviously defeats the object. To deceive the enemy, it would be necessary to send dummy messages resembling those of a tactical nature as much as possible. Some indication would be necessary to earmark such message as dummies. This could easily be arranged. For example, a pre-arranged set of 4 or 5 letters could be apportioned as dummy letters *only to be used in dummy messages*. These letters might change weekly.

Care should be taken that in the working of dummy messages exaggerated statements are not made. The game would be given away if a message read: "Please send two thousand miles of barbed wire with rations tonight". I quote from a letter from Lt-Col. Drake, G.W., addressed to Captain Hitchings on 27/5/17, in which he says that in his view,

"No attempt should be made to arrange for the sending of dummy messages containing information, false or real, with the intention of the enemy picking it up. There is always the danger that information that is false today may be correct a week hence, i.e. just when the enemy has succeeded in deciphering the message.

My intention in this scheme was to conceal

(1)   Decrease in the number of formations on any given front;

(2)   Increase in the number of formations on another front.

This I understand can be done.

As regards the sending of messages, this should be confined to messages which are more or less of a routine nature and unimportant. In no case should they contain information of movements or tactical intentions. All that is required in this direction is to lead the enemy to believe that formations which were on any given front, now unimportant, are still there, and also that no increase has been made in the number of formations on the front now of importance."

Messages of the above nature would provide sufficient practice in encoding and decoding.

From the point of view of security, messages consisting of a jumble of letters and enciphered before transmission would be most desirable. I am certain that the transmission of this kind of message in anything like the quantity of the dummy messages complained of, would make the cipher practically insoluble.

The fact that the messages are "in no way stereotyped", and "No cipher messages of importance were being sent at the time" does not lessen the danger of this practice. What I am combating is the principle involved. If operators get into the habit of sending this kind of nonsense, it will be very difficult to stop the practice when the necessity arises.

It would be interesting to hear what Signals have to say on the subject, especially as regards excessive jamming. The possibility that, as often happens, an important German message is "jammed by Wilson set" sending such a message as "My father was one of the knuts of Barecelona, and so was Ma", does not bear contemplation.

It should be borne in mind that the enciphered message has a secrecy of its own quite apart from the nature of its contents. If the Key is solved on dummy messages sent on one Corps front, it may not endanger any messages from that particular Corps, but will be the means of reading perhaps the only important tactical message of the day sent two Corps fronts away.

I should be glad if you would reply to Captain Spencer in this sense.

AIR 137/4700

5

Order by Lieutenant-General Herbert Lawrence, Chief of the General Staff, Advanced G.H.Q., 18 August 1918

O.A.D.907/4. S E C R E T

General Sir H.S. Horne, D.C.B., K.C.M.G.,
  Commanding First Army.
General Sir H.C.O. Plumer, G.C.B., G.C.M.G., G.C.V.O.,
  Commanding Second Army.
General The Hon. Sir J.H.G. Byng, K.C.B., K.C.M.G., M.V.O.,
  Commanding Third Army.
General Sir H.S. Rawlinson, Bt., G.C.V.O., K.C.B., K.C.M.G.,
  Commanding Fourth Army.
General Sir W.R. Birdwood, K.C.B., K.C.S.I., K.C.M.G., C.I.E., D.S.O.,
  Commanding Fifth Army.
Major-General J.M. Salmond, C.M.G., D.S.O.,
  Commanding R.A.F.
Lieut.-General Sir C.T.McM. Kavanagh, K.C.B., C.V.O., D.S.O.,
  Commanding Cavalry Corps.
Major-General H.J. Elles, C.B., D.S.O.
  Commanding Tank Corps.

Reference O.A.D.907/2 dated 15th August, 1918.
In order to prevent our troop movements being followed by means of our wireless activities, the following precautions will be observed:–

1. The Third Army will ensure that no additional wireless activity becomes apparent on their front.

2. The Fourth Army will maintain their present wireless activity, particularly in the case of the Cavalry Corps, Tank Corps and resting divisions.
The Cavalry Corps wireless sets necessary to represent the

presence of the Cavalry Corps in the Fourth Army area will remain with Fourth Army for the present.

3.   All Armies will ensure that the wireless activity on their front remains, as far as possible, as at present, in spite of any moves of Corps, Divisions, Artillery, R.A.F. and Tanks, which may take place.[3]
Copies:– B.G., G.S. "I".
     D.Sigs

WO 95/575

6

Order by Lieutenant-General Herbert Lawrence, Chief of the General Staff, G.H.Q., 7 September 1918

O.A.D. 817.   SECRET.

General Sir H.S. Horne, D.C.B., K.C.M.G.,
   Commanding First Army.
Lieut.-Gen. Sir C.T.McM. Kavanagh, K.C.B., C.V.O., D.S.O.,
   Commanding Cavalry Corps.
Major-General J.M. Salmond, C.M.G., D.S.O.,
   Commanding R.A.F.
Major-General H.J. Elles, C.B., D.S.O.
   Commanding Tank Corps.
Major-General Sir J.S. Fowler, K.C.M.G., C.B., D.S.O.,
   D. Signals.

1.   In order to mislead the enemy as to the direction of our next blow, the First Army will stimulate preparations for an attack on a large scale to be delivered between the River SCARPE and the LA BASSEE Canal.

2.   The general lines on which these preparations will be simulated will be as follows:–

(i)   The Cavalry Corps Wireless Sets at present with Fourth Army will be transferred to First Army and will represent the arrival of the Cavalry Corps H.Q., under arrangements which will be made by D. Signals with Armies concerned.

(ii) A certain number of Tanks will be placed at the disposal of First Army to carry out training with troops in back areas, and to make tracks as if a concentration of Tanks was taking place in the area between the River SCARPE and the LA BASSEE Canal.

(iii) Officers of the Cavalry, VII, and Tank Corps will carry out reconnaissances of the proposed front of attack. Arrangements will be made by First Army with Cavalry Corps, Second Army and Tank Corps.

(iv) Traffic and movement in the forward area concerned will be increased.

(v)   The apparent number of occupied aerodromes will be increased. There will be a slight general increase in the activity of the R.A.F. and a strengthening of our A.A. defences.

    The necessary arrangements will be made by G.O.C. R.A.F. and G.S. A.A., G.H.Q., with First Army.

(vi) Existing ammunition dumps will be given the appearance of a gradual increase.

(vii) Additional Casualty Clearing Stations will be erected under arrangements which will be made by First Army with D.G.M.S.

(viii) The artillery resources of the First Army will be so disposed and employed as to give the impression of a general reinforcement of artillery to the front in question.

(ix) Information will be given to the troops that the American II Corps is about to be interposed in front line with a view to offensive operations and that the American troops are now concentrated at, and north of, ST. POL.

3.   The above scheme will be put in hand forthwith.
Copies addressed personally to:–

Second Army.
G.S., I.
G.S., A.A.
A.G.
Q.M.G.
M.G.R.A.
E.-in-C.
D.G.M.S.

WO 95/575

7

Memorandum by Colonel R. Meinertzhagen for Brigadier-General, General Staff, G.H.Q., I., 23 October 1918

The Security Section

1. The Security Section will advise on:–
(1) The preparation, distribution, periodical changing and the safeguarding of codes and ciphers.
(2) Negative, positive and confirmatory camouflage.
(3) The prevention of leakage of information from all sources.
(4) Instruction to educational establishments throughout the Armies in the Field, in the objects of security and the means by which it can be best obtained.
(5) The constant liaison between security effort in the British Armies in France and Allied Armies, the War Office and Home Forces.

2. The Security Section will have the following organization:–
$\qquad$ B.G.I.[4]
$\qquad$ Security Officer, G.H.Q.
With each Army. $\quad$ Army Security Officer. (G.S.O. 2).
$\qquad$ Army Security Officer. (Class HH).
$\qquad$ (Army Camouflage Officer.)[5]
$\qquad$ One clerk.

With each Corps.	Corps Security Officer (Class FF).
	(2 Camouflage Officers.)
With each Division.	(Divisional Camouflage Officer) not yet
	on establishment.

3. It is left to Army Commanders to decide whether their Security Section shall function under Intelligence, Operations, or directly under the M.G., G.S.[6]

4. All security effort must be as inconspicuous as possible unless deliberate advertisement is aimed at, and in this respect the mention of a Security Section or Security Officers in orders of battle, establishments, or orders of any description is undesirable. It is known that the enemy has a Security Section and it is also known to a large extent what are its duties. This knowledge has been derived from captured documents.

Should security officers fail to safeguard the identity and scope of their appointments, they will assuredly fail in the objects of their work. The identity of officers in Security Sections should not be known outside the Headquarters of the formation to whom they belong.

5. The ultimate goal of security is to produce an element of surprise. This can only be effected by preventing the enemy divining our real plan, whilst at the same time feeding him with sufficient material to induce him to believe he is in possession of our real plan.

Whereas the primary duty of the Intelligence Section is to gauge the enemy's intentions and the means at his disposal to carry them out, in other words to pick the enemy's brains, Security feeds the enemy with material served up in as acceptable form as possible. A security officer must never lose sight of the fact that he is dealing with a trained Intelligence Officer at the enemy's headquarters and that badly prepared camouflage will have the same effect on a trained Intelligence Officer as badly served food – it will be refused or if accepted will not be digested. A study of enemy methods of security and a knowledge of the enemy's personal characteristics is a necessary basis for successful security. A security officer should constantly frame his mind to impersonate the enemy and judge of the quality and quantity of material which is likely of acceptance or rejection.

6. The prevention of leakage of information and camouflage apply equally to the enemy, to our own troops and indeed to the world in general.[7] It may even at times be necessary to induce higher formations to believe that they understand correctly our future plans, and to encourage them in this belief.

As the sole source from which the enemy can gauge our correct intentions is the Staff which frames such intentions, every item of information bearing on such intentions, when spread abroad by that Staff, becomes a source of danger from a security point of view.

Intentions should therefore be issued in such a manner that they are not recognized as such, either by our own people or the enemy.

7. Camouflage gives a wide field for an imaginative brain and can be exercised to a second and third degree; if channels of leakage and methods of camouflage are carefully controlled, both the enemy and our own troops may become so confused and gorged with material that they are unable to assimilate it. This produces a clogged and inoperative brain, incapable of seeing clearly what our plans are.

8. The effect which camouflage of all sorts has on the enemy must be very closely watched and entails the closest touch with all branches of the Intelligence Section.

Instructions for Army Security Officer

1. His duties largely consist in using existing machinery for his purposes. At times he will be doing pure Intelligence work, at other times he will be doing Operations work. The co-ordination of all his effort must therefore be his first consideration. The closest touch must be maintained with the various branches of the General Staff to which he belongs and the best relations must be cultivated between him and the various

administrative services, more especially Moves, Signals and Royal Engineers.

2. He is responsible for the safe custody and periodical changing of codes and ciphers throughout the Army and for the carrying out of G.H.Q. instructions periodically issued in this respect.

He must ensure that no unauthorised methods of cryptography are used in any unit or formation; he must also ensure that strict uniformity of signalling procedure obtains throughout the Army, in order that no unit or formation can be distinguished by its procedure.

By frequent visits to offices who hold codes and ciphers, he will become acquainted with the methods of dealing with messages. He will also visit Signal offices and will bring to the notice of the Security Section at G.H.Q. any possible channels of leakage.

He will keep in particularly close touch with wireless communication and ensure that this prolific source of leakage is effectively controlled. (See also under para. 5.)

For the purposes of this paragraph (No. 2) he is assisted by the Signal Security Officer who is responsible for all coding and decoding. Should such work be found during operations to take up all the latter officer's time to the detriment of other security work, another officer should be attached to assist. It should be a matter of pride to the Signal Security Officer that he never delegates this duty to Signal personnel.

In Divisions and Brigades, encoding and decoding is the duty of the General Staff.* Should such work become too heavy it will be necessary to attach specially selected officers to assist rather than delegate the responsibility to the Signal Service.

The responsibility for cryptography and for decision as to whether a message should go in clear or cipher, rests entirely with the General Staff, and should not be delegated to the Signal Service.

---

* For revision when the division of responsibilities in these respects has been settled.

Special attention is drawn to the Secret memoranda on codes and ciphers, Ie (c) 3030/1 of 5–10–18 and Ie (c) 3030/4 of 12–10–18.

3. He is responsible that all steps are taken to prevent leakage of information throughout the Army. This leakage takes varying forms.

4. Experience has shown that the Intelligence Services of all belligerents gain the larger part of their reliable information affecting operations from prisoners of war. No effort on our part should, therefore, be spared to control this form of leakage.

Steps are being taken in the United Kingdom whereby all ranks are instructed on their behaviour if taken prisoner.

Arrangements must be made whereby frequent lectures and instructions are given to all ranks on the obligatory questions they must answer if taken prisoner, namely – rank and name. Many Allied pamphlets on this subject advocate instructing the men in the form of answer they should give to the obvious questions: but as such replies are usually misstatements, which inevitably results in their contradicting themselves, it is better that men should be instructed to give always the same reply to all questions, either "I cannot say" or "I cannot answer questions". Prisoners of war giving false information either voluntarily or under pressure, are not liable to punishment, though it has become a practice to threaten reprisals in the hope of intimidation. Men must be warned of other methods employed by the enemy to extract information from silent prisoners, namely, dummy patients in hospital, detectophones in prisoners' rooms and camps, the "pigeon" prisoner, Army nurses employed under the enemy Intelligence Service, etc.

Instructions must also be issued regarding the removal of unit identity marks or the carrying of incriminating maps, documents or letters on the person of men whose position renders them liable to capture.

All ranks should be reminded that there is no evidence to show that harsh treatment has been meted out by the enemy to silent prisoners, though of course the direct threats are resorted to. On the other hand, preferential treatment, so often used as a bribe for information, not only never materialises but if accepted only lowers the respect shown by the enemy to the prisoner in question.

The Intelligence Section at G.H.Q. is now receiving in ever increasing quantity the results of examinations of our prisoners, from which it is not difficult to obtain evidence showing what particular man or unit has failed in their duty in this matter when prisoners. Though it is undesirable to quote this as a threat, it would be advisable to remind men that records are kept by our Intelligence Section embodying the substance of all such captured documents.

5. The Signal Service is only concerned with the actual success in producing efficient inter-communication and has not the necessary time to control messages from a Security point of view, nor the necessary Intelligence experience to judge as to how much is or might be of value to the enemy, or to know how best to use wireless as a camouflage weapon. The Signal Service is, however, vitally concerned with correct procedure and will assist Security in this respect.

From evidence produced by the Intelligence Section, it is clear that there has been considerable leakage in the past from our wireless system; due probably to:–

(1) The various arms of the service being recognized by their type of wireless.

(2) The sending of messages in "clear", when code or cipher could have been used.

(3) Incorrect use of codes and ciphers.

(4) An unconsidered ("too free a", deleted) use of wireless as a means of communication.

6. Regarding (1). Measures have already been taken to avoid any distinction in the employment of definite wave-lengths by different arms. With regard to the use of different systems of wireless, the only distinctive feature existing at present is the cavalry. Sets are already on order to remedy this defect.

In addition, it is hoped to gradually build up a "camouflage wireless group" which will represent an Army, 6 battalions of Tanks and a Cavalry Corps, which will be controlled by G.H.Q. and be treated absolutely as G.H.Q. troops. Neither the group nor any part of it will be shewn on establishments or referred to in orders.

In wireless camouflage, when it is possible to represent a formation by actual wireless sets, it would be ill-advised economy to represent any formation by anything less than its full quota of such sets.

The "camouflage wireless group" will be employed:–

(a) To represent units, formations and training areas which do not exist or misrepresent the actual location of a unit or training area.

(b) To supply extra control stations.

(c) To produce lateral wireless communication and break up the group system.

Units from the "camouflage wireless group" may be allotted to Armies as the situation demands.

7. (2). The sending of messages in clear when code or cipher could have been used.

The responsibility for this rests with the individual framing the message. It has been clearly laid down from time to time what class of messages may be sent in clear. A great number of cases still occur where wireless messages giving away valuable information to the enemy are sent in clear, where these messages under no stretch of imagination could be designated as S.O.S., and where their value would not be depreciated by the delay necessary for encoding or enciphering them.

The Signal Security Officer will therefore arrange that copies of as many wireless messages as possible are sent to him for examination. He will forward to Security G.H.Q., through the Army Security Officer, all messages which he regards as "leakage". During actual operations it will not be possible for the Signal Service to submit a copy of every message, but in normal times every effort must be made in conjunction with the Signal Service to collect all messages.

8. (3). Incorrect use of the codes and ciphers.

It is the duty of the Army Security Officer to ensure that instructions regulating the use of codes and ciphers are strictly adhered to. Any negligence in this respect or suggested improvements should at once be brought to the notice of the G.H.Q. Security Section.[8]

9. (4). An unconsidered ("too free a", deleted) use of wireless as a means of communication.

It should be accepted as a principle that the more wireless intercepted by the enemy ("in use", deleted) the more quickly are our codes and ciphers solved ("by the enemy", deleted) and the greater becomes the leakage.[9] ("Though it might be argued that the more wireless traffic we employ the less will the enemy intercept owing to his inability to cope with it; it is unsound to assume that the enemy is incapable of increasing his intercepting stations to deal with our increased volume of messages" – deleted.)

This paragraph is not intended to restrict the free use of wireless when operations demand such a course.

Therefore wireless should never be used when other equally efficient forms of communication are available.

(" 'Practice' and 'nonsense' messages must be reduced to a bare minimum and", deleted.) Army Commanders, acting on the advice of their Security Officer, should, if necessary, close down wireless altogether in emergency, after weighing the possible disruption of communications with the result at which security aims.

It may become necessary for G.H.Q. to issue special instructions with a view to exercising wireless control for special operations. ("During or previous to important operations it may become necessary for G.H.Q. to exercise absolute control over all wireless stations in respect to the volume of wireless communication" – deleted.)

10. Our telephones in forward areas are a source of leakage of information through the enemy's listening sets.

The Army Security Officer will arrange that control listening sets are from time to time established in forward areas with a view to preventing leakage to any large degree, and he will ensure by every means that instructions regarding the use of the telephone in forward areas are enforced.

The danger from this source largely disappears during battles of manoeuvre, or if a river such as the SCHELDT or MEUSE intervenes between the opposing forces.[10]

11. The counter-espionage organizations in Armies and lower formations control leakage conveyed to the enemy by his agents. It is the duty of the Security Officer to keep in close touch with such work and bring to the notice of I(b) officers any channels of leakage he may suspect. He has, however, no executive control over I(b), and can only, through the head of the Intelligence Section, make use of its machinery.

Loose or indiscreet talk will similarly be dealt with in conjunction with either the I(b) sub-section or the A.G's. Branch in the Army.

12. He is responsible for all negative camouflage, i.e., camouflage designed to conceal information, inanimate objects or troops from the enemy. Under this heading is included not only the actual concealment of dumps, gun positions and roads, but the care of lights at night, proper concealment of troops in billets, concealment of Tanks, etc.

By frequent reference to the R.A.F., the success or otherwise of this class of work can be assured.

For the purposes of this paragraph the Army, Corps and Divisional Camouflage Officers will assist. Camouflage Officers work under the Chief Engineers of the formations to which they belong. The Security Officer will advise on all matters of policy and will bring to the notice of the various Chief Engineers any ideas or alterations considered advisable.

The Controller of Camouflage works under the Engineer in Chief, and merely issues technical instructions and arranges for the supply of material.

13. Fighting troops should be employed to camouflage works when we are anxious the enemy should interpret such work as camouflage. But when our camouflage is intended to hide our real purpose, other than fighting troops should be employed.

14. He will ensure that all G.H.Q. instructions regarding positive camouflage are carried out, i.e., camouflage designed to carry false information to the enemy.

It is essential that positive camouflage be controlled by the one brain and that it be invariably in conformity with the general camouflage plan. All information derived from our efforts is eventually sifted and adjudged by one enemy brain – a highly trained Staff officer, and any flaw in the scheme will destroy the whole work and expose our methods.

It is, therefore, very undesirable that positive camouflage should be initiated by the Army Security Officer without full previous reference to G.H.Q.

15. In the main, positive camouflage will be prompted by G.H.Q., Armies being required to conform in certain details.

The various forms of positive camouflage can be summarised under the following headings:–

(a) Construction of aerodromes, hospitals, hutments, railway sidings, gun positions, dumps, etc. As far as resources permit, camouflage of this description should be real, but when dummy work has to be introduced, it must be designed to deceive our own troops as much as the enemy.

The R.A.F. should be constantly asked to report on all such work.

(b) The spreading of false news by various means.

(c) Wireless, Power Buzzer and telephone camouflage. Both dummy messages and degrees of activity have in the past proved useful camouflage weapons.

(d) Troop and transport movement, attitude and dispositions of troops of all arms, railway activity and great aerial or A/A gun display: Artillery registration.

(e) Preparation of maps and documents designed to deceive the enemy and deliberately allowed to fall into the enemy's or enemy agents' hands.

16. Confirmatory camouflage. This consists in playing on enemy apprehension and confirming any false deductions he may have made. Such camouflage should usually be initiated from G.H.Q.

AIR 1/1155

VI
Codebreaking: Organisation

These documents deal with the organisation of British military cryptanalysis during the Great War. Documents One, Two and Three discuss the size, growth and structure of codebreaking and signals intelligence in general at GHQ France during 1917–18. Document Four provides a unique inside view of the personnel and organisation of one British codebreaking bureau in the field, that attached to GHQ Iraq. Its structure was far less elaborate than that at GHQ France, because it did not have to be more so. Compared to the Western Front, in Iraq the enemy transmitted far less traffic by radio and did so through a smaller number of cryptographic systems, each of which could be attacked at any one time by every British codebreaker. There was also a notable difference in the distribution of cryptanalytical intelligence to staffs and commanders in these theatres. In Iraq, and almost certainly Palestine as well, the commander and his senior staff officers routinely saw raw pieces of cryptanalytical intelligence, because these often revealed directly the intentions and capabilities of the enemy. The sheer volume of intelligence available in France made the use of a more elaborate bureaucracy inevitable, while, after 1914, codebreaking provided less dramatic material than was the case in the Middle East. This material had to be processed and interpreted by a specialist staff in order to have any value for a commander, although, on the infrequent cases to the contrary, raw solutions appear to have been provided directly and quickly to the appropriate commander. Each of these approaches was appropriate to the local situation. Document Five discusses the reorganisation of the British Army's codebreaking and signals intelligence service throughout the Middle East in late 1917. This shows the high degree of coordination between the four separate codebreaking bureaux of the British Army (in Egypt, Great Britain, India and Iraq) which attacked the cryptographic systems used by the enemy in the Middle East. Notably, these bodies worked far less closely with the codebreakers at GHQ France, who dealt almost entirely with different systems (the exception being the German double transposition cipher, and even here the procedures for using the systems were distinct). These British personnel, instead, cooperated with American and French cryptanalysts, who attacked the same German codes. Documents Four and Five also illustrate the bureaucratic-political structures of British signals intelligence during the Great War, by which a private letter could set in motion a significant change in organisation.

I

Memorandum by Brigadier-General E.W. Cox, General Staff, G.H.Q., I., 26 February 1918

Ie/1598/2.

M.G. Organization.

(1) It has lately become impossible to make full use of the material obtained by the Wireless Observation Groups, with the Intelligence Corps personnel authorized in War Office letter No. 121/France/1304 (S.D.2), dated 8.1.18 (your O.B./2087).

Obviously, the amount of personnel required for such work depends on the developments in the German Signal Service and these developments now make it necessary to ask for an increased establishment.

(2) The original establishment of cipher personnel was based on the number of German codes in use on our front. Partly owing to the appearance of new types of stations on the Western front, partly owing to the extension of our front, and partly owing to the appearance of a new German Army, the material obtained has increased, and, in particular, the number of different codes and ciphers has approximately doubled.[1] It is impossible for one man to work efficiently at the solution of more than one code at a time.

For these reasons, an increased establishment of 3 cipher officers, 3 cipher clerks and 3 W.A.A.C. typist clerks (2 of whom should be shorthand-typists) is necessary.

This increase is considered essential on account of the importance of the results obtained, particularly during active operations. These results include indentifications of units and information of much tactical value (times of counter-attacks, warning of gas shoots, times of sending out patrols, times of relief, reports on information obtained by patrols, company strengths etc.).

In view of the increasing importance of the cipher office in the Ie. section, it is necessary that one of the Cipher Officers should be graded as a 2nd Class Agent.[2] In addition to his ordinary duties, he would act as second in command to the Officer in charge of the Section, and would take charge of the Section during his temporary absence.[3]

(3)   The appearance of long wave stations on the British front, connected with the activities of giant aeroplanes, and the appearance of stations attached to the headquarters of the higher formations, demands a further increase in establishment if the available information is to be exploited. It is not possible, at present, to allot long wave intercepting and compass stations to Armies, but these stations already exist in the G.H.Q. Observation Group, and the material can be passed to the Army concerned if the establishment of the radiogoniometric section is increased.

The proposed increase to establishment comprises 2 cipher clerks and 2 additional interpreter clerks, of whom, in each case, one should be a Sergeant.

(4)   With the appearance of giant aeroplanes using wireless and the necessity for accelerating the transmission of information regarding the positions of these fast moving machines, it becomes essential to issue all such warnings from the Headquarters of the G.H.Q. Wireless Observation Group rather than from the General Staff (I), who have hitherto issued the warnings.

In order to provide continuous reliefs for this duty, one additional Intelligence Corps Officer will be required, and in view of the important nature of his duties the Officer in charge of this Branch should be a 2nd Class Agent.

(5)   If these proposals are approved, they will involve a total increase to the present establishment of the Wireless Section of the Headquarters Company of the Intelligence Corps of:–

4 Officers (including 2 2nd Class Agents),
5 Cipher Clerks (including 1 Sergeant),

2 Interpreter Clerks (including 1 Sergeant),
3 W.A.A.C. typists (of whom 2 should be shorthand-typists)
2 Batmen (Medical Category B.1 or lower).[4]

(6) Amendments to the Intelligence Corps War Establishment, necessitated if these proposals, and those contained in this office letter No. I.C.7142/B, dated 9.1.18, are approved, are (sic) enclosed marked "A", and a summary of the proposed increase is also enclosed marked "B".

(B)

INTELLIGENCE CORPS WIRELESS SECTION HEADQUARTERS COMPANY.

Summary showing proposed increase in personnel based on the assumption that the proposals contained in this office letter No. I.C.7142/B dated 9–1–1918 (your OB/2010) are approved.

	Officers.	Other Ranks.						W.A.A.C		
	Agents	Cipher Clerks	Interpreter Clerks	Draughtsmen	Clerks	Batmen	A.S.C. (M.7.)	Assistant Administrators	Women	Total
Present organization.	10	5	10	1	5	5	1	12	4	53
New organization.	14	10	12	1	5	7	1	12	7	69
INCREASE.	4	5	2	–	–	2	–	–	3	16

Transport. Remarks.

	Motor Cars	Motor Bicycles	
Present organization.	1	5	
New organization.	1	5	
INCREASE	–	–	

WO 158/962

2

Memorandum by Brigadier-General E.W. Cox, General Staff, G.H.Q. (I), 1 July 1918

I.e. 316

M.G.,G.S. (S.D.).

(1) It has now become impossible to make full use of the material gathered by the various Wireless Observation Groups, with the personnel authorised in War Office Letter No. 121/ France/1304 (S.D.2), dated 15–4–18 (your O.B./2087). Obviously, the amount of personnel required for such work depends on the developments in the German Signal Service, which now makes it necessary to ask for an increased establishment.

(2)   The present establishment of cipher personnel was based on the number of German codes and ciphers in use on the front. The number of these codes has largely increased of late, necessitating the addition of 3 more cipher clerks (including one Sergeant) in order to keep pace with the latest developments. The importance of the information obtainable from the enemy's messages is greatest during active operations, when information of the greatest tactical value is obtained daily.

(3)   Information of great importance is also given by a close study of the material obtained by the Radiogoniometric Section. The amount of material obtained has more than doubled during the past three months, and the office is now working the whole 24 hours in two shifts of 12 hours each. To enable this to be done, much of the detailed research work has had to be neglected, causing a considerable loss of efficiency. In particular, a close study of the messages sent by aeroplanes enables the various observers to be classified under their proper flights, thus enabling the movements of these flights to be followed from one sector to another, and the comparative density of flights to be shewn in various sectors of the front.

It is particularly to be pointed out that detailed information of this kind cannot be camouflaged by the enemy by any means, and that a comparison of the results of this analysis with other indications shews clearly what the enemy wishes us to think. I consider that 4 additional P.B. clerks (including one Lance-Corpl.) are necessary for this work.

(4)   In addition, the increased use of giant aeroplanes has thrown a very great strain on the personnel on night duty who now have to issue all warnings on giant aeroplanes and Zeppelins using wireless; other branches of the work often have to be circumscribed, or even stopped, in consequence, in order to cope with the work due to the presence of these aircraft in the British area. To deal efficiently with this, 3 additional P.B. clerks (including one Sergeant) should be provided.

(5)   If these proposals are approved, they will involve a total

increase to the present Establishment of the Wireless Section of
the Headquarters Company of the Intelligence Corps of:–

3 Cipher clerks (including one Sergeant).

7 Clerks (including one Sergeant and one Lance-Corpl.)

Amendments to War Establishment Leaflet No. 1179 Part
VIIA are enclosed marked "A".

(6)   With a view to economizing man power, I would suggest
that, if arrangements can be made for W.A.A.C. typists at
G.H.Q., the 4 clerks, mentioned in para. 3 might be replaced by
6 W.A.A.C. typists (2 shorthand), and the personnel re-
distributed.

WO 158/962

3
Memorandum by Brigadier-General E. Clive, General Staff, G.S.I., 4 November 1918

M.G.G.S., S.D.   I/628

1.   With reference to I/638 of 14.8.18 and O.B.2010 of
20.8.18, temporary authority was given in the last quoted letter
for certain additions in the establishment of G.S. I(e), G.H.Q.,
and of the Intelligence Corps.

The appointment of a General Staff officer charged with the
duty of advising upon the necessary measures of "security" and
"camouflage" and the proposal to appoint special G.S.O's to
carry out these measures at Army Headquarters, as well as the
experience already gained in the working of G.S. I(e), which
deals with the security of our own signal traffic, necessitates a
revision of the whole establishment of this section.

2.   In view of the largely increased importance and scope of its
work, it is considered that this section should be organized, as
shown in Appendix I, in 4 sub-sections, under a G.S.O.2,
assisted by two clerks, as at present, dealing respectively with:–

(a) German codes and ciphers.
(b) Positions and activity of German wireless stations.
(c) Security of our own signal traffic.
(d) Positive camouflage in connection with our own signal traffic.

(a) *German Codes and Ciphers.* It is considered essential that the Officer in charge should be made a General Staff Officer, 3rd Grade. During the past year, the importance of this subsection has increased very considerably and its full establishment now consists of 9 Intelligence Corps Officers and 10 cipher clerks, together with 12 assistant administrators, Q.M.A.A.C., and 7 clerks Q.M.A.A.C. The duties of the officer in charge necessitate his being in constant touch with the corresponding staffs in French and American General Headquarters, as well as with the British and French War Offices. I am of opinion that these liaison duties and also his dealings with the various Army Headquarters would be considerably facilitated, if he were made a General Staff Officer, and I strongly recommend his appointment as G.S.O.3.

(b) *German Wireless Stations.* Owing to the recent changes in the enemy's methods, the work of this sub-section has increased considerably, and the present establishment of clerks is altogether inadequate. At present, 14 of the clerks are working in two 12-hour shifts of 7 clerks each, day and night, but it is found that these hours are more than the personnel can cope with and the medical officer reports that they are being overworked. In these circumstances, I have no alternative but to request an increase to the establishment of 4 interpreter clerks and 2 clerks (including 1 sergeant), which will enable the work to be carried out in 8-hour shifts.

The work and responsibilities of the officer in charge of this sub-section fully justify his being raised from 2nd to 1st Class Agent in the Intelligence Corps, and I recommend this increase.

(c) *Signals Security.* To deal with the large increase of work which will result from the use of control wireless stations at Corps, Army and General Headquarters (authorized in War Office letter 121/France/2755 (S.D.2), dated 15.9.18) one G.S.O. 3rd Grade and 3 Intelligence Corps officers, 2 cipher clerks and 7 clerks will be required. War Office authority already exists for 1 Intelligence Corps officer and 2 clerks, and temporary authority for 2 Intelligence Corps officers and 4 clerks (including 1 sergeant) was sanctioned in O.B.2010 of 20.8.18.

The sub-section will deal with all questions concerning the security of our own signal traffic and of our own codes and ciphers. It will also estimate the effect produced on the enemy by our normal signal traffic and our camouflage operations, based on data supplied by the D.Signals and Armies.

The work falls into 2 main categories:–
(i) Security of our codes and ciphers.
(ii) Signals security and results of camouflage.

It is proposed that (i) be carried out by an Intelligence Corps officer (1st Class Agent), assisted by an Intelligence Corps officer (3rd or 4th Class Agent) and 5 clerks (2 cipher clerks, including 1 sergeant, and 3 clerks, including 1 sergeant and 1 corporal).

The signals security work (ii), which will entail the study of a very large number of reports, will require the services of 1 Intelligence Corps officer (2nd Class Agent) and 4 clerks (including 1 sergeant and one corporal).

I strongly recommend that the officer in charge of the whole sub-section shall be a G.S.O.3, as his very important duties necessitate his dealing direct with various senior officers of the Signal Service. Army Security Officers and Allied sections which fulfil a similar role. An additional reason for this grading is furnished by the fact that he necessarily acts as deputy for the General Staff Officer in charge of I(e), during the latter's absence.

(d) *Positive Camouflage.* In order to be able to deal with the very important question of positive camouflage as applied to the Signal Service, and particularly to wireless, it is essential to increase the establishment of G.S.I(e) by one other G.S.O.3.

This officer, who must have had wireless experience, would be attached to Signals for a period of 2 or 3 months in order to make himself thoroughly acquainted with the actual conditions under which work is carried out by the Signal Service, both in forward and in training areas. His duties would consist in applying the knowledge thus gained towards assisting the general (positive) camouflage scheme; without thorough knowledge of the minutest details, no positive camouflage scheme could be made to appear convincing to the enemy.

3. I think the time has now come when the officer in charge of G.S.I(e) should be advanced to G.S.O.2. Since this appointment was first made in January, 1917, the scope of the section has enormously increased, entailing increased responsibilities on the officer in charge. He has direct dealings with nearly all branches of the Staff at G.H.Q. and is in constant communication with General Staff Officers at Army Headquarters and with Allied Staff. I am strongly of opinion that this officer's position and responsibilities necessitate his being appointed a G.S.O.2.

4. The proposals will necessitate an increase to the War Establishment of General Staff, Intelligence.
(a) As laid down in War Office letter 121/Staff/4863(S.D.2) of 14.3.18, amended by 121/France/2146(S.D.2) of 14.6.18, 121/Staff/5554(S.D.2) of 24.8.18 and 121/France/2880(S.D.2) of 9.10.18, of the following General Staff Officers:–
   1 G.S.O. 2nd Grade.
   2 G.S.O's 3rd Grade.
(b) As laid down in War Office letter 121/France/2350(S.D.2) of 12.7.18, amended by 121/Staff/5554(S.D.2) of 24.8.18

and 121/France/2813(S.D.2) of 8.10.18, of the following clerical staff:–

1 Sergeant.

1 Corporal.

3 O.R.'s.

(Temporary authority for 1 sergeant, 1 corporal and 2 other ranks has already been given in O.B.2010 of 20.8.18. The net increase in numbers would therefore be 1 other rank.)

The above proposals will also necessitate an increase to existing establishments of the following personnel which, I submit, is fully justified by the great importance of this section for the success of future operations:–

2 Intelligence Corps officers (1st Class Agents),

4 Interpreter clerks.

2 Cipher clerks (including 1 sergeant),

2 Clerks (including 1 sergeant).

(Temporary authority for the 2 Intelligence Corps officers has already been given in O.B.2010 of 20.8.18.)

A table showing the amendments to War Establishment leaflet No. 1179 (Intelligence Corps), as amended by War Office letter No. 121/France/2278(S.D.2) of 11.6.18, which will be necessary under these proposals, is given in Appendix II.

INTELLIGENCE "E"
G. S. O., 2nd Grade.
(a) 2 clerks (1 Sergeant, 1 Corporal).

SIGNALS SECURITY.

GERMAN CODES AND CIPHERS.

G.S.O.3.

1 G.S.O., 3rd Grade.
9 I.C. Officers.
  (1 – 1st Cl.Agent;
  3 – 2nd Cl.Agent:
  5 – 3rd or 4th Class Agents).

1 I.C. Officer
(2nd Cl.Agent).

(a) 4 Clerks.
(including 1 Sergt. and 1 Corporal).

10 Cipher Clerks.
  (including 2 Sergeants).
12 Assistant Admini-strators, Q.M.A.A.C.
7 Clerks, Q.M.A.A.C.

2 I.C. Officers.
(1 – 1st Class Agent and 1 – 3rd or 4th Cl.Agent).
2 Cipher Clerks.
(including 1 Sergeant and 1 Corporal).

(a) 3 Clerks.
(including 1 Sergeant and 1 Corporal).

POSITIVE CAMOUFLAGE.

GERMAN WIRELESS STATIONS.

1 G.S.O., 3rd Grade.

4 I.C. Officers.
  (1 – 1st Class Agent;
  1 – 2nd Class Agent;
  2 – 3rd or 4th Class Agents).
16 Interpreter Clerks.
  (including 3 Sergeants)

POSITIVE CAMOUFLAGE.   GERMAN WIRELESS
STATIONS.
7 Clerks.
(including 1 Sergeant and 1
Corporal).
1 Draughtsman.

(a) Borne on establishment of G.S. (Intelligence).

APPENDIX II.

WAR ESTABLISHMENT LEAFLET No. 1179 (Intelligence Corps). (As amended by War Office Letter No. 121/France/2278 (S.D.2), dated 11.6.18.)

Headquarters Company.
  Under Wireless Section:–
    Amend number of officers to read "16".
    Amend number of sergeants to read "6".
    Amend number of other ranks to read "23".
    Amend number of clerks to read "1 Sergeant and 6 rank and file".
    Amend number of batmen to read "8".
    Amend totals accordingly.

Note (q).   FOR "of whom 1 may be 1st Class" SUBSTITUTE "of whom 3 may be 1st Class".

Note (r).   DELETE, and SUBSTITUTE:–
(r). Distribution of employment:– Cipher clerks 12 (including 3 sergeants); interpreter clerks 16 (including 3 sergeants); draughtsmen 1.

WO 158/961

4
Letter from Gerard Clauson to Lieutenant G.G. Crocker, 9 October 1917

Personal & Secret   *Baghdad*

My dear Crocker,[5]

Your letter came at a most providential moment. I am temporarily laid on the shelf, in other words am in bed with a sore belly. I gave a lifelike imitation of the village pump for 3 days & then went to the doctor who gave me a dose of castor oil, which spurred me on to further efforts hither to unimagined, & then filled me up with some powders which have reduced me to the state of the Scottish wild-cat.

Later. However God is good & with the help of a little hot tea & firm determination not to take No for an answer I have managed to produce quite a satisfactory little bit of piece work. Incidentally since writing the above I have solved another of our local brand of cipher, the 9th of its kind. I don't know how the Devil I can send you my notes on solving these ruddy things. I think I'll cut it up and send it to you in 3 installments each lot being sent twice. Then if one assignment gets torpedoed there'll be another lot 3 weeks later. I imagine there's no absolute cast iron hurry for it, & if they only know the loop-holes in the system, Allah Kerim! It's easy enough to make cast iron. How they can be such awful mugs as to make a system as complicated as a double transposition on 2 different keys & then use it so that it can be got out in anything from 23 hours to 6 days entirely defeats me & I can only put it down to the direct intervention of God on the side of the Entente.

We are at last properly organised for our side of the show here, thank God, have our own little room (though as a matter of fact I work in the main room so as to be near master) & our own subsection, known as the A.R. Section, from your own phrase "absolutely reliable." As you probably know the show here is run by a B.G.G.S. Next to him comes a G.S.O.I., who is the immediate father of the A.R. Section. All translations are put up to him & he notes them up & puts them up to the General who puts (deleted – "them straight") about 30% of them straight up to the Army Commander, so we are as you see rather more favoured by the lords of the land than they seem to be in France.

Our staff at present is three officers, (deleted – "Capt sic Campbell) all Special Service Officers[6] graded as G.S.O.III. (1) Campbell Thompson, the Assyriologist, a curious old bird with a most amazing inverted brain; (deleted – "& at certain") sometimes I think him the most impractical thing God ever made, (deleted – "but") he has hordes of minor detail about all sorts of people (he keeps the Who's Who of our foes, enemy agents etc. on this front) & will serve you with masses of useless information if you ask him who so-&-so is, & will probably miss all essentials completely, & yet on (deleted – "one") occasions, he puts up a real slap-up job of work. He has just sorted (deleted – "out") through some old papers & put up a really fine contre-espionage piece of work, & has also specialized in finding the words of the enemy keys on this front & has found the German of most of them to his own satisfaction (but not quite of mine, I think there are too many possibilities) hence recent frenzied telegrams to you on "Perseran in Mitteleuropa",[7] which I am inclined to think the finest hare ever started. As long as you can solve them on the 'one down, 'nother come along' principle I don't think the somewhat fugitive assistance of finding a sentence which is broken up into sections to form the various keys is likely to be any real help. However that's as it may be.

(2) There is Hony, Levant Consular Service, late Consult (sic) in Mosul, a gentleman & a dam' good fellow with a real brain. He is nominally a Turkish interpreter & is a good bit better at Turkish than I am. He arrived in July & I have now taught him about as much as I know regarding the technical side of solving, all he wants is a little practice in word-building etc. & he takes that whenever he can, so practically now our controls here are all trebled.

We have also an Army Schoolmaster, a Warrant Officer, quite a decent fellow to do all the hack work of transposing.

We organize as follows, German originals come to the W.O. who transposes them & hands them to any one of us. If he gets at all behind (which he doesn't at present) we take some off him. We then translate them appealing to Maj. Blaker (who is German by descent & speaks it like a native) if we get held up by them. We note them up & then put them up to G.S.O.I. etc. Turkish originals come to Hony or me & we transliterate & translate them etc. as before. Turkish messages in new keys we can all tackle. C.T. holds the record having downed one with only 113 groups to work on; they rarely present any difficulty. Germans we all tackle, comparing notes as we work, so often the result is a product of our united efforts, tho' actually I have given the 'coûp de grâce' to all so far. Messages from Syrian stations we tabulate & send a list of to Egypt daily, so that if we get any they miss we can send it to them. They do the same for messages from Mesopotamia. We have reduced the reporting to a fine art with code names for the addresses etc. & the whole thing works quite smoothly.

As regards volume of stuff, Turk messages are very rare confined practically to occasional messages from the now safely captured Euphrates Group. Germans vary usually 30–40 a day (deleted, "without") (counting each part of a multiple part message as a separate message) but rising substantially when there's any fuss on.

Besides translating the messages we send the W.O. any snappy bits we get by wire; & also of course, we send any new keys etc. that way. We also summarize all messages & index them under various heads in the A.R. Summary which is a manuscript work used solely for reference. We do not send written reports out at all. Apart from wires to the W.O. nothing leaves the section in recognizable form & nothing is put in our Intelligence Summaries, but the information is of course used to check and coordinate other information.

The only people who know of the existence of the A.R. Section are the A.C., C.G.S., Operations & Intelligence G.H.Q. only, the Chief Political Officer (personally only) & the Wireless blokes who take the stuff in. After all no-one else need & it makes one absolutely cat to see how Egypt splash it about in printed summaries & things, but that I think is stopped now thank God.

The latest news regarding D.F.'s[8] is not quite so good but improving. Coxon is a bloody old ass & f——ing awful nuisance. He has done nothing except stand on his dignity, put up distinctly 2nd rate intercepts & then try & get work taken away from the Anzacs who do thundering well. He could think of nothing except trying to pinch more personnel & material & give a minimum of bearings. Everyone was getting bloody sick of him when your merciful offer to replace him arrived. One station is actually going & the other will in a week, so with Lefroy coming here to give things a start proper & with another fellow vice Coxon we should do well.[9]

I wrote to Colonel French[10] 2 months ago suggesting that if he had any other work for me in the spring, I hoped he would let me know. I suggested the Russian front but that don't look too good.

The dead rock bottom fact-of-the-matter is that there is literally nothing doing here in the summer; I love the place & the people I work with more than its possible to imagine & I'd hate leaving them, but Falkie's bunt, if he makes his mind up to have one is bound to come before March & once made I very much doubt whether there'll be anything doing here at all. I even doubt their leaving the German stations here. And here I shall be 6 weeks from home with a fiancée in England who wants to get married almost as much as I do & nothing to do. What would really be best would be for you to require my presence at home for a month to confer with you; then I could come back here for next winter campaign, if there is a next winter campaign. I have been away from home about 15 months now & I'm getting pretty tired of it. I suppose Cork St.'s pretty tedious,[11] but wait 'till you've done a clean point of nearly 11 months without a single ruddy half holiday. Mind you not for worlds would I have missed it & not for worlds would I leave it as long as there's a show on, but even when there's nothing doing you still spend every day in the office only there's less work to do & it's all dull. At present every day you have one or more genuine pinches & feel you've earned your 30/- when you go to bed. So enough of this grouse, p'raps I shall get marriage leave in the spring or the war may be over; I don't much like the leave idea though, so many good fellows deserve leave more than me. I wish to Gawd you'd send some of your private secretary brand of clerk out here, we could do with one to furnish the A.R. room.

Your remarks on cipher on other fronts are a great help, as you know we telegraphed for something of the sort some little time ago to deal with possible eventualities when the German Corps of the YILDERIM Army Group rolls up.

The Salonika system sounds pretty bloody. I suppose they can down it all right tho! Do they do anything on the Italian front? You get nothing from Russia I imagine & aren't likely to with the present sods running it.

I seem to have written you a most inconscionable lot of Balz, D.U. to-morrow I will get onto the real work of the letter the technical side.

IWM, Sir Gerard Clauson Papers

5
Telegrams to and from General Headquarters, Mesopotamian Expeditionary Force, October and November 1917

From Dirmilint[12]
To General Baghdad
No. 43793 Cipher
Dated 23/10/17.   Rec. 25/10/17.

Most secret. I am anxious to obtain closer coordination between the branches dealing with cryptography on the Mesopotamia, Egypt and Salonika fronts. It is suggested that advantage be taken of the presence of Major LEFROY in Mesopotamia to discuss how this co-ordination can be effected. I am inclined to think that this might be done by making an Officer responsible for this and putting him in Egypt, his position to be analogous to that of LEFROY who is responsible for the technicalities of wireless interception and co-ordination on these three fronts. If you can spare CLAUSON to undertake this work I shall be very glad and will send full instructions in a subsequent telegram.

Intld. by W.F.B. 25/10/17 [13]

L.O.

From Dirmilint
To Genl. Baghdad
No. 45240 Cipher. M.I.
Dated Novr. 10th 1917.　　　　　Rec. 11/11/17.

It is proposed to send an Officer to Egypt to hold position analagous to that of Major Lefroy as regards wireless in order to coordinate work of branches dealing with Cryptography. G.O.C. Egypt is asked to send Lieut. Jolawicz who has good knowledge of German to Mesopotamia to replace Captain Clauson and G.O.C. Mesopotamia is asked to spare Captain Clauson for the above appointment. So that he may inform me direct where any additional personnel will be useful, Clauson should be given all necessary facilities to study problems on spot.

Rep. India and Egyptforce
Intld. by W.F.B. 11/11/17.

L.O.

From Dirmilint London.
To General Baghdad.
No. 45822 Cipher.
Dated Nov. 16th 1917.　　　　　Rec. 12.35 p.m. 17/11/17.

Following for Captain CLAUSON to be read in conjunction with my telegram No. 43793 Cipher Octr. 23rd and 45240 Cipher Novr. 10th.

As *soon as you can be spared* you should proceed to Egypt and later to Salonika. You are to take charge of all deciphering and translating work on the 3 fronts with Headquarters in Egypt. Please send as soon as possible, first, briefly by telegram, your observations on present situation, your ideas on need for additional personnel and provision of weekly reports from all fronts. You should also get into communication with Colonel JEFFERY,[14] Army Headquarters India, with regard to improving if necessary existing liaison with him. Full draft instructions for your remarks are being sent by mail to Egypt. Please report your arrival there. You will work in the closest possible touch with Wireless Intelligence. This is an absolutely essential part of scheme. (No other addresses)[15]

General Baghdad.
To Dirmilint London.
No. I(a) 3325 (X–4846)
Dated 18th Novr. 1917.   Des: 1.10 a.m. 20/11/17.

Following from Captain Clauson. Begins. Your 45822 dated 16th. Date of my departure from Baghdad is dependent on reply to General Baghdad's No. X–4800 of November 16th. Am getting into touch with Col. Jeffrey. Am already close touch Major Lefroy. Understand my draft instructions will clearly define our respective spheres of responsibility in Egypt, a point for settlement being whether as hitherto Lefroy shall control cryptography as well as wireless technical matters in Egypt or whether I as cryptographer shall be directly responsible to War Office and not to Lefroy with whom however I would always be in closest touch. Early answer on this point would be advantageous. Regarding distribution and requirements personnel three fronts, will report when in position to do so. Re weekly reports on other fronts will report later. Following is situation here. Cryptography Section and Wireless Intelligence Section are in close touch but report separately and direct to G.S.O. one Intelligence. Responsibility of Cryptography section confined to distribution of cryptographic information to other fronts, plus decipherment and translation of intercepts plus furnishing of references to former deciphered messages. Wireless Intelligence Section is responsible for location of enemy stations by D.F. plus interception of enemy messages plus co-ordination and registry of all intercepts taken in by his own stations and by other friendly stations and for passing them to cryptography section. Wireless Intelligence Section Iec is given by Cryptography Section all information regarding comparative accuracy of intercepts and regarding locations and technical details obtained from text of intercepts, but has not access to files of translated messages. G.S.O.1 coordinates information obtained by both sections with other sources of information, being assisted in this when required by cryptography section. Results appear satisfactory.

Re solution on this front, unsolved residuum is of 3 classes (1) German political mission in Persia's figure code (2) Yilderim cipher, apparently transposed Huber type (3) new M.D.R. figure and letter code presumably naval. Quantity small about 2 or 3 messages each sort per week.

Am bringing all unsolved material with me and also a massed experience this section in decipherment, which I hope put on paper during voyage.

Re cryptography sections of reports from Mesoptamia, in view possibility mails being robbed on Tigris or elsewhere suggest all that is required is weekly despatch hence of copies of all unsolved messages plus separate cipher letter containing remarks and any available assistance towards solution. If any new cipher system is solved or other experience gained, full written report should be sent Egypt by hand of some Officer. Similarly any papers on decipherment from myself or other sources should be sent to Mesopotamia by hand as required. Current changes of cipher key are reported by telegram. Considered that any written reports extra to those above quoted are not repaid by risk they involve, and that circulation of translated texts is beyond sphere of cryptography section. Above embodies views of staff here. Is it correct?

Am arranging special ciphers for use between myself and Mesopotamia.

Will report by wire when I leave Baghdad and Basra. Ends.

IWM, Sir Gerard Clauson Papers

VII
Codebreaking: Techniques

These documents discuss the techniques used by military code-breakers during the Great War. They reveal clearly the processes of logic and intuition by which cryptanalysts attacked their prey: how a knowledge of vocabulary, grammar and colloquial usage shaped one's attempt to grasp the structures of language hidden by a code; how guesses, guided by instinct and experience, determined which of several possible lines of inquiry might first be pursued; how any and every kind of fixed relationship between parts of speech and code groups could be used as a lever to unhinge a cryptographic system. Document Two (along with Documents Six to Eleven, Chapter Four) reveals the techniques used to break codes on the Western Front during 1917–18. Since this issue, as against the solution of ciphers, has received little attention, these documents are of general interest – a similar, if more sophisticated approach, was used to attack diplomatic codebooks during the nineteenth and twentieth centuries. Document One is a treatise on British techniques of attacking enemy ciphers in the Middle East. It illuminates the state of that art during the Great War. The bulk of this document is devoted to a description of the attack upon one of the most sophisticated cipher systems used by any army in the field, double transposition ciphers. Such was the development of cryptography that by 1943 the British Army defined these simply as middle grade systems, for use between the commanders within a division. Both of these documents provide incidental material on the information which the British Army derived from codebreaking and, indirectly, explain why no army of that period maintained a high level of cryptographic security.

I

Memorandum on Code Breaking Techniques in the Middle East, 1917

The GERMAN Wireless Stations at present in IRAQ belong to the 151st FELD FUNKER ABTEILUNG, which consists of 6 (or possibly 7) field stations with 3-letter calls of which the first letter is "S" and one Receiving station. The S-group consists of 2 stations of a size roughly corresponding to our Pack-sets, normally working on 800 metres, and 4 sets corresponding to our Wagon-sets and normally working on 1200 metres. The old BAGHDAD station had the call S T K and this was adopted in its turn by the new big BAGHDAD Station. This latter was destroyed by the Germans on our capture of *BAGHDAD* and the old set with the old call retired to SHURAIMIYAH where it was occasionally heard till sometime in April since when it has not been mentioned and its survival is doubted.

The official numbers and locations (on 10.1.18) of the other S-stations are as follows:–

No. 1. (Pack) S X Y at KIPRI.
No. 2. (Pack) S D L
        S.W.W. of SHERCAT.
No. 3. S M R at KIRKUK.
No. 4. S T M at AL HUMR (on the TIGRIS).
No. 5. S A Z at HADITHA (on the EUPHRATES).
No. 6. S B A at MOSUL.

The Receiving set's call is O D; it receives messages generally from S M R and S B A on 1800 metres.

TIMES OF WORKING

As a rule all sets except O D now keep a 24-hour watch.

OFFICERS

The whole FUNKER ABTEILUNG is under the Command of Captain SALZMANN. The remaining Officers are one Oberleutnant or Leutnant per station.

PERSONNEL etc.

The stations have German technical personnel both N.C.O's and men, there being generally one Offizier Aspirant as 2nd-in-command and one Vize-Wachtmeister for cipher duties or two Vize-Wachmeisters with each station, and about 20 operators and mechanics and one medical N.C.O. or man. There are also about 40 Turks attached to each station, presumably as escort, orderlies, sweepers etc. and with the transport. The transport at any rate in the case of the heavy Stations appears to be principally oxen or buffaloes, with the two light sets probably ponies and mules.

ORIENTIERUNGS OFFIZIER

There is an officer called LEHMANN (the son of a Prussian Lt-Col:) who was mentioned under this title (either in full or as OROFF) several times during August and September. He reached MOSUL in August and went down to TEKRIT and thence to KIFRI where he now is. When the O.C No. 2 station went sick and O.C No. 3 station went out on a road reconnaissance he temporarily took over command of both stations. His exact function is uncertain. It is probable that he is merely an Intelligence Officer in addition to his Wireless duties, but if so it is curious that he never sends in any reports. It is therefore considered possible that he may have something to do with Direction-finding, but this is highly improbable, and the word "ORIENTIERUNGS OFFIZIER"[2] has not been used for some time past.

CLASSES OF TRAFFIC

The following classes of messages are transmitted by the S-stations.

A: Double-transposition cipher messages in German. These

form the great bulk of the messages.[3] They fall into the following groups:–

1. SERVICE MESSAGES[4]

Messages regarding requirements in personnel and material; strength returns; cash returns; instructions regarding procedure, working hours etc; orders for changing cipher and so on.

These messages are prefixed "KIF". All other messages are prefixed "CHI".

2. FLYING CORPS MESSAGES

Reports of movements of aeroplanes, reconnaissance reports (rendered to O.C. Flying Corps and C.G.S 6th Army after each flight), strength returns of planes in working order, rendered every Saturday; miscellaneous orders and reports etc.

3. LOCAL PURCHASE MESSAGES

There were German Local Purchase Officers on the KIFRI Line and at HADITBA, the former SCHUNNMANN working to supply the Turkish 13th Corps, the latter SONKROON, working it is suspected, to build up a reserve of supplies for the ASIEN-KORPS,[5] FALKENHAYN's projected striking force on the EUPHRATES; he met with a great deal of Turkish opposition and did not succeed in doing very much.

Both these Officers used to send in reports to and get orders from the ARMEEKASSENAMT 6th Army (AKA SECES) (sic)[6] but nothing much has been heard of them lately.

4. Messages dealing with the acitivites of the German intrigues with PERSIA, NIEDERMAYER, DRUFFEL, FRICK and the rest.

5. Messages dealing with German intrigues with the tribes in ARABIA, the ANIZAH, SHAMMAR and DILAIM and especially with AJAIMI of the MUNTAFIK. Most of these messages have been to or from Lieut: PREMMSER the representative at HADITEA of MISSMONT (= probably the Mission MONTETON, which is presumably the German organization which manages these intrigues. Captain Count DIGHON VON MONTETON was a

Staff Officer of the old DEUTSCHE IRAQ GRUPPE at BAGHDAD and subsequently at MOSUL).

6. TACTICAL MESSAGES.
These are common only during operations, or when the telegraph lines are interrupted.

7. MESSAGES TO YILDERIM
JILDERIM (sic) is the code address of the H.Q. FALKENHAYN Army Group and as such is the addressee of many of PREUSS-ER's messages and of HALIL's[8] daily reports etc. The latter are as a rule intercepted only when HALIL is on one of the fronts and out of direct telegraph with ALEPPO and beyond.

There is a special YILDERIM cipher, which cannot at present be deciphered.[9] It is not used by the S-stations for internal inter-communication, but is used for communication with HZR (ALEPPO) and the other SYRIAN Stations. PREUSSER has unfortunately adopted it for his reports to H Z R and it is sometimes used for forwarding HALIL's reports by wireless from S B A, the messages being re-enciphered at MOSUL. We have therefore got the original en clair of a few of these messages, and also the encipher in the YILDERIM cipher.

8. PRIVATE MESSAGES.
A certain number of private messages from Officers of the various stations are sent to MOSUL for transmission to GERMANY.

9. There is a small unclassified residuum of miscellaneous messages, instructions to the Post office etc.

B. Messages in the YILDERIM Cipher. Vide above.

C. Messages in the old HUBER Disc substitution cipher (vide W.O. telegram of 1.4.17 giving the decipherment of this cipher). This has been used in 4 or 5 messages only to or from O D.

D. The Germans intriguing with PERSIA have two or perhaps 3, 5-figure and 4-and 5-figure numerical codes which are occasionally used between S B A, S M R, S X Y and O D.

Regarding these codes we have made very little progress.

In the first the message begins with a 3-figure groups (sic) indicating the number of the message followed by a 5-figure groups (sic) indicating the date. In some cases this is followed by one of about 5 3-figure groups believed to mean "In reply to" or "in continuation of", followed by another number and date. Next comes a 5-figure group which always begins 92. There are about 10 such groups known. The message then proceeds in a medley of 4 and 5-figure groups the range being roughly 1000–29000 and 89000–99999.

The code group series representing the numerals has been reconstructed. It proves that the groups for the various series 1, 11, 21, 31 and 2, 12, 22, 32, and 3, 13, 23, 33 etc fall into groups of 3-figure numbers each beginning with the same digit; i.e. the numerals from 1 to 10 are represented by 10 3-figure groups each beginning with a different digit. These are increased by 8 or 18 to give the group for the figure 10 higher; i.e. 416 is the group for 1, 416 + 8 = 424 is the group for 11, 416 + 8 + 8 = 432 is the group for 21 and so on. When it is impossible to add another 8 without going into another 100, the 8 is added but 100 deducted so that the group still begins with the same digit; e.g. 692 = 9, 600 = 19, 618 = 29 and so on.

The second of these figure codes is a 5-figure code with a range roughly from 10000 to 37000. No conclusions have been reached regarding it.

4. TURKISH 4-FIGURE CODE MESSAGES.
These are occasionally intercepted when operations are on, or the line is down.

5. TURKISH 2-FIGURE CIPHER MESSAGES.
In recent months these have been confined to occasional messages between the EUPHRATES station and AL BUSH on the subject of local purchase.

ON THE DOUBLE TRANSPOSITION CIPHER USED BY THE S-STATIONS.
When the S-stations came East in the early winter of 1916–1917

they brought with them a number of cipher keys, probably 6. These keys were known by the names of different kinds of grain and are therefore known as the "GRAIN" series. They are the usual sort of transposition key; i.e. a long word or short phrase, the letters of which are represented, according to their alphabetical order, by figures to give the key on which the transposition takes place. The system is identical with that of our own transposition cipher, but in this case after the message has been transposed once instead of being written out at once in groups of five for transmission, it is first transposed again on a key formed by the same phrase with the first or last 3 letters cut off. When the "GRAIN Series" was originally used it was always the first three letters that were cut off. With the "METAL Series" (vide below) it was always the last 3 that were cut off. Now however when a key is taken into use it is described as "ARIE" or "SERIE" the former meaning that the first 3 letters are cut off to form the shorter key, the latter that the last 3 are cut off.

As in decipherment[10] the shorter key is used first we have become accustomed to calling the shorter key the "First Key" and the longer key the "Second key" and these terms will be adhered to here.

Of the "GRAIN Series" we have solved 5 keys, the others if they existed having been early abandoned, as from March 23rd at any rate, to September 6th these 5 keys were used alternately, in no particular order, the period of use for each key varying from 5 days to 5 weeks. The change was ordered by a message sent about 48 hours before the change was to take place reading "VOM—TEN NITYAGRAB—", the first blank representing the date and the second the name of the key to be taken into use.

The following are the keys in the "GRAIN Series" which have been solved:–

"HAFER"   2, 7, 5, 1, 18, 4, 8, 6, 3, 11, 9, 10.
(1st key in HAFER ARIE, 1, 9, 3, 5, 4, 2, 8, 6, 7,
   "   "   "   SERIE, 2, 7, 5, 1, 9, 4, 8, 6, 3)
"GERSTE"   11, 10, 8, 9, 4, 8, 6, 3, 11, 9, 10.
"MAIS"   8, 9, 10, 2, 11, 6, 3, 13, 14, 4, 1, 12, 15, 6, 7.
"ROGGIN"   4, 14, 8, 3, 6, 15, 11, 12, 7, 1, 9, 13, 2, 5, 10.

"WEIZEN" 10, 2, 6, 13, 4, 8, 14, 3, 7, 17, 1, 9, 18, 15, 16, 11, 12, 5.

This series was dropped on September 16th and a new series adopted called after the names of Metals; of this series the following 7 keys have been solved:–

"KUPPER" 2, 8, 5, 10, 9, 12, 3, 6, 13, 4, 1, 11, 7, 14.
"SILBER" 8, 2, 9, 12, 3, 10, 16, 15, 4, 11, 13, 14, 1, 6, 5, 7.
"STAHL" 6, 4, 10, 11, 2, 5, 3, 12, 9, 7, 8, 1.
"ZINN" 1, 3, 12, 7, 5, 9, 4, 13, 11, 8, 10, 6, 2, 15, 14.
"MESSING" 1, 13, 9, 12, 2, 6, 11, 5, 3, 10, 7, 4, 8.
"GOLD" 9, 1, 12, 5, 8, 16, 2, 13, 3, 17, 6, 14, 10, 4, 11, 15, 9.
"EISEN" 1, 6, 8, 3, 2, 4, 7, 9, 11, 5, 10.

Keys are now chosen indifferently from either of the two series and are seldom kept in use for more than 8 days. The last *new* Key "EISEN" was taken into use on 13.11.17. It will be noticed that in the metal series the keys are all of different lengths, ranging from 11 to 17 letters.

It is to be hoped that they have now completed the cycle of keys of the METAL series and will continue to use these keys for some time to come.

It is quite clear from the way in which they use the double transposition cipher that the enemy have not the vaguest idea of the normal methods for solving such a cipher. There are briefly 4 in number–

(1) By getting a message in which a mistake has been made in the first transposition and of which a corrected version has been subsequently transmitted.
(2) By the method of the perfect rectangle.
(3) By the method of the semi-perfect rectangle.
(4) By anagramming.

(1) This is the best method by which a totally unknown form of double transposition cipher between stations, whose messages have not hitherto been read, can be solved. The way in which it presents itself to the solver is that he gets two messages almost identical *but not quite.* Two examples have occurred in MESOPO-TAMIA.

One solved ANNA (independently to the EGYPT and W.O. solution). In this case the encipherer got two of his columns misplaced in both transpositions, and subsequently sent the message again correcting his error. In this case comparing the two messages, which were each, as far I remember, about 100 letters long, two blocks of 9 letters each were transposed about the middle of the message and every 8th or 9th letter either one or two letters were different, however a count of the two messages showed that exactly the same letters were present in each message. This looked like a double transposition on the same key with 2 columns near the middle transposed, and after the two messages had been reconstructed in the figure formed after the second transposition had taken place so that the two columns of the original transposition (which appeared of course as parts of lines in the 2nd transposition) were in one order in one case and reversed in the other case, the key automatically appeared by numbering the columns and the cipher was solved, as in this cipher both transpositions were on the same key.

The other mistake solved "GERSTE" the first S-station key solved in MESOPOTAMIA. (One was previously solved by the War Office but only 2 months after it had gone out of use and it was not then realized that it was likely to come into use again; it was however useful to this extent that after the first key of the new cipher had been solved by this mistake as described below, it was assumed and proved to be the case that with the new cipher as well the second key was 3 figures longer than the first key).

In this case two messages were picked up with the same number and beginning but with the former containing one letter less than the latter. The count proved that they contained practically the same letters, but when the messages were put side by side 8 or 9 letters identical were followed by 4 or 5 letters different then another 8 or 9 letters identical and so on.

This looked like a double transposition in which one letter had been dropped in writing out the message after the first transposition and before the second. The two messages were therefore divided into columns and arranged so that the identical top halves of each column came in the same position in the figure while the bottom halves of the columns in the longer message were one column to the right of the corresponding bottom halves of the short one. Before very long the two figures were complete and it proved that the encipherer in writing out the message after the first transposition omitted one of a pair of I's on the first occasion.

The first key having been thus discovered and proved to be 10 letters long it was taken as a working hypothesis that the second transposition would be 13 letters long, a message of 91 letters was taken and transposed on the first key, and the result was divided into columns of 7 and written on little slips of paper which were easily re-arranged to form a message (with the help of a few CH's[1] Z U's etc, and a certain amount of trial-and error word building). This method of solution depends entirely on mistakes in encipherment being made and as a matter of practical fact almost no messages containing such mistakes have been picked up in this country except the two mentioned above.

(2)   THE METHOD OF THE PERFECT RECTAGLE (sic) is the simplest and most expeditious method of solving a double transposition cipher. It has proved effective with the majority of keys solved in MESOPOTAMIA but depends of course on a perfect rectangle being forthcoming.

A message in a perfect rectangle is one of which the CHI number, i.e. the number of letters in the message, is the multiple of the number of figures in the first key and the number of figures in the second key. Where 3 is the difference between the length of the 1st key and the length of the 2nd key the following are the likeliest perfect rectangles:–

88(8 × 11) 108(9 × 12) 130(10 × 13) 154(11 × 14) 180(12 × 15) 208(13 × 16) and 238(14 × 17).

The following is an example of such a solution which actually occurred in practice.

Shortly after the key changed to "HAFER" the following message from S B A to S M R, S X Y and S D L CHT 108 was intercepted:–

SAARX XNXXS NMUXX HBTXS OTJCL   TVNIX   EXMXO RAAGX
SODRE NGBRV MEFXI NTTIT   DTBXI UXZHA EANNL XEADS
MXZXT XUSSB IEHSC   WUXXS XLYDI   TMX

The CHI number, 108, being the product of 9 and 12, this message would be a perfect rectangle if the second key contained 12 letters and the first or preliminary key therefore contained nine letters.

To test whether this is so divide the message into groups containing the same number of letters as the longer key, i.e., in this case 12.

Write these groups out as lines, one below the other so:–

                  SAARXXNXXSNM
                  HXXHBTXSOTJC
                  LTVNIXEXMXOR
                  AAGXSODRENGB
                  RVMEFXINTTIT
                  DTEXIUXZHAEA
                  NNLXFADSMXZK
                  TXUSSBIEHSCW
                  UXXSXLYDITMX

If the message is a perfect rectangle each of the lines above will contain a section of the original untransposed message transposed on the key which has to be discovered.

To see whether a prima facie case has been made out the message should be examined to see if the C's in the message are accompanied by an H or K in the same line in all or most cases.

In the message above there are 2 C's accompanied in each case by H's in the same line (lines 2 and 8).

To strengthen the prima facie case the lines should be examined in turn to see if they contain a reasonable proportion of vowels and consonants to make words. The searches in this case need not be extended beyond the first line, which so obviously contains the words ANSXMRXXANXS(XY?) as to make the theory that the message is a perfect square almost certain.

To reconstruct the key write out the message in blocks of twelve as above but with the columns spaced out to catch the eye and numbered from 1 to 12, so:–

1	2	3	4	5	6	7	8	9	10	11	12
S	A	A	R	X	X	N	X	X	S	N	M
U	X	X	H	B	T	X	S	O	T	J	C
L	T	V	N	I	X	F	X	M	X	O	R
A	A	G	X	S	O	D	R	E	N	G	B
R	V	M	E	F	X	I	N	T	T	I	T
D	T	B	X	I	U	X	Z	H	A	E	A
N	N	L	X	E	A	D	S	M	X	Z	X
T	X	U	S'	S	B	I	E	H	S	C	W
U	X	X	S	X	L	Y	D	I	T	M	X

These columns must now be fitted together to make words. A start may be made by putting together 12 and 4 containing MR in the top line and CH in the second so:–

12	4
M	R
C	H
R	N
B	X
T	E
A	X
X	X
W	S
X	S

To make S M R this must be preceded by 1 or 10; 1 looks more promising, (sic) try it. Also put CH in the line 8 together

1	12	4		11	9
S	M	R		N	X
U	C	H		J	O
L	R	N		O	M
A	B	X		G	E
R	T	E		I	T
D	A	X		E	H
N	X	X		Z	M
T	W	S		C	H
U	X	S		M	I

3 obviously comes before 11, 9 making ANX in the 1st and

VOM in the 3rd line, 10 must therefore follow it to make AHXS(XY) in the 1st line. Put the other AN in the tope (sic) line together as well

3	11	9	10		2	7
A	N	X	S		A	N
X	J	O	T		X	X
V	O	M	X		T	F
G	G	E	N		A	D
M	I	T	T		V	I
B	E	H	A		T	X
L	Z	M	X		N	D
U	C	H	S		S	I
X	M	I	T		X	Y

The whole can now be fitted together

2	7	5	1	12	4	8	6	3	11	9	10	
A	N	X	S	M	R	X	X	A	N	X	S	1
X	X	B	U	C	H	S	T	X	J	O	T	2
T	E	I	L	E	N	X	X	V	O	M	X	3
A	D	S	A	B	X	R	O	G	G	E	N	4
V	I	F	R	T	E	N	X	M	I	T	T	5
T	X	I	D	A	X	Z	U	B	E	H	A	6
N	D	E	N	X	X	S	A	L	Z	M	X	7
X	I	S	T	W	S	E	B	U	C	H	S	8
X	Y	X	U	X	S	D	L	X	M	I	T	9

The first over the top give the second key; to find the first key number the lines and write the message out again in its original untransposed order:–

A	N	X	S	M	R	X	X	A	N	X	S	1
X	Y	X	U	X	S	D	L	X	M	I	T	9
T	E	I	L	E	N	X	X	V	O	M	X	3
V	I	E	R	T	E	N	X	M	I	T	T	5
A	Ⓒ	S	A	B	X	R	O	G	G	H	N	4
X	X	B	U	C	H	S	T	X	J	O	T	2
X	I	S	T	W	Ⓘ	E	B	U	C	H	S	8
T	X	I	D	A	X	Z	U	B	E	H	A	6
N	D	E	N	X	X	S	A	L	Z	M	X	7

The accuracy of the solution can be checked by the fact that the first key

1, 9, 3, 5, 4, 2, 8, 6, 7.

is obviously the second key.

2, 7, 5, 1, 12, 4, 8, 6, 3, 11, 9, 10.

With the first 3 letters cut off.

(3) THE METHOD OF THE SEMI-PERFECT RECTANGLE is suitable only in certain favourable cases. It falls into two parts (a) that in which the semi-perfect rectangle is smaller than the perfect rectangle (b) that in which the semi-perfect rectangle is greater than the perfect rectangle.

(a)   If the number of figures in the first and second keys have a common denominator, then if the number of figures which would be contained in the perfect rectangle (i.e. the number of letters in the first key × the number of letters in the second key) be divided by that common denominator a CHI-number favourable to solution will be obtained.

This method has been efficacious in solving one cipher key out here.

In this case the key lengths were actually 12 and 15 and a message containing 60 letters was intercepted. It was for various reasons assumed that the key lengths might be 12 and 15 and the message was tackled on this basis, and came out.

It is obvious that such a message when originally written out to be transposed would be in 15 columns of 4 letters each. Then written out for the second transposition this would be re-arranged in 5 lines of 12 letters each, each line containing exactly 3 columns of the original message. Therefore the message as finally written out for transmission contains 12 groups of 5 letters each group being 1/3rd of the jumbled letters of one line of the original message before transposition; therefore if three such groups can be put together and anagrammed out into one or more words the other groups can be placed underneath them and similarly anagrammed out, the letters in the same relative position to each other in different lines before anagramming being also in the same relative position to each other after anagramming.

This somewhat complicated explanation can best be understood by taking a 12–15 key and writing out and transposing a 60-letter message according to it, writing each line (i.e. quarter) of the original message before transposition in a different coloured chalk or a different alphabet.

Practically the only two favourable CHI numbers for this method which are likely to be met with are CHI 60 when the key is 12–15 and CHI 90 when the key is 15–18. The procedure being the same in both cases, to exemplify the method we will take a CHI 60.

The following message was actually intercepted from S B A to S M R.

EFBOF	KXXAX	TIGHS	TINBG
ENUHN	IREII	AXNZE	TSKRB
RXFOF	ELROF	ENAAX	KNLXX

The first step is to write it out with the groups well spaced out so as to catch the eye, much as the message is written out above only more widely spaced out.

Various hypothesis must now be made regarding words which it might contain. The principal feature of the message is the 3 K's, large number of F's and lack of C, D, P.

The lack of D excludes "DRUFFEL" which is recommended by its 2 F's, the absence of F knocks out "TRANSPORT" and "FTTAPPE", and therfore (sic) by implication renders "KERKUK" less likely an explanation of the 3 K's. On the other hand the presence of 2 L's and a number of F's makes a message from "KOFL" to "FLIEG" a probability.

The message will of course be one of 4 lines each containing the letters of 3 of the groups in front of us, the letters in each line being re-arranged in the same relative order as in the others as compared with their original order in the original groups.

If the message is from "KOFL" to "FLIEG", the "FLIEG" must be the beginning of the top line and "KOFL" the end of the bottom.

Take a piece of squared paper and draw two rectangles of 15 × 4 squares one below the other.

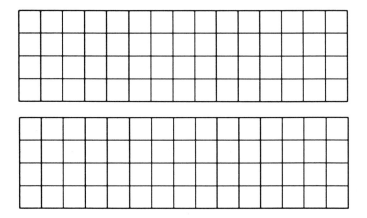

Now as there are only two L's in the message it is obvious that one group containing an L will be in the top line and the other in the bottom line; as the groups (sic) "ELROF" contains most of the letters of the word "KOFL" we will assume that it is in the bottom line.

Put the two groups in the top rectangle and the words "FLIEG" and "KOFL" in the bottom rectangle, so:–

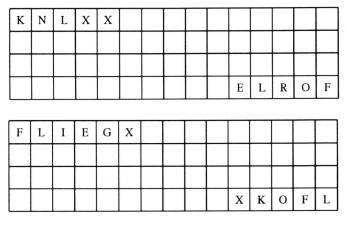

The top line is now deficient of F, I, E and O, and the bottom of K and X.

Try the following:–

K	N	L	X	X	E	X	F	G	F	I	R	E	I	I
K	X	X	A	X						E	L	R	O	F

F	L	I	E	G	X					X	K	L		R
	X									X	K	O	F	L

This suggests the word "KIFRI" over "KOFL" and this can be obtained by putting "EFBOF" in the bottom line,

K	N	L	X	X	E	X	F	G	F	I	R	E	I	I
K	X	X	A	X	E	F	B	O	F	E	L	R	O	F

F	L	I	E	G	X					X	K	L	F	R
B	X	$E/_F$	$E/_R$	O	$A/_F$					X	K	O	F	L

This started well but does not look promising. On the other hand "KIFRI" is a good idea and is very likely to follow immediately on "FLIEG". Take the 3 groups in the top line and see what can be made of the letters in them.

We get FLIEGXKIFRIXX and only NE remains over. Put them in the rectangle again therefore but put the "ELROF" in the bottom line so that the L is under the N in the top line, as it is obviously the last letter or the last letter but one. When this is tried it appears that O and F come under X and X, L therefore under N must be the last letter but one and must be followed by an X.

K	N	L	X	X	E	X	F	G	F	I	R	E	I	I
E	L	R	O	F										

F	L	I	E	G	X	K	I	F	R	I	X	X	N	E
												O	F	L	X

We now require groups to fit under "EXFGF" and "IREII" in such a way that we get K under I and X under E. These are easily found

K	N	L	X	X	E	X	F	G	F	I	R	E	I	I
E	L	R	O	F						K	X	X	A	X

F	L	I	E	G	X	K	I	F	R	I	X	X	N	E
	R	A			E	X			X	K	O	F	L	X

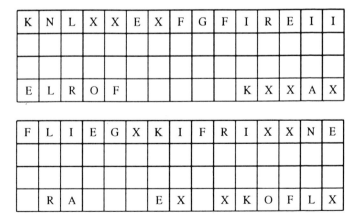

Next an X as 3rd or 5th letter of a group seems required to give the obvious ending XXXKOFLX. This is found and gives us the bottom

K	N	L	X	X	E	X	F	G	F	I	R	E	I	I
E	L	R	O	F	W	N	A	A	X	K	X	X	A	X

F	L	I	E	G	X	K	I	F	R	I	X	X	N	E
A	R	A	W	A	N	E	X	X	X	K	O	F	L	X

By reconstructing the word KARAWANE we place the group TSKEB and it is a matter of comparative ease to allocate the remaining groups and we get the complete text.

FLIEGXWIFRIXXNE   called *FIGURE "A"*
UNZEHNTENXABGIN
GBETRIEBSSTOFFK
ARAWANEXXXKOFLX

We have now anagrammed the text but have still to find the key. This is done as follows.

Write the message out in columns of 5 side by side, thus forming a rectangle of 12 × 5 letters, and number the columns off from the left.

1	2	3	4	5	6	7	8	9	10	11	12
E	K	T	T	R	I	A	T	F	E	W	K	called *FIGURE "B"*
F	X	I	I	N	R	X	S	X	L	N	N
B	X	G	N	U	E	N	K	F	R	A	L
O	A	R	B	H	I	Z	E	G	O	A	X
P	X	S	G	N	I	E	B	F	F	X	X

It will be observed that each line of Figure B contains the jumbled letters of 3 columns in Figure A; e.g. the top line contains columns 4, 7 and 11, and the second line columns 6, 10 and 14. Anagram the figure therefore into 3 columns, each line of each column being a column of Figure A, so:–

(a)				(b)				(c)				
12	4	1	10	9	5	3	11	6	7	8	2	
K	T	E	E	F	R	T	W	I	A	T	K	*FIGURE B.2.*
N	I	F	L	X	N	I	N	R	X	S	X	
L	N	B	R	F	U	G	A	E	N	K	X	
X	B	O	O	G	H	R	A	I	Z	E	A	
X	G	P	F	F	N	S	X	I	E	B	X	

The 3 groups of figures form the 1st, [deleted in original, "called 1st because it is 1st deciphering",] (shorter) key, but it is not yet certain in what order the groups are to be placed to do so. This can be fixed by taking advantage of the fact that the 1st key is merely the 2nd (longer) key with either the first 3 or the last 3 figures cut off and the remainder adjusted accordingly.

Write out Figure A and underline the 3 groups in the top line of Figure B in red.

F	L	I	E	G	X	K	I	F	R	I	X	X	N	R	*FIGURE A.2.*
U	N	Z	E	H	N	T	E	N	X	A	B	C	I	N
G	B	E	T	R	I	R	B	S	S	T	O	F	F	K
A	R	A	W	A	N	E	X	X	X	K	O	F	L	X

Now if (a) in figure B.2 comes first then KTRE must be numbered 1 in the key of figure A.2, but it is the 7th column and therefore bears no relation to the key of figure B.2, in which 1 comes on the 3rd column if (a) comes first.

Again if (b) in figure B.2 comes first than 1 comes 4th in the key of figure A.2, whereas the 4th column in Figure B.2 with (b) first is 7 or 11.

Therefore (c) must come first. In that case 1 in figure A.2. is the 11th column. Similarly if we arrange the groups as (c), (b), (a) in B.2, 1 is also the 11th column. Similarly, 2 is the 4th column and 3 the 7th column in both.

The whole of the 2nd key can be easily reconstructed by numbering the columns in the order in which they come in the reconstructed Figure B.2 (in the order (c) (b) (a)) and the cipher is solved, with

6, 7, 8, 2, 9, 5, 3, 11, 12, 4, 1, 10
as the first key and

8, 9, 10, 2, 11, 5, 3, 13, 14, 4, 1, 12, / 15, 6, 7
as second key.

(b)   If the key lengths are very short it is possible that a double rectangle 176 (with an 8–11 key) 216 (with a 9–12 key) or 260 (with a 10–13 key) may be met with. This is tackled in lengths of 22, 24 or 26 as the case may be, each containing 2 disjointed phrases, and the procedure is much the same as with a perfect rectangle.

4.   ANAGRAMMING PURE AND SIMPLE is the pis-aller of the solver. It again falls into two parts,
(a)   Anagramming a single message
(b)   Anagramming two or more messages of identical length.
   On this front (a) has proved effective once and (b) twice with 2 and two or three times with 3 messages of identical length.
   (a) is obviously unlikely to occur often as a message sufficiently short in a formula sufficiently well known to make the anagramming sufficiently certain is seldom met with.
   In the case in point it was provided by the message changing the cipher. This occurred regularly every 8 days at that time and at about the time when the changing message was due the following message was intercepted, CHI 66 from S B A to S M R and S A Z

ENUZA	GAATS	NOZNB	NVSUG	XSEDA
IXSAF	XWTNX	ARSOI	ELXAA	INSMS
NTZXZ	RLMNM	WXTHX	D	

   It was reasonably obvious that this was to be anagrammed into the following:–
AN SMRXUNDSAZXVONZWOURDZWANZIGSTENXMITTAGS XABXSTAHLXSERIEXXSALZMANN
the only point admitting of real doubt being the exact distribution of the X's.
   For various reasons connected with other messages which had been examined it was highly probable that the lengths of the key to be discovered were 13 and 16. The anagrammed version

was therefore written out in lines of 16 letters in its assumed original form:–

1	2	3	4	5	6	7	8	9	10	11	12	13	14	15	16
A	N	S	M	R	U	N	D	S	A	Z	X	V	O	N	X
Z	W	O	U	R	D	Z	W	A	N	Z	I	G	S	T	E
N	X	M	I	T	T	A	G	S	X	A	B	X	S	T	A
H	L	X	S	E	R	I	E	X	X	S	A	L	Z	M	A
N	N														

It is obvious that when the message is written out for the second transposition in a quasirectangle called "the intermediate figure" what appear in the figure above as columns will re-appear as parts of lines; i.e. the columns

A	and	N
Z		W
N		X
R		L
N		N

will reappear as AZNHN and NWXLN

But this figure in which these lines occur can be reconstructed by cutting up the original intercepted cipher messages into 1 column of 6 and 12 columns of 5 letters (the CHI number of 66 being fortunately a particularly favourable number giving an almost perfect rectangle for the intermediate transposition). The problem therefore is to cut the original cipher message up into columns and fit these together in such a way that the columns of the deciphered message can be read across it as parts of lines.

For convenience of reference, number the columns of the deciphered message.

Now our only fixed points are the lat (sic) 5 letters of the cipher message which must occur in the 1st, 2nd, 3rd, 4th and 5th lines of the intermediate figure. Similar (sic) there is a strong probability (12 to 1) that the last 5 letters of the message occur in the 1st, 2nd, 3rd, 4th and 5th lines of the intermediate figure. Now it will be noticed that of the last 5 letters of the message the H is the only H of the message and occurs in the 1st column of the decipher and the D must be one of the 2 D's occurring in the

6th and 8th columns respectively. Therefore to follow the column

X
T
H
X
D

we must find a column in which N is the 3rd and T or W the 5th letter. The 5 letters immediately preceding the last 5 give us such a combination. We therefore reconstruct

XL
TM
(AZN)HN
XM
DW(GS)

As for the other combinations it will be noticed that XL occurs in the 2nd and 13th columns and TM in the 15th; XM does not occur but there is an M at the top of the 4th column, and X at the bottom of the 3rd, 9th and 10th.

We therefore assume

W or G	X L
T	T M
N	H N/
M or S or X	X/X
?	/D S

This suits the 32nd to 36th letters, we therefore reconstruct

W X L
T T M
N H N
X X/M
A/D W

and assume

I N) W X L (N/
I N) T T M/
/A Z) N H N/
A N) X X/M (V I S/
A or B, A/D R (G E/

We get NOANE in the 11th to 15th letters of the cipher. This suggests that we have got the X's in the top line of the decipher wrong and that it should read ". . . UNDSAZXXVON".

It is now a purely mechanical process to reconstruct:–

```
X G X L/N W X L N/R N T E/
S A S X/O T T M/V S S Z/N
E A A/A Z N H N/S O M X/U
D T R/A N X X/M U I S/Z Z
A S/X I B A/D W G E/N Z A
I
```

which contains all the columns of the decipher divided up as shown. If the columns of this intermediate figure be numbered according to their original occurrence in the cipher message (i.e. the first 5 letters of the latter be number 1 and 30) we get the first key

5, 2, 6, 9, 3, 7, 13, 12, 4, 8, 10, 11, 1.

To obtain the second key write out the columns of the decipher in the order in which they occur in the intermediate figure; i.e.

```
X N R
G W N
X X T        and so on
L L E
N
```

number them from 1 to 16 and then put the appropriate numbers over the text of the decipher. This gives

8, 2, 9, 12, 3, 10, 16, 15, 4, 11, 13, 14, 1, 6, 5, 7.

This checks with the 1st key if the last 3 figures are cut off.

(b) Anagramming with 2 or more messages of identical length is too simple to need much explanation. The messages are written out in lines one below the other on a long slip of paper with the letters exactly underneath each other and then cut up into narrow slips each containing 1 letter of each message and these are sorted till words appear in all messages. Finally the complete text of both or all three or more messages (as the case may be) is recovered.

When this has been done the most expeditious method to

recover the key is to represent the letters as arranged in the anagrammed message by the figures from 1 to (the total number of letters in the message) and substitute these for the letters of the cipher message as received and then to take the first five letters (figures) of the cipher message, say 17, 5, 23, 69, 38. Write these in a column and add 12, 13, 14, etc, to each in turn, i.e.

	+12=	+13=	+14	
17	29	30	31	
5	17	18	19	
23	35	36	37	etc:
69	over length of message.			
38	50	51	52	

Now take each of these other columns in turn and see if it occurs *figure for figure* in the rest of the message, supposing 31, 19, 37, 7, 52 does, then it may be taken as certain that 14 is the length of the 2nd key and the rectangle will soon be completed.

13	17	31	45

IWM Sir Gerard Clauson Papers

2

Memorandum by Intelligence (E), Ciphers, General Headquarters, January 1918

"Enemy Codes and Their Solution"[12]

SOLUTION OF CODES

INTRODUCTION

As the following brochure is primarily intended solely for the purpose of showing the methods adopted in solving the codes used by German Field Wireless Stations, it is not proposed to enter into a long explanation of the nature and solution of codes in general. It is obviously impossible within the limits of a short treatise to treat exhaustively all the aspects of code solution, nevertheless, a few preliminary remarks on the subject may well fall within the particular scope.

DEFINITION OF A CODE

A code is in essence a conventional dictionary used for the purpose of translating, by means of combinations of letters or figures, a secret communication into such a form that it cannot be deciphered by anyone not in the possession of the code book.

In codes used by German Field Stations certain groups of letters are allotted to the words and phrases most frequently used in conveying information of a military character, as well as to numbers and to the most frequently used spelling groups.

A number of groups are also allotted to the various punctuation marks and grammatical signals such as

HAUPTWORT, MEHRZAHL, GEGENWART,
MITTELWORT DER VERGANGENHEIT,

and several groups are definitely set aside as dummy groups to be inserted in frequently recurring phrases and in short passages of a more or less stereotyped character.

The advantages of such a system of secret correspondence are obvious. Encoding and decoding are easy and rapid; the encoded message is generally much shorter than the original text; the comparison of one message in code and in clear does not enable another message in the same code to be read; and the measure of security is high if not absolute, unless the code book falls into the enemy's hands, or has been in use for such a long time that a sufficiently large amount of material has been intercepted to enable the enemy to solve it.

QUALIFICATIONS FOR THE WORK

In order to undertake successfully the reduction of a code certain preliminary qualifications are essential. Much time and much labour must be devoted to the work if any useful measure of success is to be obtained.

The would-be solver must possess a thorough knowledge of the language employed, not only from the point of view of vocabulary but also from that of a knowledge of all the peculiarities of its grammar, syntax and idiom, and of the peculiar phraseology, diplomatic, commercial or military, in which the messages are likely to be couched.

He should possess a lively intelligence, the faculty of imagination tempered by a highly developed critical faculty, the power of analysis, a high degree of a certain natural flair or instinct for the work, untiring patience and perseverance, in a word, the qualities of genius, defined as an infinite capacity for taking pains.

He will need a dogged obstinacy, which however must not render him incapable of discarding a supposed clue, once it has been discovered not to lead anywhere; a highly trained visual memory which will help him to remember the look of a code group, to recognise it on its reappearance, and to remember where he has seen it before, what its sequences were, and what theory, if any, he had formed about it each time it occurred.

He must possess the faculty of keeping anything from a dozen to twenty theories in his mind in order to build up a chain of coincidences and reasoning until each link fits into its place and forms a coherent whole.

IMPORTANCE OF METHOD

In addition to the above qualifications, however, a right method, and a clearly defined system of attack on a new code are necessary. It is the purpose of this brochure to try and lay down the main principles of a logical method, such as enabled the first code to be solved without the aid of previous analogies, and the more or less adventitious assistance of a knowledge of all the pecularities of phraseology and procedure adopted by certain stations or groups of stations.

At the same time, however, as much reference as possible will be made to all analogies which may lead to a successful attack on a new code when its general outlines, scope and procedure are known.

FIRST STEPS

At this stage a tabulated summary of the most essential steps to be taken will perhaps be most useful. Later on a more detailed elaboration of these steps will be brought in under the various sections as they occur.

(1)   The first step to be taken is to collect all the material that has been accumulated and have it typed out in such a way that the maximum amount of material can be brought under the eye at any one moment.

The material should be sorted as far as possible into sections showing the sender and receiver, and keeping as close together as possible all messages from the same station or group of stations.

Any indication in clear at the beginning or end of messages should be shown, such as sender, receiver, time group of transmission, Chi or Zif numbers showing the number of groups etc.

All pages should be numbered consecutively, and each separate message on a sheet should be given a serial letter. This will enable reference to be made to any particular code group or message by giving the number of the page and the letter of the message, i.e. 21B, 36K, etc. etc.

(2)   A book should now be prepared in which the letter or figure groups can be arranged in order, after which every group that occurs in the code should be indexed in the book by giving its reference as above.

In proportion as the signification of any group is discovered, its indexing should cease, and the meaning should be inserted opposite to it on the line. A sample page of such an index is shown in Appendix (2).

This book will then serve as a decoding or "Entzifferung"

book as well as an index. It will be well at the same time to mark the initial and final groups of each message in some distinctive colouring on the index, so as to facilitate the study of these particular groups, and to aid hypothesis as to their function when they should be frequent.

(3)   The index will soon begin to show the frequency of the recurrences of the various groups employed.

Attention should be concentrated on the initial and final groups which might indicate the address or signature respectively, or the word "an" "addressed to" or "intended for".

If the sequence of the first two groups should show any tendency to be at all constant it will be extremely probable that the first = "an", and the second = "unit" or person addressed.

Any outside knowledge as to the nature of the possible unit, or the rank, designation or name of the possible person may well aid hypothesis at this stage.

Very soon it should be possible to identify the various groups for "Division", "Brigade", "Regiment", "Kampf-Truppen-Kommandeur",[13] "Funken-Telegraphie-Station"[14] etc. etc.

When the study of numbers, treated in detail elsewhere, has resulted in identifying the groups which must be numbers, although as yet their actual value is not known, we have now reached a very fruitful stage for hypothesis as to the numbers of the possible units mentioned.

INITIAL AND FINAL GROUPS

(4)   An analysis of the most frequent final groups in each message should now lead to the discovery of signatures, of Punkt = Full stop, or of Fragezeichen = Note of interrogation. The last mentioned is very frequent in short messages such as "Wo Bleibt Abend Meldung?"[15] or "Wie ist die Lage dort?" etc. etc.[16]

A comparison of initial and final groups will now often show that the same group occurs at the beginning of some messages and at the end of others. This will point fairly conclusively to the fact that these groups represent the units or person sending or receiving the message.

Any outside indication as to the possible sender and receiver in each case will now be useful in forming an hypothesis as to the signification of these address and signature groups.

At this stage, as in fact at nearly every other, analogy with previous messages sent by the same station in codes already known or solved should be studied as far as possible.

A knowledge of the possible subject matter of messages sent at stated times, or under circumstances about which any outside or collateral information can be obtained should always be sought for, and will invariably and inevitably assist in experiment and hypothesis.

INTERIOR GROUPS

(5) We now approach the most difficult part of the solution, namely that of the inside portion or text of the message. This it is proposed to undertake by a separate treatment of the several kinds of groups which normally occur in the text of messages.

These may be usefully treated under the general headings of phrases, words, spelling groups, (used for spelling out words or names for which there is no equivalent group in the code), punctuation marks and grammatical signs.

Of these, for reasons to be explained later, the numbers are, in the early stages of the code, the most important, and their study shall therefore be treated first.

It must be remembered however, that it is almost impossible to separate one portion of the work of solution from others, and as stated earlier on, the efficient code solver must possess the faculty of keeping many possibilities and collateral theories in his mind, even while endeavouring to concentrate on some one particular aspect of the work.

The whole problem resolves itself into a coordination of hypotheses, separately obtained by analysis, theory and imagination, but linked together by every possible means until the whole chain of reasoning is found to be complete.

NUMBERS

Importance of numbers
In the days when cipher was employed to the exclusion of code, there was no necessity to concentrate on numbers apart from their context. The key once discovered, the whole message and all succeeding ones were immediately decipherable in their entirety.

Now however that code has taken the place of cipher the verification of numbers assumes a much more important aspect.

As it is obviously impossible to solve the two thousand odd groups which exist in a code until they have been used in messages, or even then until some of them have occurred sufficiently often to enable one to analyse their sequences and positions, the code has to be built up little by little, in proportion as material comes to hand.

It becomes necessary therefore to concentrate on what will be most immediately useful, and one of the most important pieces of information that we can obtain from enemy wireless messages is the identification of units in the German lines on any particular portion of the front, for the purpose of ascertaining what is the strength of the enemy forces opposite to our own.

For this reason we will begin with the solution of numbers, and consider this problem from the double standpoint of solution by analogy and solution on first principles, combining the two methods whenever the necessary progress has been made.

An essential preliminary is a knowledge as complete and detailed as possible of the constitution of the German Army and of the German order of Battle.

(1)   SOLUTION BY ANALOGY[17]

In these codes numbers are used in the following ways:–
(a)   In mentioning Units, Divisions, Brigades, Regiments etc.
(b)   In mentioning dates and times of day.
(c)   In giving map references after Karten Punkt and Plan-quadrat.

(d) In giving numbers of shots, casualties, Funken-Telegraphie Station accessories.

(e) Number of messages sent and received,
e.g. "3 Fundsprueche geschickt, 4 empfangen."[18]

(f) In giving tabulated reports of the day's activity under various headings.

(g) Chi or Zif numbers and time of groups of messages answered or referred to,
e.g. "Chi 17 an KS nicht verstanden"[19]
"Funkspruck 1806 erledigt"[20]
"Wer hat Funkspruch 1037 gegeben?"[21] etc. etc.

A sample message including most of the above uses might run as follows:–

"An Division 105. Abend Meldung 18 – 2 – 17. (1) Von 10 Uhr 25 Morgens bis 3 Uhr 30 Nachmittags 40 Schuesse schweren Kalibers auf Kartenpunkt M2 Planquadrat 5209. (2) Feindliche Flieger Taetigkeit gering, 5 Flieger ueber Abschnitt 7A. (3) Wetter gut, sickt klar (4 bis 7) nichts. (8) 2 Unter-Offiziere und 7 Mann schwer verwundet, 10 Mann leicht verwundet. (9 bis 10) nichts. Gezeichnet Bataillion II / 316."[22]

The form of these report messages varies with each sector and group of stations, but the same station has the tendency to send the same form of stereotyped message at certain stated times each day, and a careful analysis of previous messages from the same station in an old code will often be of material assistance is solving a new code.

One of the most essential things therefore in starting to solve a new code is to study as carefully as possible all previous messages, with reference to matter, form, and station procedure with all its varying peculiarities, and to analyse and experiment on the new messages to find out any analogies which may exist.

It has often been possible to make a start on a very limited amount of material when the same stereotyped form of message is still being transmitted by the same station.

It frequently happens however, that with a change of code or a change of unit, these messages are no longer sent in the same stereotyped form. Some messages rarely mention units, others rarely give the date, and some use letters instead of numbers in sending tabulated reports.

In one code certain stations regularly sent messages of this type.

"2 geschickt, 5 empfangen.",[23]

but with a change of code such messages ceased altogether.
In the same code one station regularly sent a message in the following form;–

"Regiment b' Morgen Meldung b' (1) etc."[24]

with a tabulated report on stereotyped lines.

When the code changed the form of these reports changed absolutely and no analogy could be observed. These changes were most possibly due to the transference of the particular Difua to another sector of the front.

When the form of procedure thus changes and analogy breaks down we are thrown back on solution by first principles, just as when the first code was solved without the help of previous knowledge of station procedure and phraseology.

(2)   SOLUTION BY FIRST PRINCIPLES

In solving a code without the aid of analogy there is a tremendous amount of preliminary spade work to be done.

(a)   by indexing,

(b)   by analysis of frequent groups and their sequences,

(c)   by a study of what may be called in a general way stationary groups, i.e. Punkt, Uhr, An, Von, Bis, Meldung, etc., and mobile groups, i.e. numbers, spelling groups and words,

(d)   by a search for groups which have a tendency to recur in pairs.

These are explained more fully elsewhere.

In earlier codes the problem was rendered much easier by the fact that there was only one group for Punkt, Komma, Uhr etc., and by the fact that each number up to nine was represented by only one group.

This meant that to encode compound numbers such as 15, 23, or 103, the single numbers were used, and to encode 17th or 21st the single cardinals were written followed by "te" or "st" etc.

In the present codes unfortunately the tendency has been to increase the number of groups for each cardinal up to 10, to give groups for compound numbers from 11 to 20, and 20 to 100, and to allot groups to all ordinals up to 12th, and to frequentatives for "einmal" to "Zehnmal".

But in spite of these increased difficulties it is possible to lay down a certain number of first principles such as may help in elucidating numbers.

As numbers tend to be some of the most frequent groups apart from Satzzeichen, the preliminary spade work should have resulted in spotting certain frequent groups.

By marking these groups in distinctive colours as shown in Appendix (1) it will be noticed that some of them have a tendency to attract each other, and to hunt in couples, threes, and occasionally fours.

Now groups which invariably appear in couples, *in the same order*, will most probably be nouns or verbs followed by "Mehrzahl" or "Mittelwort der Vergangenheit" etc., station calls, or stereotyped phrases such as "Morgen Meldung", "Abend Meldung", "KTK A" or "KTK 3" etc.

Groups which invariably run in threes or fours, or more, *in the same order*, will most probably be spelling groups, and might give P– O– ST, L– AM– P– E, S– A– TZ– B– U– CH, etc.

But when groups tend to appear generally in bunches of two, three or four, *and not always in the same order*, most if not all of them will turn out to be numbers.

Thus if A, B, C, D, E, F should represent half a dozen of these frequent groups they might occur in the following orders;– A B or B A; A C E, E A C or F C A; B A D C or E A B D etc. It will then be safe to presume that these groups represent numbers.

By tabulating the sequences before and after any one of these groups they will soon be seen to attract others, until anything from 12 or 20 of them can safely be presumed to be either numbers or some word or letters which frequently accompany numbers, such as Unit, Uhr, Komma, Planquadrat, von, bis, zwischen, und etc., or one of the letters of a station call such as K 3, 9 D, M 4, etc.

Bearing in mind at this stage what was said above about stationary and mobile groups, it should now be possible to discover that some one frequent groups, not a number, frequently precedes two or three mobile groups, and might be Division, Brigade or Regiment, or comes always second or third in the sequence, when it might be Uhr or Komma used instead of Uhr.

If the presumption is in favour of the stationary group being Uhr, a tabulation should now be made of all the groups preceding and following it, going for instance four backwards and four onwards in each case, and keeping the stationary group always in the same perpendicular column. This is shown in Appendix (1b).

If the presumption in favour of Uhr should be correct, this group should practically invariably be preceded by and most frequently followed by one or two numbers although as yet the latter may remain unidentified.

It should now be possible to discover von, bis, zwischen and und, bearing in mind the usual formula as shown in the sample message above.

This is best done by concentrating on the most frequent group (not obviously a number) which almost invariably precedes the one or two mobile groups (numbers) followed by the stationary group (Uhr). If there is any such frequent group it should be "bis." The discovery of "von" follows logically.

As certain Satzzeichen such as Punkt, Komma, or Bindestrich, and certain frequent words such as "und" and "von", occur often in close proximity to numbers, it is well at this stage to try and separate these groups from those representing numbers. This is best done by the system of distinctive marks, as explained above.

When the groups coloured in a distinctive way tend to occur in other parts of the messages away from numbers, and in certain more or less easily recognisable positions, they are probably not numbers themselves.

For instance "Punkt" will occur frequently at various parts of messages and often at the end; "und" will of course appear in many places where none of the presumable numbers are around it.

Punkt, Komma and "und" moreoever will not have appeared immediately *before* the Uhr which has been analysed and its recurrences and sequences tabulated.

By proceeding on these lines it becomes possible to sort out many groups which though they have a tendency to go with numbers are not numbers themselves.

Having now arrived at the stage where we are practically certain of having discovered several groups which must be numbers, there are two or three ways in which it will soon be possible to allot values to them.

It is very useful at this stage to colour or underline distinctively all presumable numbers, not necessarily in different ways, but by giving a uniform mark to distinguish it as a number.

It will then be possible to concentrate on any agglomeration of numbers which occurs at the beginning or at the end of messages.

This should result in identifying the groups representing units, especially if a careful analysis of all initial groups of messages has resulted in a presumable "an".

By studying the daily Intelligence E (c) summary (cf.App.3) to see what units are connected with the station concerned, it will be possible to conjecture numbers of Divisions, Brigades or Regiments.

By comparing one conjecture with another and noticing points of similarity, it will soon be easy to give definite values to the numbers of units. This is done in the following manner.

If one address or signature should be in the order X.Z.Y., and another in the order V.Y.W., and if there were Regiments connected with those stations with the numbers 245 and 356 respectively, this would easily lead not only to the conjecture that the group Y = 5, but also that X = 2, Z = 4, V = 3 and W = 6. It might then be possible to find an address

"an (Unit) X.W."

which might quite well fit as Brigade 26 in the sector concerned.

By a system of check and cross-check on these lines many numbers will be identified.

Having got so far it will now be well to concentrate for a time on the numbers before and after "Uhr". Here certain definite assumptions may be made.

The numbers preceding Uhr must range from 1 to 12. If by good fortune there are two numbers in front of Uhr, the first must be *one* and the second 0, 1 or 2.

This was very easy to ascertain in the former series of codes, but unfortunately in the recent ones the compound numbers 10, 11 and 12 are practically invariably used.

If there is only one number after Uhr this will practically certainly be 5, 10, 15, 20, 30, 40, or 50. Of these by far the most frequent is 30. When there are two numbers after Uhr the first will range from 0 to 5, and the second will almost invariably be 5.

These hypotheses may now help the checking and cross-checking of unit numbers, and may lead to more identifications.

At this stage much valuable assistance will result from an analysis of all messages containing "von — bis —" Here the second number will obviously be higher than the first, except in such a case as

"von 9 Uhr 15 bis 9 Uhr 45"

when it will have the same value.

There are other frequent uses of "bis" besides those in connection with times of day

i.e. "20 bis 30 Schuesse"[25]

"5 bis 8 nichts" (in tabulated reports)[26]

"vom 4ten Abends bis 5ten Morgens"[27]

which however are now almost invariably ordinal numberals, etc.

There are other clues which may lead to the comparative size of a number. A very frequent request is as follows;–

"Sofort einen Mann nach KW schicken."[28]

Here the number is nearly always "eins"

In asking for wireless apparatus and accessories one of the most frequent messages is

"Bitte ( ) Akkumulatoren"[29]

where the number is always relatively low, 1, 2 or 3.

In reporting the number of messages sent and received, in the form

"— geschickt, — empfangen"

the numbers are also relatively low, ranging generally between 1 and 8.

In the case of a message which mentions a Chi or Zif number, or the time-group which is always prefixed to each message, it is often possible to discover the message referred to.

For instance in a message from KS to MD, we might discover a group of four numbers, obviously referring to the time group.

Example: "Funkspruch — — ohne Sinn"[30]

By referring to previous messages on the same day, we find one from the same station timed 1309. The presumption is very strong that these are the four numbers referred to, and if we have already identified two or three of these numbers we can now determine the value of the remainder.

A still more satisfactory discovery is that of a serial report, such as the one quoted above, where the numbers will obviously be consecutive, and will sometimes give the whole series from 1 to 10.

Occasionally numbers can be identified by their inclusion in spelling groups. Of such numbers "ein" is by far the most frequent, the group for this syllable frequently serving the double purpose of spelling group and the number "eins".

More rarely we have examples such as

"2 Mann RE – *VIER* krank."[31]

"Erhoehte Funken-Telegraphie Bereitschaft, gut *acht* geben"[32]

"Es besteht *zwei* – F E L darueber."[33]

METEOROLOGICAL REPORTS

Meteorological reports are often extremely useful in assigning values to numbers previously unidentified. A characteristic code message would run;–

"Wetter Meldung von 26–12–17. Boden Wind hundert, null, sechs; zwei hundert, null, acht, fuenf; hundert, null, zwoelf; eins, fuenf, null, null; Barometer 03,6. Temperatur minus 3 : 6. Feuchtigkeit 92 prozent. Luft gewicht 171,30."[34]

GERMAN WIRELESS PRESS

Another fairly frequent type of message is an extract from the wireless press[35] dealing with number of prisoners and guns captured in some theatre of war. For instance at the time of the Italian debacle we frequently had code messages of the following types;–

(i) "A und B Kompagnie. Hundert achtzig tausend Gefangenen, hundert Geschuetze; an einem Tage sechzig tausend Mann und vier hundert Geschuetze. Gemona ist gefallen."

(ii) "Gefangenen Zahl am Isonzo erhoehte sich auf sechzig tausend und 450 Geschuetze."[36]

A study of our own meteorological reports for the same date and time, and a study of the day's German wireless press will be very useful. By comparing the code message with the clear it will often be possible to see exactly what the right translation should be.

REPORTS ON FLOODED AREAS

One of the most interesting and at the same time useful types of message is one which appears twice daily on the flooded sector of the Yser. By opening the dams at certain places the Germans are able to flood certain districts.

At the above stated times each day a certain station sends a code message dealing with the height of the water above and below the dam in question.

As these messages are very stereotyped in form they are extraordinarily useful in identifying numbers far more quickly than would have been otherwise possible.

A typical example runs:–

"late Reserve Pioniere 13. Wasserstand 6 Uhr

Abend OB – ER – STROM 4 ; UNTER–STROM 3,65 Meter."[37]

These things are of course only adventitious aids to the solution of a code, and are of most use when the solution has already reached a certain stage, i.e. when some of the more frequent spelling groups and words have been identified.

By continual analysis, hypothesis and experiment on all the above lines, employing analogy where available and first principles when that fails, leaving no stone unturned, and pursuing a perpetual system of check and cross-check, we at length reach the satisfactory stage of verifying all the numbers.

This is obviously a much more difficult task than in the previous series of codes, where it was only necessary to identify one group for each number, but even with the current series the problem is not incapable of solution.

WORDS AND PHRASES

By the time that numbers have been identified, or at any rate a certain proportion of them, many odd words will have been discovered simultaneously. Of these the most probable discoveries will have been von, bis, zwischen, und, Uhr, times of day, and possibly more or less definitely fixed values of the various synonymous expressions for Schuss, Flieger, Akkumulator, etc.

Having arrived at this stage, further hypothesis becomes more easily possible, and we may be gratified by a leap forward in the solution, and a considerable number of obvious identifications for groups will occur to us.

It is at this stage however that it is necessary to make haste slowly, as there is always a tendency to assume that a certain group must have a certain meaning because of its context in one particular message.

It is here that the critical faculty should step in, and this should be aided by the use of the index which has been made. Before asserting that the meaning of a group is such as we presume it to be on the one example, it is absolutely essential to find all its references in the index, and to assure ourselves that the presumed meaning will fit in all the places in which the group occurs.

Having proved this by at least four or five occurrences we may then find that the group in question occurs in messages where none of the surrounding groups are as yet identified. When this is so it forms the basis of conjecture as to the probable meaning of the groups before and after it.

For this reason whenever the meaning has been proved without a shadow of a doubt it should be written over the groups wherever it occurs, and all the surrounding groups should be exhaustively analysed.

The best and safest method of doing this is to write the group in question on a separate sheet, and to write out its sequences, going backwards and forwards for at least four groups. When the meaning of any of the surrounding groups is determined, the translation of them should be given.

The same process should be gone through with any group that is being experimented on. It will then frequently become possible to form a chain of reasoning so secure that we can safely assume the meaning of the group to be correct on only one occurrence instead of having to wait for its repetition several times to assure ourselves of its correctness.

The basis of reasoning becomes almost Euclidean or algebraical, i.e.

If $A = Z$, then B should $= Y$; if $B = Y$, C should $= X$, if $C = X$, we may by this time be fortunate to find a sentence in which the whole chain is found to be sound and the sentence will read coherently.

It is at this stage of solution that the faculty mentioned above of being able to keep a dozen or twenty groups in one's mind at a time, with their sequences and context whenever known, and any theories that may have been formed about them when first encountered, will be most invaluable.

It is obviously impossible to treat this process at all fully without taking a score or two of pages in a code, and reconstructing all the mental processes, all the hypotheses, and all the clues, fruitful or otherwise, which have led to the complete reduction of the code.

A few examples may however serve to illustrate the meaning of what has been said above. When a sufficient number of spelling groups had been identified in one particular code to spell out V I Z E — W E B E L, very little additional evidence was necessary to supply the missing group "Feld".

In previous messages a certain group by its position and possible function in the sentence partly decipherable seemed to be a preposition.

By inserting the word "Feld" wherever its equivalent group occurred, it was found in one or two instances to follow the above preposition.

In another case this same preposition proceded a time of day. The assumption was very strong therefore that the preposition was "vor", giving "Vorfeld" in one case, and "Vor acht Uhr Abends"[38] in the other.

In another case it came followed by "und". This led to the assumption that the group after "und" was "hinter". The assumption proving correct led to the discovery of "Vor-und Hinter-Gelaende",[39] which fitted in excellently with a patrol report, and led on by successive steps to more and more identifications.

Returning once more to the group for "Feld", it was seen to occur after two unknown groups, where it might be part of a place name or of the territorial designation of a unit.

The two unknown groups referred to, (let us call them X & Y) were also discovered close together in a sequence of groups as follows;– (W) L U E — (X) W IE (Y), where W = another group previously unidentified.

By comparing the two messages we discovered without undue difficulty that the last mentioned sequence spelt out

SCH–LUE–SS–EL SCH–IE–BER

i.e., a sliding alphabet ruler, and that the place name was EL–BER–FELD. By inserting with the aid of the index the identifications SCH, SS, EL and BER wherever their groups occurred many more spelling groups, were discovered and these in their turn led to others, until most of the spelling groups were discovered.

SPELLING GROUPS

At this stage it is necessary to discuss the use of spelling groups and to know how their solution may be obtained.

In the initial stages of the solution of the codes used by German Field Wireless Stations we were absolutely in the dark as to the nature and extent of the employment of spelling groups.

In many codes, when it is necessary to spell out a word for which there is no equivalent in the code, the custom is to employ spelling groups solely for individual letters.

This means that when the characteristic recurrences and sequences of simple substitution occur, the presumption is that spelling groups are being employed.

By applying the principle of the solution of simple substitution to the particular parts of the messages where these peculiarities are noted it is a fairly simple matter to discover the groups used for individual letters.

This is especially the case when any outside knowledge of the probable subject matter of the message, or of the names of persons or places likely to be mentioned, is obtainable.

It would, for instance, be fairly simple to spot the translation of the sequence X Q V P Q V (where these letters stand for the code groups employed), as L O N D O N, of W B Z Z B D L B as C A R R A N Z A, of L J C F Q C F M as T H O U R O U T, of X Q S S Y A Y Z Y as Z O N N E B E K E, of M D Q QH Y-A D Q Q M I Q Y Z as D R O O G E B R O O D H O E K, etc. etc., if these were likely to be referred to in the text.

As in many codes it is customary to insert a "Buchstabier-Gruppe" i.e. "spelling begins", "spelling ends", before and after a word spelt out, it is frequently possible to identify this group by the period of its recurrence, and when once discovered it leads in its turn to the knowledge that the groups within its two repetitions are spelling groups, even if it is impossible at an early stage to identify their exact meaning.

In the code under consideration there are certain frequent words or abbreviations spelt out. Among these the most frequent of the easily identifiable ones are the abbreviations K–T–K = Kampf Truppen Kommandeur, and R–I–R = Reserve Infanterie Regiment.

They sometimes occur with a Punkt or Bindestrich between them, and sometimes without any separating group.

In the early stages of experiment on these codes, one of the things which led to the eventual solution of the code was the very frequent repetition of a sequence of groups which ran as follows;– BS WK RJ WK BS. Variations of this procedure were noted such as BS RJ BS alone; WK BS WK RJ WK BS WK etc.

Before noticing these various peculiarities the tendency was, on the analogy of simple substitution, to imagine that the first form mentioned above was such a word as N E U E N, N E B E N, S T E T S etc., but when, later on, the second and third variations were discovered, it eventually became evident that the WK = Punkt or Bindestrich, and that the BS RJ BS = either R–I–R or K–T–K.

This was apparently a very slender thread with which to unravel a whole code, but in codes it must be remembered that "c'est le premier pas qui coûte", and upon this slender foundation the whole code was eventually reconstructed.

In the code under consideration there were groups for spelling far in excess of the 26 single letters of the alphabet. There were modified vowels, double consonants, frequent diphthongs such as au, ei, eu, ie etc., and frequent combinations of two, three or even four letters such as BL, GR, SCH, HEIT etc.

This made the problem of solving spelling groups more difficult, and it was not until this fact was realized that further progress was made. There still were however certain characteristics in the sequences of certain groups, which pointed to the fact that they must be spelling groups.

As was seen above there were sequences in the code which might be spelling such words as "neuen", "neben" or "stets" which turned out to be K–T–K with Punkt or Bindestrich interspersed, but having thus obtained a very possible punkt it became possible to block out the messages into groups representing phrases or more or less self-contained sections of the text.

It was mentioned in the section above which dealt with the solution of numbers that when the code was analysed with a view to marking in some distinctive way sequences of groups which occurred very frequently in the same order, but with different groups before and after them, the presumption was in favour of these sequences representing words or names spelt out in full.

It would be too great a stretch of the long arm of coincidence if on different dates, at different times of the day, and from different stations, there should be same (sic) repetition of four or five groups which would stand for the same numbers before and after Uhr, or for exactly the same sequence of words in a stereotyped phrase such as for example

"25 Schuesse auf Abschnitt"[40] or

"Waehrend der Abend Stunden Flieger Taetigkeit gering"[41]

Therefore by collecting several of these frequently recurring sequences, analysing and comparing them, and noticing certain clearly defined characteristics, and at the same time conjecturing what some of the most frequently spelt out words or names would be, it became possible to determine the value of a good many spelling groups.

This process was materially aided by the fact that several of the most frequently used spelling groups were also capable of being used as single words, e.g. in, an, ich, ist, es, da, ein, acht, und etc.

As a fair proportion of these were capable of being discovered by other methods, such as by their recurrence in certain definite places in a message such as "an", or by analysis having proved some of them to be numbers such as "ein" and "acht", we were already on the right road to find out some of the single letters and spelling groups.

Such words as ES–T–AM–IN–ET, L–AM–P–E, W–ACHT–ME–IST–ER, FL–AN–DER–N became gradually capable of solution. Having, as explained above, discovered the values of the groups for K and T from K–T–K, we were very soon able to identify such a word as T–A–K–T–J–SCH or more easily still K–O–N–T–A–K–T.

This "premier pas" had started us off on the high road to success, after repeated failures, "culs de sac", and the inevitable preliminary gropings in the dark which characterise the first attempts at code solution.

One of the most interesting words which helped in beginning to get out the spelling words in a new code was a sequence of groups in the order Q W X Q W X W. This turned out to be B A R B A R A, useful as the code name of a certain unit.

The fact that the same word was spelt out in a succeeding message as B–AR–B–AR–A gave us the group for "ar".

Having got a possible "S" in the word P–O–S–T in another part of the code, we were soon able to identify another group as S–A–TZ–B–U–CH. From this point all was plain sailing.

As the tendency in recent codes, however, has been to increase not only the number of groups for single letters, and short words such as "an", "in", "ist" etc., but also to add groups for less frequent spelling groups such as NG, CHT, RS etc., the difficulty of solving spelling groups on first principles has increased. The difficulty even then is not as great as it might otherwise seem to be, if the analysis is searching and thorough enough.

For instance it is possible to notice that the same sequence of groups sometimes occurs practically identically, but with one group varying in the different sequences.

When it is noticed that of these repetitions of an almost similar sequence two may be in the form

X K K X Q X T

and the third in the form

X K K W Q W T

the presumption is very strong in favour of the groups represented by X and W being equivalent to the same spelling group or letter.

When a little thought has resulted in this sequence suggesting the word A P P A R A T we not only have definite values for the P, R and T but also the value of two groups representing A.

At this stage it will be as well to repeat what cannot be too frequently insisted on, namely that, when any value is discovered for a particular code group, this value should be immediately transferred to it every time it occurs in the code.

The mere fact that there are a few odd words, spelling groups or letters hanging in the air in a message, will lead to new theories, which can be proved or disproved by reference to their context, and then carry on the chain.

Spelling groups having been shown above to possess certain characteristic sequences when carefully analysed, it is now possible to determine with more or less accuracy what groups are spelling groups, and apply certain principles of frequency to them.

The frequency tables used in solving substitution ciphers will obviously not apply when, as in the particular type of code we are studying, there are groups for compound letters, in addition to these for the single letters.

For example the letter E which is the most frequent letter in most languages will in this code tend to become one of the less frequent groups owing to its forming part of so many spelling groups.

For all single vowels excepting O in this code there are two code groups, and as O only occurs in two words which can be used as syllables, namely "WO" and "SO", and as moreover it is a fairly frequent letter it should assume importance if analysed among spelling groups.

It eventually becomes possible to discover a relative frequency of initial and final spelling groups, although this can not be done with anything like the mathematical degree of certainty as in cipher. E, EN, ER, ST will be frequent final groups; GE, SCH, ST, ER, BE, VER will be frequent initial groups.

Of single letters at the beginning of words some of the least frequent in cipher, or in spelling in code when only equivalents for single letters are used, will tend to become much more frequent, owing to the fact that their relative infrequency in clearly defined spelling groups causes them to be employed alone.

Thus D, F, K, M, P, W and Z will rise to a much higher rate of frequency among letters than they reach in cipher.

STATION CALLS

In these codes many valuable identifications of single or modified letters may be obtained owing to their use in station calls. Each German Field Wireless Station uses a particular call sign, and this consists generally of two single or modified letters with an occasional number.

Some stations are in the habit of putting these station calls into code, and when dealing with messages from such stations, bi-groups between "Punkts" or at or near the end of messages should be looked for.

A list of call signs of the groups of stations concerned together with that of the adjoining ones should be referred to, and if one letter of a call sign is known the other will be readily found.

Compare the following message with list of calls:– "WO BLEIBEN GEGENWART STATION MELDUNG MEHRZAHL VON PUNKT sj mo PUNKT rt ab PUNKT mo ne UND rt ne PUNKT."[42]
List of calls. BD – NT – KS – MO – FR – SG – FG.

A glance at the above will show an important point namely that the final group of one bi-group is the same as the initial one of another e.g.

sj <u>mo   mo</u> ne

By consulting the list of calls it will be found that two of them have the same peculiarity

K <u>S   S</u> G

From the above sj mo were assumed to be K S and mo ne to be S G. This again gave rt ne as F G which gave a further identification viz, rt sb as F R.

Having now arrived at the stage where a great many spelling groups have been discovered, we are in a position to discover many short words, which are at the same time used as spelling groups, but which if inserted into their respective places wherever they occur as single words, fix a valuable basis for conjecture as to the meaning of their context. Some of these have been mentioned above, but there will be no harm in recapitulating a few of them.

The spelling M–E–IST–ER gave "ist", which is a vary valuable word in a sentence. GE–WO–R–DEN gave WO and DEN, both extremely useful single words.

The spelling of P–I–RE–ALLE–R, a place not far from St. Quentin, constantly referred to in artillery reports, verified "alle", which led to the phrase "an alle Stationen".

KOMMA–N–D–O definitely established "KOMMA" as distinct from Punkt or Bindestrich.

ACHT–UNG proved the conjecture for the number "acht" to be the right one.

Leutnant NEU–MANN and other proper names ending in "Mann" eventually helped in the discovery of TOT, VERWUN-DET, KRANK etc.

BE–T–H–MANN–HOHL!WEG (sic) established WEG as distinct from GRABEN or STRASSE, and also gave us HOHL.

The average German operator is not very particular about correctness of spelling as shown in the above mis-spelling of the Chancellor's name: some of his mis-spellings, involuntary or jocular, have given us many valuable short words, and at the same time caused us a certain amount of amusement.

A place called Itancourt, near Pirealler frequently referred to in connection with artillery reports was spelt out by one sportsman as I–T–AN–C–UHR–T. Uhr also appeared once in UHR–L–AU–B.

B–U–K–O–WIE–N–A gave "wie", which with "ist" and "wo" quoted above, helped in the discovery of Fragezeichen, as we noticed that interrogative sentences nearly always had a characteristic final group which had previously puzzled us.

SCH–MIT for Schmidt was valuable in proving "mit".

TEL–E–F–O–NIE–SCH and even NIE–CHT for "nicht" gave much help.

On the occasion of the promotion of one wireless operator to be a Funker, a comrade at another station sent the message

"ICH GRAD–U–L–IE–RE"

It seemed almost too good to be true that the group between ICH and – ULIERE should be the word "Grad", but this was confirmed by the use of the index, as we discovered that it came in a meteorological message referring to temperature, and also in GRAD–AUS for "gerade aus".

FR–OE–H–LICH–E WEIN–ACHT–EN gave the group for "Wein".

SCHON–EN DANK was also useful in verifying the possible identification for "schon".

The gem of the whole collection however was "E–SS–EN" (sic)

"E–SS–EN (gegenwart) Abloesung schon da",

which reminded one of the old Latin catch of one's schooldays

"Mea Mater est mala sus!"

A more or less complete list of such short words appears in Appendix (4).

It must be remembered, however, that such helps as these only come when a code has begun to reach a fairly advanced stage of solution.

None of these things which seem so simple and help such a lot at a later stage can take the place of a proper method of attacking a new code, and a firm grasp of the general principles of code solution, coupled with a long and exhaustive analysis on the lines laid down above.

Analogies with previous codes, and as much outside information as may be obtainable, must be worked to their utmost extent, but when the nature and structure of a code change, or when previous station procedure is no longer adhered to, it is necessary to start working on first principles.

As in the course of the preceding treatment of the solution of spelling groups frequent reference has been made to the principles of Simple Substitution Ciphers, code solvers should make themselves familiar with the main principles of the solution of this form of cipher.

It would take up too much space in this pamphlet to discuss at the requisite length the methods adopted in this process, but information on this subject together with examples for practice, will be found in the "Manual of Cryptography".

A few dozen examples worked out, and a study of the tables of frequency of the language used in the code, and of its characteristic sequences, will prove very useful as a preparation for the study of the solution of codes.

HILFS-SIGNALE

In the particular code under consideration there is a recognised procedure in regard to "Hilfs-signale", and the discovery of these is often of great use towards the complete solution of a code.

Some of these have already been referred to, but at this stage a detailed consideration of their nature and use will be of value.

"Hilfs-signale" are grammatical groups placed after certain words to alter their meaning wherever necessary. The most frequent of them are indications of the tense or number in which a verb is intended to be translated, or of the number of a noun.

They will each be treated separately under their various headings, with an example of their respective uses, and the method of discovering them explained wherever necessary.

(1) *Hauptwort.* (Noun) This group is placed after a verb or an adjective when the corresponding noun does not exist in the code.

e.g. "C.O.S. ist der drabtlose arrufen (Hauptwort) (i.e. Anruf) eines Schiffen das sich in groesater Gefahr befindet."[43]

"Walche Wellon-lang (hauptwort) (i.e. Laenge) gebracht die Station?"[44]

The context is often sufficient to determine the function of this group. Inserted at each recurrence by the aid of the index, it is often very useful in conjecturing the actual meaning of the preceding group, hitherto unidentifield.

(2) *Einzahl.* (Singular) This is used to indicate the singular of a noun, of which only the plural form exists in the code. i.e. after "Kerzen", (inserted in the code in the plural because of its frequent use in speaking of candle power) or after "Kontroll-schuesse", "gelbe Leuchtkugen", "Granaten" etc., of which only the plural form is given.

It is also used after verbs to indicate the use of the singular number, i.e. "We (sic) bleiben (Hehrzahl) Abend Meldung.?"[45] and even occasionally to convert a verb into a noun, i.e. "Reihen folgen (Einzahl)" "Reihenfolge."

(3) *Mehrzahl.* (Plural). This is one of the most frequently used grammatical groups. It indicates the plural number of a noun referred to, and is very frequent after Schuss, Kompagnie, Akkumulator, Funkspruch, Graben, Flieger etc. etc.

Example, "30 Schuss (Mehrzahl) auf Graben (Mehrzahl) westlich von (Place name)"[46]

Owing to the frequency of this symbol it can often be very easily discovered. When beginning to analyse a code, all groups which have a tendency to occur in pairs should be specially marked, and the two groups bracketed together. It will then be found that one of them is invariably the second one of the bi-group.

When this second group occurs frequently as the second member of several bi-groups it will frequently turn out to be "Mehrzahl". Conjecture as to this may be facilitated by a consideration of the position of these bi-groups in the message.

This often helps to discriminate it from "Mittelwort der Vergangenheit" (past participle) which is also a very frequent "Hilfs-signal".

As it is exceedingly useful in guessing the meaning of a whole sentence to know that a certain group is either a noun or a verb, any group which has the newly discovered "Mehrzahl" after it, should be bracketed to it, and should be noted as a noun.

This noun, although as yet unidentified, should be noted as

such, by the aid of the index, every time it occurs even when not accompanied by the plural sign.

(4) *Eigenschaftswort.* (Adjective). This is comparatively rarely used, but many (sic) serve to turn a word which only occurs as a noun in a code book into an adjective when discovered, its occurrence should be similarly noted, as for "Mehrzahl".

(5) 1 ste Steigerungs form. (Comparative)
    2 te   "   "   (Superlative)
These two symbols, as their name implies give the degree of a comparison in which an adjective is to be translated.
e.g. "Feindliche Artillerie Taetigkeit ruhig (1ste Steig.form) (i.e. ruhiger) als am Abend vorher."[47]
       "Gross (2te Steig.form) (i.e. groesste) Gas bereitschaft."[48]
Any symbol followed by one of these degrees of comparison must be an adjective, and its occurrence, singly as well as accompanied by the degree of comparison, should be noted, and its function inserted, even where it is as yet impossible to define its exact meaning.

(6) *Zeitwort.* (Verb). This group serves to indicate that a word which is only given as a noun in the code must be translated as a verb. Its use is therefore the converse of "Hauptwort", and it should be treated accordingly.

(7) Gegenwart. (Present Tense.)
     Vergangeheit. (Past Tense.)
     Mittelwort der Vergangenheit. (Past Participle.)
     Zukunft. (Future.)
     These serve to indicate the tense of a verb.
     Example. "Regiment melden (Gegenwart) (i.e. meldet) dass Feind in unsere vorderen Graeben eindringen (Mittelwort der Vergangenheit) (i.e. eingedrungen hat)[49]
Any occurrence of these tense symbols should be noted and treated in a similar manner to Mehrzahl or 1ste or 2te Steigerungs form as described above.

(8) *Buchstabier Gruppe.* (Spelling begins or ends.)
The use of this symbol has been described above when treating of spelling groups and their solution.

SATZ-ZEICHEN

For the very lucid and stimulating treatment of the various Satz-zeichen used in German Field Wireless Code in the section which follows we are indebted to Lieut. D. Macgregor, whose collaboration has been a very great service to us in clearing up knotty points.

It would be very good practise for the beginner in code work to take the examples he gives, and endeavour to solve them before referring to the key which follows.

"A beginner in code solution is apt to fancy that punctuation marks are a very unimportant branch of his subject. This is quite wrong. They are of paramount importance; and any neglect of them, or any slipshod identification, not only bar the way to many valuable discoveries, to which their accurate identification would have led, but obstructs and obscures the whole work of solution. The mistake, if a fatal one, is still natural."

Given a complete, intelligible sentence, if often matters little if a colon be put for a dash or a stop, comma for brackets, or say an exclamation mark be left out.

But the code solver is not dealing with complete or intelligible sentences. At the start he is dealing with wholly unintelligible sentences, and even after a months' work he is hampered by unknown groups, by Morse errors, manuscript or typescript errors, and nearly every kind of doubt and difficulty which can be conceived. Here it is that the Satz-zeichen play their part.

At the start, thanks to the mechanical unintelligent pedantry of the German, they are themselves, some of them, readily discoverable, and they lead directly to solution of the preliminary difficulties; later, they act as guides to the sense, giving form and construction to the unintelligible, guiding and controlling the conjectures of the investigator.

In a word the study and discovery of these signs is not a mere scholarly refinement, a finishing touch to the work of solution; it is an integral and indispensable part of that work.

The following notes and examples are intended to illustrate this point, and to indicate a few of the technical uses which the solver can make of the Satz-zeichen. But it must not be forgotten that the "rules" given below are not laws of nature or even grammatical canons. "Anforderung" is not always followed by "Doppelpunkt", most often it has no punctuation at all; sentences frequently follow each other without a "Punkt" between them; "8–30" is often written "830". Some codes scarcely punctuate at all. Nevertheless in any code where punctuation is regular it will be found to follow the lines indicated, and a full knowledge of these will be of incalculable value.

(1)   *Punkt*

(a)   Separating sentence from sentence; normal and frequent, not infrequently at the end of short, single sentence messages.

(b)   As the mark of abbreviation;

> "GE–SCH–AE–F–T–S–Z–Punkt"
> "ST–RE–ICH–H–Punkt."
> "K–Punkt–T–Punkt–K–Punkt"
> "R–Punkt–I–Punkt–R–Punkt"

Note especially GE–XYZ–Punkt, where XYZ should always be tested for FR, giving GE–FR. = Gefreiter.

(c)   With figures; very frequent. Betweeen a number and the unit to which it applies:

> "An 8 Punkt Infanterie Brigade."
> "1 Punkt Kompagnie."

Very frequent is (sic) tabulated messages, before and after (more commonly only after) figure or letter headings:

> "3 Punkt Anschluss vorhandon 4 Punkt Sicht dunkel
> 5 Punkt nichts etc. etc.[50]

Rarely = Uhr. "2 Punkt 30" (see under Komma)
Regular in dates: "12 Punkt 1 Punkt 18 Punkt"

(d)   After the "address to" and before "address from:
> "Brigade Punkt Lage ruhig Punkt Unterschrift K–T–K."[51]

The following pair of actual messages affords an excellent example of various uses of the Punkt and of the incalculable value of the Punkt in the initial stages of solution. On the basis of these messages alone some 15 identifications can be made. The beginner should try his skill on these. The identifications are given below.

(A) TL v LQ 0245 GR 12) ufk rur kni ult rwl rur ufo kqt khy rnd rst uvg

(B) LQ v TL 0245 GR 48) ufk uvg kqt rof kni knw uuo rqw rur rwl ult kni rur rwl ujq rfp uiw kld kni rzt uzm ujm rwl rtq rsp kni kwr kvt kni kpg rzt rzi kbd ulg kgd rwl rur rtz ryp ult rbz kni rzt uzm rur ult rur

In passing, a word or two on the "Punkt (nicht das Satz-Zeichen)"

This is used in the following ways :–

(a) Topographical:

"Zwischen Punkt L and K im Planquadrat"[52] etc.

Frequently preceded by "rot" or "blau".

(b) As a word or part of a word "Zeit-Punkt" "Punkt-lich"

(c) As the "Satz-zeichen". This is naturally very rare, but is commoner than might be supposed and has frequently been exceedingly useful.

In general, Punkt (nicht das Satz-zeichen) is a very valuable group and demands great attention. It must on no account be called "Kartenpunkt" or its other uses will be obscured, and the colour identifications (a very difficult subject, the investigation of which is still in its infancy) to which it often gives the first clues, will be hampered and delayed. "Kartenpunkt" for which there is a separate group is probably very uncommon.

(b) Between Battalion, Company or Battery and Regimental numbers.

"1/116" = Bataillon 1 Regiment 116;

"12/94" = 12th Kompagnie Regiment 94 and so forth.

But the usage does not stop here. The following is a pretty "Bruchstrich identification" ;–

"KGG / Kiel" (presuming that KGG is known not to be a number) = Bataillon I II or III Regiment Kiel.)

Or take the following equation (signatures of corresponding Meldungen on successive days):

"RMO/RSJ" = "2/RSJ" — solve for the two unknowns RMO & RSJ!

Clearly RMO = "Bataillon II", RSJ = Regiment so & so — the Regimental number is obtained from the order of battle maps. (Note: the equation RMC XYZ RSJ = 2 XYZ RSJ, is of course, easily soluble for the three unknowns in the same way, so that the previous knowledge of the Bruchstrich was unnecessary here. But this is an exceptionally simple and lucky case and usually one is dependant entirely on the Bruchstrich for this kind of identification. Of course in the later stages of a code the group for Battalion I II & III are quite clearly recognisable on other grounds.)

The value of the Bruchstrich, as of the other Satz-zeichen, belongs mainly to the initial stages so far as *direct* identification is concerned.

(c)   In Machinengewehr OB/15.

(d)   In the various phrases "Empfang 2/2" "Hier 1/1" etc.
(XYZ 2/2
(Flieger Taetigkeit XYZ rege[53]
where of course XYZ = beiderseits.

(e)   Sometimes in map references.

V.   *Trennungestrich.* This overlaps with Bindestrich in many uses and until recently was confused with the word "Unter-schrift."

(a)   Separating "address to" and "address from" from the text. In this use it is seldom (? never) preceded by Punkt. "Unterschrift", which is very common, naturally only sepa-rates "address from" from the text and may or may not be preceded by Punkt. In Caesar RIW was called Tren-nungestrich although this left UUD, a palpable Satz-zeichen, at a loose end. The former was, it is now clear, "Unterschrift".

(b) As a dash or "Gedankenstrich" in sentences its use is quite normal. Sometimes preceded by Punkt.
"Besatsungen gesund Punkt Trennungestrich Satzbuecher erhalten."[54]

(c) = bis. (cf. Bindestrich.)

(d) See Komma (e). (Trennungestrich and Bindestrich are much commoner in this connection than Komma.)

VI. *Bindestrich*

(a) Normal use as hyphen:
"Artillerie-Schutz-Stellung"
"Funken-Telegraphie Bereitschaft"
"Infanterie-Schutz"
"Strasse Messines-Wervicq"

(b) = bis. (cf. Trennungestrich.)

(c) See Komma (e)

(d) With figures, in giving strengths of units, (note position of Punkt — see Punkt (c)

"1 Punkt Kompagnie 2 Bindestrich 8 Bindestrich 5 4 2 Punkt Kompagnie 2 Bindestrich 15 Bindestrich 7 3 3 Punkt Kompagnie, etc. etc."

i.e. No. 1 Company, 2 Officers, 8 N.C.O's and 54 men etc.

A run of numbers in this form may easily yield identifications, such useful words as Kompagnie, M.G. Kompagnie, Minenwerfer, Bataillon, and others, which the following example illustrates;–

"uqv kso kza 12 ker Bindestrich 32 ruv Bindestrich 292 rzs kjv kza 2 rze rlc"

Identify kao kza ker ruv rzs and, with the help of the following — uqv kjv *and* rlc ;–

"Streufeuer auf den hinteren uqv mehrzahl"[55]

"Sofort dringend ein Wagen fuer ein leicht und 2 rlc."[56]

VII. *Fragezeichen.* Frequent and normal in use, but very often omitted where there is no ambiguity. Very occasionally followed by Punkt at the end of a short message. Its importance for the discovery of other groups — ist, sind, was, wie, warum, etc., —

is plain. The following should be tackled. A reasonable conjecture can be – and was – made for the four underlined groups on
these messages alone; it proved correct, and was of great use in
solution when more material came to hand. (The Fragezeichen
is omitted in these messages.)

Dec. 12th 69 v ZB Zif 3	rrr kzj ure
" " ZB v 69 Zif 9	ure etc. etc.
" " NQ v OY GR 2	ure rkm
" " LQ v GU GR 9	ukt &c. &c. rkm

VIII. *Ausrufungszeichen*
Commoner than might be supposed. Comes after commands,
urgent and reproachful questions (We bleibt Vorpflegung![57] &c)
and, of course, "verboten". Not of great help to the solver, but
sometimes gives a useful clue since it indicates the general nature
of the preceding message. Negatively, its discovery is a great
advantage; for it is a thorn in the side so long as it rests unidentified.

IX. *Klammer*. Rare and elusive. Is usually given away by a
foolish operator using the same group for the beginning and the
end of the parenthesis – after that the way is smooth. Generally
useful when found; unidentified it is a most treacherous and
dangerous will o' the wisp.
(a) Normal – for any parenthesis.
(b) Very rarely enclosing the heading numbers in tabulated
      messages. Fill in the blanks in the following:
"Zwischen – – C und D im – ZD 36c – 1 Doppelpunkt 10 –"
Solutions to examples:–

1. (a) An K Punkt T Punkt K Punkt mitte bitte morgen
         Meldung Regiment.[58]
    (b) An Regiment mitte eine Punkt maessig (– feuer (–
         Kaliber K Punkt T Punkt K Punkt Bindestrich rfp
         Haus zwei Punkt ohne Aenderung drei Punkt verhan-
         den vier Punkt dunkel fuenf Punkt Ablessung ohne
         neu-ig-keit sechs Punkt K–A–L–T sieben Punkt ohne
         Aenderung K T K.[59]

The identifiable groups are underlined in red, these for which a vague but valuable guess as to their general nature could be made in blue, – e.g. KQT of which it can only be said that it is say rechts, mitte, links, nord, sud, etc. – a valuable narrowing of the field of search.

It may be objected that UJP might be zwei – it follows a Punkt after K T K. This is quite fair; and the figure identifications should perhaps read ROF eins, UJP ?2, KLD ?2 or 3 etc. The difficulty however would be cleared up very quickly.

II.   *Komma.* Less frequent and, on the whole, markedly less useful to the solver than the Punkt.

(a)   Normal use – separating parts of a sentence.

(b)   With figures = Uhr or decimal point – Very common.

(c)   *Very* rarely for Punkt after an abbreviation.

(d)   "KOMMA–N–D–O" used to be frequent, but seems never to be used now.

(e)   In tabulated messages occasionally used as follows;–
"3 Punkt vorhanden 4 Punkt dunkel 5 Punkt Komma 6 Punkt unveraendert" etc., where evidently Kommas stands for "nichts" or the like (also Bindestrich & Trennungestrich) or means that 5 and 6 are "unveraendert".

III.   *Doppelpunkt.* Quite normal in use. The locus classicus is after "Anforderung" but it is frequent after any heading;
"Meldung Doppelpunkt" "Eigene Tactigkeit Doppelpunkt" "Verluste" etc. etc.

Also found in map scales. (See example given under "Klammer") It naturally overlaps sometimes with Trenungestrich.

e.g. "Losungswort : Deinz" and "Losungswort – Deinz" are equally correct.

IV.   *Bruchstrich.* Not frequent but easy to identify and enormously useful. But it must be identified exactly; under no other name does it smell so sweet. A vague rendering such as Strich or Komma hinders, not helps.

(a) "1/4 Stunde" – not common, but it must not be thought that an example of this use is necessary to prove the identification. The use and value of the Bruchstrich was discovered independently of this simple case; and the identification can now be made and used with absolute confidence in any code without a thought of fractions.

VI. Graben Staerke Doppelpunkt 12 Offizier Bindestrich 32 N/Offizier Bindestrich 292 Mann Verluste Doppelpunkt 2 Mann schwer verwundet.[60]

VII. Wo bleibt Anforderung   ⎫ These of course are only
      Anforderung &c.&c.[61]   ⎬ "reasonable conjectures" not
      Anforderung ?   ⎪ certain identifications.
      1st &c.&c. ?   ⎭

IX. Zwischen Rot or Blau Punkt C und D im Planquadrat VD 36C (1:10 tausend)"[62]

GENERAL HINTS AND SUGGESTIONS.

It cannot be too frequently insisted upon, at this as at every other stage of code solution, that work on back messages should go on concurrently with that on the new material which continues to come to hand.

In fact it is often far more useful to concentrate on a dozen or more back messages, where there are frequently some which contain only a few untranslateable groups, or at any rate, some which have reached a sufficiently advanced stage of progress to enable the general meaning of the whole message to be conjectured.

It is necessary to dig deeply as well as widely in the process of code solution, and one message, if worried as a dog worries a bone, will sometimes yield more marrow than several pages discursively scanned.

It is well never to insert a conjectural translation into the code sheets, until it has been definitely proved. This is a dangerous proceeding and leads either to preventing the right meaning of the group being discovered, or to wrong conjectures being made about the surrounding groups. All theories still in the air should be written on a separate sheet and kept until verified or disproved.

DISTRIBUTION OF WORK

When there are several people working on one code – and the more, not only the merrier, but also very much the faster – it is well to divide the work among them in the following manner.

One should sort all material as explained at the beginning according to place of origin, destination etc., others should type all messages received in the manner laid down earlier on.

Several copies of each sheet should be made for distribution to those who have to work on them.

All sheets should be clipped together in such a manner that they can be easily handled, and should be kept in consecutive order, so that their subject matter may be chronologically arranged.

Others should be responsible for keeping an up-to-date index of all groups occurring in the code.

One person should be responsible for recording all identifications of code groups in a special index, correcting wrong or insufficiently specified meanings as the right meaning is discovered.

The rest of the available staff should be the actual solvers.

One person should be the controlling mind of the whole work of the code. He should check all theories, be personally responsible for the accuracy of every identification inserted in the index, suggest fruitful lines for experiment, and distribute any possible clues discovered among the remainder of his staff for separate experiment.

When one clue seems likely to be a fruitful one, everybody should work at it until it either proves to be the right one or is definitely discarded as leading nowhere.

All those engaged at work on the same code should work in harmony and conjunction one with the other.

No personal motives, and no jealous desire to keep possible clues from others, in order to have the credit of discovering or proving it, should be allowed to enter into the work.

Every mind should be bent towards the same end, namely the finding of the first identification to start building on, and the complete reduction of the whole code at the earliest possible moment.

Two heads are always better than one, and mutual discussion of possibilities will lead very far on the right road.

Nevertheless after a certain stage has been reached it is often well to divide the work more or less roughly on the following lines. One person might concentrate on initial and final groups, another on an exhaustive study of numbers, another on spelling groups, another on common words and phrases, another on Hilfs-signale, and another on the discovering of the exact function of all the various marks of punctuation.

At the same time, as the code is an entity, it is obviously impossible to lock up these various things in water tight compartments.

The discovery of a group for a particular unit will help in that of numbers, the discovery of a note of interrogation will assist in finding frequent interrogative words, and so on in every aspect of the work.

In conclusion enough has been said to prove that no code ought to be insoluble, given a sufficient quantity of material, a proper method of work, the necessary qualities in the would-be solvers, and sufficient time between the changes of the code-book to admit of the reduction reaching such a stage as to yield information even if only fragmentary.

In code as distinct from cipher a certain length of time must elapse before complete or even partial reduction is possible. The time taken is directly proportionate to the amount of material to work on, to the amount of outside information or of analogy with previous codes available, and to the number and experience of those engaged on it.

In a cipher a fortunate shot may result in the finding of the system, periodicity or keyword on the very first message, or at any rate on two or three, and the key once discovered all material enciphered on the same system is immediately decipherable, whereas with a code, the translation of one message does not render the other messages decipherable.

Cipher deals, moreover, with the more or less mathematical arrangement of 26 letters, while code deals with anything from two to three thousand words.

It is obvious to the meanest intelligence that no meaning can be conjectured for a code group until it has been used in messages at least once, and frequently not until it has been used sufficiently often to enable its sequences to be experimented upon.

A code is not solved in a day, nor even in a week, not even by a miracle. Complete reduction of a code can only be attained when every group existing in it has been used in messages.

Nevertheless it is often possible, as shown above, to obtain a certain amount of very valuable information, even when only about a hundred groups are solved, especially if several of these are the groups for numbers and units.

With the aid of the numbers, dates, times of day, and identifications of units are discoverable.

One final word. The fundamental principles of science and inductive logic hold good in code solution as in any other similar study. The material having come to hand, the phenomena are present.

Observation, experiment, hypothesis, verification are the links in the chain, and when the chain is complete in every link, a certain feeling of gratification may legitimately exist as the result of "something attempted, something done", which may help to shorten the war if only by one day.

APPENDIX 1

The three adjoining sheets, comprising pages (a) and (b) of Appendix (1), give a collection of sections chosen from an actual code, arranged so as to show the theories of numbers and the method of attacking their reduction.

All the groups representing numbers are underlined, and it will be apparent that their sequences are as characteristic as was explained earlier on in the section dealing with numbers.

The tendency of numbers to attract each other, and to occur in twos, threes or fours, but never, or very rarely, in the same order, is strikingly exemplified.

The examples shown are chosen from a series of messages ranging over about a week, so as to show that in a weeks' time if not before, sufficient phenomena are available for the faculty of observation, followed by the necessary hypotheses, to come into play.

The first two pages give all sorts of numbers used with units, with "Uhr" and with "Planquadrat" indiscriminately.

The third page shows the method of attack when a presumable "Uhr" is discovered.

We will give the identifications of a few frequent words on these two pages, after which it is suggested that those who wish to prove their mettle should endeavour to identify as many numbers as possible and also "Brigade", "Regiment", "von" and "bis", working on the lines explained at length in the course of this pamphlet.

We will also give the numbers of the units mentioned, so that there should be a possibility of finding where they are mentioned, identifying their numbers, and applying them to the groups surrounding "Uhr".

Regiments 31, 35, 73, 92, 93, 107, 115, 210.

Brigades 24, 34.

rib	=	*An*	ral	=	*Nachmittags*
klu	=	*Uhr*	uev	=	*Schuse*
kxy	=	*Punkt*	kig	=	*Planquadrat*
rtq	=	*Komma*	uic	=	*Karten Punkt*
kyv	=	*Und*	rvy	=	*Bruchstrich*
ugw	=	*Vormittags*	ksw	=	*Bindestrich*

APPENDIX 1(a)

(A)	rro	use	rtq	rro	ktd	kyv	use	rro	rtq	khf	rvp	key	kor
	ude	rro	khe	rtq	kwr	ktd	ufj	uku					
(B)	ule	rvp	kho	rtq	rro	kho							
(C)	kho	ujt	khe	kqo	kop	khe	rub	use					
(D)	rny	rub	khe	kyv	rny	kae	upt	---	---	rhy	uim	khe	---
	---	---	khe	rve	ryl								
(E)	rib	rny	khe	kxk	---	---	rix	khe	kxk	rnn	rny	khe	kxk
(F)	uug	rro	rvp	kop	khe	rvp	---	---	---	---			
(G)	uln	uuk	rbb	kkr	ujy	rah	khe	khf					
(H)	uzy	kan	rro	kxy	uah	upj	khe	kxy	uus	rib	kda	kwr	kxy
	ule	klp	uyf										
(I)	rhn	khe	rny	uop	rtq	kwr	rro	kyv	upt	rvp			
(J)	kke	khe	kqo	kxy	rub	kxy	kwl	kxy					
(K)	uuk	kdt	kkr	rtf	kae	rvp	rtq	ujy	rvp	uso	kyv	rwi	keg
				rtf	uqw	rvp							
(L)	rlo	khe	kxk	kwl	ral	ryp	klu	uln					
(M)	rlj	ulr	khf	rvp	kuv	kof	uiy	ubi	kwr	uin	rbe		
(N)	rib	rny	rub	kwr	kyv	rny	kae	kwr	---	---	kwr	rve	ryl
(O)	kpj	rro	use	kop	kho	rbe	rve	rtq	uln	kop	rvp	kle	
(P)	usi	kly	ktd	ulv	khf	kre	rzj	kjq	rqw	ube	rmr	umm	
(Q)	kar	rno	rca	kae	khe	kae	kjm	kdy	rmn				
(R)	khe	rvp	ray	rwe	uyy	raz	rro	kae	ufj	kae	kqe	udi	rmr
	rro	rro	rvp										
(S)	rio	nny	rar	kae	kyv	rny	rro	use	rvp	---	---	---	
(T)	uwk	rqi	uge	kwr	rro	rvp	ktk	rtq	kwr	rro	khe	kae	rtq
	kwr	rro	khe	kqo									
(U)	klh	ukr	kkr	rwi	ktm	kig	rvp	ktk	ktd	ktk	kyv	uvd	kig
	rvp	urh	res	kae	kyv	rdu	ktm	kig	rvp	kae	ktd	ktk	kyv
	rvp	kae	ktd	kae									
(V)	rib	rry	rro	ktd	kae	kxy	rer	kve					
(X)	kwr	klu	uln	kop	rve	---	rve	kop	kae	uln	uic	uan	
	kig	rvp	kae	ktd	rvp	kxy	kqe	uln	kop	rro	ral	kop	
	kbm	kig	rvp	uqw	ktd	rvp	kxy	rve	kop	kae	uln	kqr	
	uic	uan	rro										
(Y)	ugl	ktk	uln	ksw	ucw	uln	klu	uln	uev	kkr	kbn	rtq	
	kxk	klu	kve	uev	kfg	kkr	kbn	rtf	klu	uln	kxk	uev	
	kkr	kkm											
(Z)	klh	ksg	uln	rvy	kwr	rro	knb	ksg	ktk	kop	rub	uic	
	uan	kyv	ktm	uic	ulv	kas	ros	rvp	kyv	kjq	uib	rvp	
	ucw	ros	ktk										

APPENDIX 1(b)

(A)	---	kit	kbq	kae	klu	uln	kya	rel	kao
(B)	ksg	rvp	kop	kae	klu	kai	uov	rte	kkr
(C)	uke	uer	ulz	kae	klu	khf	rvp	kop	rro
				uno	klu	ral	uan	kvv	uop
(D)	ksg	kae	kop	rub	klu	uwd	kae	uaw	uif
(E)	ktk	rtq	kwr	ktd	klu	urr	rqu	kur	ksw
(F)	kop	kho	rbe	khf	klu	uln	kop		
				ulv	klu	uqt	kkw	kwz	udm
(G)	kag	ulv	kop	ktk	klu	uln	upj	ukr	kkr
(H)	---	---	kag	uqw	klu	kve	kop		
				uqw	klu	uln	kar	rze	rea
(I)	kag	ktk	kep	ktk	klu	uln			
(J)	kxu	ker	kag	ujy	klu	uln	kop		
				ktk	klu	rah	ral	rnn	kgk
(K)	---	kbj	kma	ktk	klu	ral	koi	kki	kbn
(L)	ktk	kly	kop	rtf	klu	uln	ral	rlh	uaz
(M)	---	kdr	kit	kxk	klu	khp	rrt	khf	rvp
(N)	khf	ugw	kop	ktk	klu	ral	rsr	uev	upa
(O)	---	rib	rsi	kqe	klu	khf	rvp	kww	upt
(P)	ksg	khf	kop	ulv	klu	ral			
(Q)	udm	rvv	rrt	ujy	klu	uln	kop		
				rro	klu	ugw	rgj	kei	kdt
(R)	---	ktz	kag	khf	klu	ujy	kop	rvp	upz
(S)	---	---	krq	rvp	klu	kxk	uhv	rll	keg
(T)	rdu	kqo	rbe	rub	klu	ugw	kte	rtq	kqk
(U)	kag	rub	kop	rtf	klu	khf	rvp	rro	kyx
(V)	kag	rrc	kop	kho	klu	rka	kxa	ruc	kkr
(W)	---	---	kms	kwr	klu	uln	ral	uhj	kxa
(X)	ryl	uzy	ksn	urh	klu	uln	kop		
				uqw	klu	rhf	rvp	ugv	rgj

APPENDIX 2

Specimen page of index. R Q A — Z

R Q A	$\dfrac{72}{C}$	
R Q B	$\dfrac{24\ \ 39\ \ 39}{B\ \ H\ \ Q}$—X	VORGELAENDE
R Q C	$\dfrac{49}{E}$	
R Q D	$\dfrac{9\ \ 10\ \ 28\ \ 33\ \ 45}{E\ \ A\ \ G\ \ R\ \ B}$—X	FUNKER
R Q E	$\dfrac{6\ \ 5\ \ 5\ \ 8}{B\ \ C\ \ L\ \ H}$—X	ANRUFEN
R Q F	$\dfrac{1\ \ 3\ \ 8\ \ 9\ \ 12\ \ 13\ \ 15\ \ 17\ \ 18\ \ 22}{I\ \ A\ \ FO\ \ A\ \ U\ \ L\ \ B\ \ F\ \ A}$—X	VORMITTAGS
R Q G		
R Q H	$\dfrac{9\ \ 53\ \ 74}{L\ \ H\ \ L}$	
R Q I	$\dfrac{7\ \ 79\ \ 91}{G\ \ A\ \ B}$	
R Q J	$\dfrac{9}{E}$	
R Q K	$\dfrac{28\ \ 32\ \ 45\ \ 76\ \ 69}{A\ \ G\ \ M\ \ K\ \ A}$—X	KAMPF
R Q L	$\dfrac{21}{H}$	
R Q M	$\dfrac{2\ \ 2\ \ 2\ \ 3\ \ 4\ \ 9\ \ 15\ \ 17}{K\ \ K\ \ K\ \ E\ \ H\ \ K\ \ K\ \ F}$—X	AR
R Q N	$\dfrac{1\ \ 10\ \ 74}{K\ \ O\ \ O}$	
R Q O	$\dfrac{2\ \ 8\ \ 11\ \ 11\ \ 29}{H\ \ I\ \ J\ \ K\ \ D}$—X	BATTERIE
R Q P	$\dfrac{7\ \ 8\ \ 11\ \ 17\ \ 34\ \ 37}{G\ \ F\ \ R\ \ B\ \ H\ \ G}$—X	GEHEN
R Q Q	$\dfrac{25\ \ 66}{F\ \ F}$	
R Q R	$\dfrac{2\ \ 7\ \ 18\ \ 32\ \ 35\ \ 37\ \ 41}{F\ \ G\ \ O\ \ A\ \ R\ \ G\ \ D}$—X	NEUN
R Q S		

R Q T	$\dfrac{20\ \ 22\ \ 30}{\text{N \ C \ F}}$ —X———————————	ERFOLGEN
R Q U	———————————————	
R Q V	$\dfrac{15\ \ 17\ \ 20\ \ 26\ \ 30\ \ 31\ \ 36\ \ 37}{\text{H \ H \ K \ K \ F \ L \ N \ C}}$ —X————	FUER
R Q W	———————————————	
R Q X	———————————————	
R Q Y	$\dfrac{1\ \ 1\ \ 3\ \ 10\ \ 10\ \ 25\ \ 30\ \ 48\ \ 53}{\text{F \ Q \ C \ C \ M \ D \ A \ L \ E}}$ —X——	EMPFANG
R Q Z	———————————————	

APPENDIX 3

(Specimen page)

Serial No. 96 Int. E (c) St. OMER.

Intelligence E (c) Summary of Information.

Group. Div.		Brig.	Regts.	Call Signs.
	3N		1mar–2mar–3mar	
	2N	4N	2m–3m–5m	
	88R	15/16BR	19BR–22BR–23BR	
160	54R	108R	246R–247R–248R	RO ! UJ XZ ZF
	187		187–188–189	
180	26R	51R	180–119R–131R	CJ GW O'A SQ WC XO' UQ
185	35	87	61–141–176	FZ KF KN MP O'W IX
190	41	74	18–148–152	CS GK OG RF DF G3
	58	116	106–107–103R	
200	239	239	466–467–468	O'D TU' WN XL ZW FD B9 D7
205	16	30	28–29–68	ON RP VS VX DG GL 5K
210	12R	22R	23R–36R–51R	DK DY FL LP WB
213	36R	69R	54–5R–61R	CL GH QF RJ XD
220	7	14	26–163–393	DX FW O'B RG TF VF WK YT ML
	214	214	50–358–363	
	1BR–2	1BR	1BR–2BR–3BR	
290	Artillery Stations			A'F DA' IW LX
315	8	16	72–93–153	CQ DW NU O'Q SF VU XK YS QW

Group.	Div.	Brig.	Regts.	Call Signs.
320	32	64	102–103–177	EI KB
330	5B	9B	7B–19B–21B	BX CZ MA RS WV ZA' TF ZK
350	4	8	14–49–140	DJ FW LA UC VA' U'N TL
360	38L		77L–78L–79R/85L	AW BH EA' LO NX RZ
	44R	87	205R–206R–208R	
	39	61	126–132–173	
415	6B	11B	6B–10B–13B	DV MY LK UG KZ ZD
445	207	99	209–213–98R	JM ZF A'F GT HS NU QU UR WB
	220	4G	190–55R–99R	
	17	34	75–85–89	
470	5BR	9BR	7BR–10BR–12BR	ES FU' UT WN XG ZX FK YO
	236	236	457–458–459	
505	24	89	133–139–179	BA' IZ JC XO' TH EU' JH D_7
510	221	1RE	41–60R–1RE	LN TO U'I O'W MU' DY' IW G_2
515	234	234	451–452–453	AU ON PI IO A'C CH O'_2
517	16B	9	11B–14B–21B	BI DA LD UK U'A EN ZW J_6
520	20	40	77–79–92	IB JF LE SI FA O'E
525	30	60	GrnFus–Ihr–90R	MH PU QR WE
530	24R	48R	104R–107R–133R	EZ HR IU UY ZG SD
534	16R	31R	20R–30R–68R	EA IQ KH RX UZ U'N V_9 W_1
537	50R	99R	229R–250R–231R	EG LY NI O'X SR TW U'X Z_9
540	9R	18R	395–6R–19R	CT JW O'A RI UF ZS SJ
543	Artillery Stations (?)			OW GY NG ND
545	107	213	52R–227R–232R	IK HU RM SU' WU' XH GR V_6
550	208	185	25–135–65R	BT ID RC RT UN TJ
570	183	33R	184–418–440R	ET HA OW SW XM
	9BR	17BR	3BR–11BR–14BR	
575	206		339–394–4RE	HQ KE KS XK IG 2_J

Intelligence E (c)
St. OMER

(Signed) T. Hitchings
Captain, O.i/c.

APPENDIX 4

List of words which contain complete words capable of being used as spelling groups.

EIN–J–AE–H–R–IG	W–ACHT–ME–IST–ER
EIN–BR–U–CH	ST–RE–ICH–H–OEL–ZER
EIN–DR–U–CK	BU–K–O–WIE–N–A
EIN–W–EI–S–UNG	NIE–DER–LAGE
ES–T–AR–IN–ET	P–I–R–E–ALLE–R
L–AM–P–E	P–O–L–DER–H–O–E–K
FR–AN–K–RE–ICH	AUF–NAH–ME
FR–IE–D–R–ICH	GE–WO–R–DEN
GES–SCH–AE–F–T–Z–IM–MER	END–G–UE–L–T–IG–E
GES–SCH–AE–F–T–Z–IMMER	GEGEN–W–AE–R–T–IG
GES–UND–HEIT–S	RUECK–W–AE–R–T–IG–E
G–UM–MI–R–IN–G	BE–SEIT–IG–EN
FELD–FL–A–SCH–EN	BE–SICHT–IG–EN
VOR–FELD	UNTER–WEG–S
VIZE–FELD–W–E–B–EL	GE–WES–EN
FL–AN–DER–N	ZU–SATZ
L–AN–DEN	BISLER–IG–EN
R–U–F–N–AM–E	VORHER–GEBEN–DEN
AUF–P–A–SS–EN	BEI!–R I SCH
KOMMA–N–D–O	Regiment KIRCH–BACH
HERZ–LICH–EN–DA–MK	L–O–K–O–M–O–TIEF:–EN
PR–O–ST–NEU–JA–H–R	UHR!–L–AU–B
HAUPT–S–AE–CH–LICH	SCH–MIT
JE–DEN–F–A–LL–S	etc.etc.etc.

APPENDIX 5

Notes on topographical indications, points of the compass, colours etc., (together with an easy way of identifying "und").

1. Much valuable information may be obtained by a careful study of the topographical indications in these codes, directly valuable in locating wireless stations, command posts, ammunition dumps etc., and indirectly in elucidating different messages, thus leading to further identifications. It is necessary for this purpose to compare what hints are vouchsafed with German maps, especially those with map squares; this should not fail ultimately to clear up the compass points etc.

POINTS OF THE COMPASS etc.

It is often possible to say that certain groups represent points of the compass, or directions such as "rechts and links", without it being possible in the early stages to give their exact value.

These indications have a great tendency to occur in pairs, e.g. "Windrichtung zwischen Nord-Ost und Ost, K T K Nord und Sud, Feuer auf Abschnitt rechts and links."[63] etc.

This tendency gives a certain amount of valuable assistance in spotting "und" in the early stages, even before we know the values of the above words.

Whenever we see two groups which have a tendency to be repeated in the same order with one intervening group, and certain other pairs of groups with the same intervening group it is always useful to assume that this group may be "und", and experiment accordingly.

This conjunction is sometimes also very easily identified when it comes between two groups with a "pochs" or modified vowel, or between two groups with a different initial consonant from those generally used in the code.

For instance, when the initial letters generally used are K, R and U we sometimes see this sequence occurring.

"gkr kyv gbq"

Here the groups beginning with "G" are place names or unit names and the connecting group is almost certainly "und".

COLOURS

These stations do not invariably use the compounds such as "rote Leuchtkugeln" but frequently the two separate groups.

Example "Ab 12–1–18 Sperrfeuer rot, Vernichtungsfeuer grun etc. etc ...... Leuchtkugeln."[64]

The different kinds of gas shells also furnish a useful check on colour.

APPENDIX 6

When, as frequently happens, we have identified certain prefixes or affixes, either as separate groups or spelt out letter by letter, it is very useful to prepare lists of the words discovered, or known to exist in the code, which might follow or precede these particles.

A rhyming dictionary is a very useful adjunct at this stage.

A few examples are tabulated below.

Ab-fahren	be-arbeiten	Ver-aenderung
fallen	fehlen	brennen
feuern	finden	fahren
fliegen	kommen	folgen
fuehren	schiessen	hinderlich
gehen	zitzen	sehen
hang	stehen	sicherung
lassen	stellung	stellung
marsch	stuermen	suchen
marschieren	suchen	etc.etc.
schissen	wegen	Vor-aus
schuss	sicht-(ig-en)	bereiten
senden	kaempf-(ung)	feld
stehen	etc.etc.	gehen
stuerzen	er-bitten	ruecken
etc.etc.	fahren	teil
an-dauern-(d)	geben	ueber
geben	halten	zug
halten	innere	etc.etc.
kommen	warten	Zer-stoeren
melden	etc.etc.	stoerung
etc.etc.		streuen
Befehl-s-(Stelle)	gang-bar	(ver)-antwort-lich
bereit-s	nach-	augenblick-
Erkundung-s-(Gefecht)	sicht-	a(e)usser-
Gefecht-s-(Taetigkeit)	(un)-mittel-	eigen-(t)-
Sanitaet-s-(Kompagnie)	etc.etc.	bekannt-
Vergeltung-s-(Feuer)	moeglich-st	feind-
vernichtung-s-(Feuer)	eilig-	frei-
Wirkung-s-(Schiessen)	a(e)usser-	ga(e)nz-
etc.etc.	ho(e)ch-	ku(e)rz-
Rest-les	la(e)ng-	neu-
Wirkungs-	etc.etc.	pu(e)nkt-
Wolken-	Ausfuehrlich-keit	ta(e)g-

Ziel-	Betriebsfaehig-	flu(e)ss-ig
etc.etc.	Brachbar-	nebel-
Dunkel-heit	Deutlich-	Sta(e)nd-
eigen-	Gueltig-	Sumpf-
Frei-	Richtig-	trotz-
Klar-	Taetig-	Wind-
Krank-	etc.etc.	Zeit-
Sicher-		bisher-ige
Unklar-		ein-
etc.etc.		dort-
		sofort-
		sonst-
		etc.etc.

APPENDIX 7

In addition to the usual military abbreviations, which can best be studied in "Vocabulary of German Military Terms and Abbreviations", the following is a list of the more frequent signs used by German Field Wireless Stations at the beginning and end of messages.

A R	....	Schluse
A S	....	Wait
B'	....	Break sign
B F	....	Ready to receive
B P Z	....	Am closing down
C H I	....	Chiffriert. Only used with messages of a tactical nature.
D D	....	Thanks
D Z	....	Dienstliche Zusaetze
F A	....	Answer follows
F O'	....	Message deciphered
F S	....	Jamming
H H	....	Changing to higher wave
I M I	....	Query
K R	....	Urgent message (Kriegstelegram)
M G	....	Increase power
M I M	....	Exclamation mark
M R	....	Motor trouble (Motor Stoerung)
O A	....	Send in higher note
O I	....	Send in lower note
N F	....	Nichts mehr zu funken (message ends)
N V	....	Nichts verstanden
O S	....	Communication meaningless

N N	....	Change to lower wave
U D	....	Query
U M	....	End of message (Change over)
U S	....	Atmospherics
V E	....	Verstanden
W D H	....	Wiederholen
W G	....	Report
W P G	....	How are signals!
W R	....	Wait for my call
X X	....	Must dismantle
Z I		
Z I F	....	Ziffer—only used with technical messages or those which simply concern the working of the F.T. Stations.

APPENDIX 8

German Morse Alphabet

A great deal of the difficulty in solving these codes depends not only on the jamming out of whole groups by other stations, but also on the bad sending and receiving of operators, which causes letters to be mistaken one for another. It is very useful therefore to know the German morse equivalents for the letters and numbers, and a list of them is accordingly given below.

a .-	Adolf	o ---	Otto
a .--.-	franz.a(a)	p .--.	Paula
b -...	Berta	q --.-	Quelle
c -.-.	Caeaar (sic)	r .-.	Richard
d -..	David	s ...	Siegfried
e .	Emil	t -	Theodor
e ..-..	franz.e(e)	u ..-	Ursula
f ..-.	Friedrich	v ...-	Victor
g --.	Gustav	w .--	Willy
h	Heinrich	x -..-	Xantippe
i ..	Isidor	y -.--	Ypsilon
j .---	Jakob	z --..	Zacharias
k -.-	Karl	ae .-.-	Adolfemil (ae)
l .-..	Ludwig	oe ---	Ottoemil (oe)
m --	Moritz	ue ..--	Ursulaemil (ue)
n -.	Nathan	ch ----	Caesarheinrich

1 .----	1		6 -....	6
2 ..---	2		7 --...	7
3 ...--	3		8 ---..	8
4 ....-	4		9 ----.	9
5	5		10 -----	10

APPENDIX 9

We will now give a selection of specimen messages actually intercepted and deciphered within the last twelve months.

These messages will serve a double purpose; firstly of showing the value to be obtained from the labours of the solvers, and secondly of showing the general character and subject matter of the messages sent by German Field Wireless. They will act therefore as a direct incentive to the solver, and as a basis for analogy in solving new codes.

When the key of a cipher was discovered, or when the code had reached a sufficiently advanced stage of solution, these messages were decipherable immediately on interception. In other cases a certain delay was inevitable until the key was discovered. In the majority of the following cases, however, the information contained in the messages was known to us as soon as to the enemy recipient.

The messages numbered consecutively from 13 to 25 are of very great interest. They were all received and deciphered in the course of the great German retirement in the Somme district in March 1917, and give direct indications, not only of the fact of the retirement, but in many cases of the actual places to which various units were ordered to retire.

As the exact location of all the German Wireless Stations was known to us, and also the units to which these stations were attached, the orders to dismantle stations and erect them again at places further back from the line, gave an exact indication of the course of the great retreat.

The following examples are only a few of many hundreds received and deciphered, although obviously not all of them contained information of such direct importance, or of such immediate value.

(1)   11/9/17 (sic)An Gruppe Thomas. Lage. Feind im Abschnitt E und linker Fluegel Abschnitt eingedrungen. Eigene Artillerie soll in Richtung Pappelschnur zukurz geschessen haben. A.V.O.[65]

(2) 11/2/17 Gruppe. Gegen 6 Uhr macht Infanterie bei Pappelschnur Gegenstoss. Unterstutzfeuer wird noetigenfalls angefordert. A.V.O.[66]

(3) 11/2/17 An Gruppe D. Schuesse in Richtung Pappelschnur liegen noch zu kurz. Um eigene Verluste vorzubeugen musste unbedingt zugelegt werden, nach Aussage eines Infanterieoffiziers. A.V.O.[67]

(4) 17/9/17 (sic) An 32 Infanterie Division. Von Stosstrupp drei schwarz und vier rot. Fuehrer gesund und am Bein verwundeter Englaender gefangen. Kampf Bataillon 177.[68]

(5) 18/2/17 Gruppe Thomas. Stark Truppen Ansammlungen bei Moulinruine. Mit Angriff ist zu rechnen.[69]

(6) 18/2/17 Schwytz loest Vaux Wald ab. Schubert.[70]

(7) 18/2/17 Regiment Caesar. Wird die Nacht vom 21–22 zwei Bataillon abgeloest.[71]

(8) 19/2/17 Abschnitt E. Ist Abloesung des ersten Bataillon 231 durchgefuehrt? Wie gliedert sich das erste Bataillon 230? 99 Reserve Infanterie Brigade.[72]

(9) 21/2/17 An Regiment Schaakholz. Sofort Verstaerkung. Sonst Stellung unhaltbar.[73]

(10) 21/2/17 Mit allem Garaet um 2 Uhr zum Abmarsch fertig sein. Ich schicke drei Leute. Keinen Klartext geben.[74]

(11) 22/2/17 An erste Garde Division. Vorposten Stellung durchlaufend mit Truppen. 5 Machinen Gewehr, 5 Granatwerfer besetzt. Anschluse rechts und linke erfolgt erst heute Nacht. Zweite Garde Reserve Division.[75]

(12) 10/3/17 8 Uhr 30 vormittags raeumt Regiment Bremen Irles. Die Vorposten der Garde bleiben stehen zur Sicherung unseres Anschlusses. Mit der Garde haben Vorposten zu bleiben. Sicherung des Gefaehrdeton rechten Fluegels hat ohne Verstaerkung der Vorposten stattzufinden. Nicht erforderliche Machinengewehre sind aus den Vorposten herauszuziehen. 2 F Anstellungsbataillon II Ferdinand.[76]

(13) 10/3/17 Station setzt sich Morgen 4 Uhr mit vollstaendigen Infanteriegeraet nach Moislains in Marsch. Naeheren Befehl. Leutnant Muhlank.[77]

(14) 12/3/17 Heller kommt nicht, da Ladestation nach Templeux geht.[78]

(15) 13/3/17 Wann Kommen unsere Lebensmittel? Wir haben nichts mehr.[79]

(16) 14/3/17 Im Laufe der Nacht abbauen. Wagen 6 Uhr dort. Wachtmeister Deter.[80]

(17) 14/3/17 Station Schluss. Abholung Morgen frueh. Welp.[81]

(18) 15/3/17 V P stuendlich Abbau zu erwarten, laut Befehl von K.T.K.[82]

(19) 15/3/17 L D baut morgen ab. Gegon Tragen nochmals verspre-chen. 7 Uhr 30 Fahrzeug. 9 Uhr Kirche Equancourt.[83]

(20) 16/3/17 Offizier Stellvertreter Remagen. Sofort Armee-Kommande-Funk in Marsch setzen.[84]

(21) 17/3/17 Leutnant Hein. Heute Abend abbauen. Auto halb acht Ostausgang Fins-Gouzeaucourt. Leutnant Cullmann.[85]

(22) 17/3/17 Station abbaut 12 Uhr. Aufbau Caudry etwa 8 Uhr.[86]

(23) 21/3/17 Gestriger Versuch, welcher 4 Uhr wiederholt werden sollte, wird heute 10 Uhr wiederholt.[87]

(24) 21/3/17 Morgens Divisionsstab zurueck. 111 Infanterie Division Detachement Bernstorff. Befehl ueber Aufloesung vom 203. Marschziel fuer zweite Radfahrer Bataillon 1 Bellingcourt.[88]

(25) 22/3/17 Husaren 14. Ham von Feinde besetzt. Kavallerie der 35te Infanterie Division geht auf Aubigny und Bray St. Christophe. Gefechtsstelle des Husaren 13 melden 11te Infanterie Division. Selbst Kavallerie 221 Infanterie Division bei Forest. Radfahrer im Kampf mit feindlicher Kavallerie. 11te Infanterie Division weicht auf Etreillers ueber Roupy. Melden wo Anschluss rechts und links. 221 Infanterie Divison.[89]

(26) 6/5/17 Auf K T K (A) Sofortige Aufklaerung ueber Lage an Brigade. Englaender sollen in Bullecourt sein. Noetigen-falle sofort Gegenstoss. Brigade.[90]

(27) 5/6/17 Division Messines. Morgen Meldung. Keine Verbindung mit K T K 6. Abloesung glatt verlaufen. Brigade Messi-nes.[91]

(28) 7/6/17 Division. Unterstuetzung dringend erforderlich auf der ganzen Linie.[92]

(29) 19/9/17 Die Stellung fuer die neuen Batterien ist auf Strasse Zonnebeke-Droogenbroodhoek.[93]

(30) 3/10/17 Es war abgehoert, dass Englaender morgen auf breitem Front angreifen will.[94]

(31) 4/10/17 Bataillon 3 Bayr. Res. 5 von Paschendael zum Regiment Nord in Marsch setzen. Rest soll in Bereitschaftsstellung vorgehen. Brigade.[95]

(32) 4/10/17 Abschnitt Nord Bayr. Regiment 5 macht Gegenangriff von Paschendael auf Zonnebeke. Eine Bataillon Bayer unter allen Umstaenden ist nach Droogenbroodhoek vorgescheben und stehen zu Gegenstoes zur Verfuegung. Brigade.[96]

(33) 21/11/17 Gasangriff nicht 1 Uhr 30 sondern 3 Uhr 30.[97]

(34)	22/11/17	Vordere Linie Liegt unter Stoerungsfeuer, Infanterie erbittet Stoerungsfeuer auf Friedhof.[98]
(35)	2/12/17	Sofort melden Lage der eigenen vorderen Linie. Vorfeld ist sofort in alte Linie vorzutreiben.[99]
(36)	2/12/17	Vorfeldlinie 895 zurueckgenommen. Hauptwiderstandslinie in unserer Hand. Verlust nicht bekannt. Dringend Munition fuer leicht Maschinengewehr.[100]
(37)	11/1/18	Von 8 Uhr 30 bix 11 Gasbereitschaft. Eigener Gasschiessen.[101]

ADM 137/4660

VIII
Codebreaking in the Middle East, 1916–17

These documents illustrate the types of material derived from crypt-analysis, their effect on British operations and the different forms in which codebreaking reports were produced. They pertain to, perhaps, the most complex task of intelligence of the entire First World War – the collection and assessment of material on the Turkish Army in the Middle East. This theatre was vast and the needs for intelligence exceptionally precise. The Turks had small forces fighting the British but large reserves in Anatolia, and the unexpected arrival of merely 20,000 Turkish soldiers could overthrow the balance at arms in Iraq or Palestine. Precisely this was the proximate cause for the British disaster at Kut-al-Amara in 1915–16. Even if one could acquire perfect knowledge of the enemy's order of battle and intentions and determine the location and movement of every single Turkish division, further problems were at hand. Turkish formations were often identified only by the name of their commander. 'So-and-so's force' might be a regiment or a corps, and change its identification without warning. The Turkish Army, moreover, was organised with less regularity than those of western Europe. Agonising discrepancies existed between the real and nominal strength of Turkish units and between the military quality of Anatolian and Arab and of regular and reserve formations. One 'division' might consist of 10,000 Anatolian regulars, another of 2,000 Arab reservists. One 'division' of the former sort might have greater military power than an 'army' of the latter.

Not surprisingly, in December 1915, the British commander in Egypt wrote that 'All calculations as to what the Turks & Arabs can or cannot do generally are wrong; it is impossible to get any information of what is being done in regard to preparations'.[1] One year later this was no longer the case, and largely because of codebreaking. Britain, of course, had other sources of intelligence in the Middle East. While each of these produced as much material as codebreaking, only one of them, the Aaronsohn (or 'Nilli') network in Palestine, was useful, reliable and trusted. Other agent networks and prisoners of war were regarded as untrustworthy; other technical sources of intelligence were less well developed and useful than on the Western Front. Codebreaking was the most valuable and valued source of them all, as indicated by its code name – 'absolutely reliable' information. Even when, as was often the case, it merely corroborated the material provided by other sources, this at least proved such reports true or false. Thus, codebreaking could serve as an absolutely reliable check on the accuracy of other sources of intelligence, such as the reports from the Arab forces in the Hejaz. The evidence suggests that from October 1916 onward, the British read on a current effective basis most Turkish and German radio messages transmitted in the Middle East. This was a higher degree of access than was the case with Ultra during the Second World War, although of course the volume of traffic was smaller.

The Documents in this chapter include examples of the various forms in which reports based on cryptanalytical intelligence survive. Documents Six to Eight and Ten to Thirteen are original Turkish and German messages as solved and translated by codebreakers and provided to commanders or senior staff officers. Document One is a copy of an original report sent from one British command to another. Documents Two and Three are paraphrases of such reports handled in that fashion. Document Four includes summaries made during 1916–17 by the intelligence assessing personnel of the Egyptian Expeditionary Force of the raw solutions provided by cryptanalysts. Document Five, a weekly report by codebreakers at GHQ Iraq, contains raw solutions of several Turkish messages. Presumably such reports were produced on a weekly basis by all British cryptanalytical organisations in the Middle East. These documents, and the notes attached, reveal the problems involved both in interpreting and using intelligence at the time and in judging its effect after the fact. Even first rate and absolutely reliable information may be intrinsically misleading or susceptible to misinterpretation – and, perhaps, cause more harm than help. Even when important intelligence is received, believed and correctly assessed, it may not significantly affect military operations. Even a mistaken assessment may lead commanders to take correct action.

This material shows that, on occasion, codebreaking provided several months warning of the most significant of Turkish intentions, whether their hope to launch a major offensive in Iraq or proof that local commanders doubted that they could defend Palestine. Such information, however, was of limited value: Turkish intentions might change or prove impossible to realise, while commanders might disobey the orders of their superior officers. Erroneous conclusions, moreover, could easily be drawn from the vague and often politically motivated language used by enemy commanders when making declarations of intent or participating in a debate about strategy. The British often did make errors of this sort. Conversely, this material at least denied the Turks the advantage of strategic surprise against the British, which was no small accomplishment. While of obvious importance, intelligence on the enemy's strategic plans and perceptions actually appears to have been less useful than a steady stream of reports on its operational capabilities and dispositions. Under the circumstances of 1917–18, the British could treat Turkish intentions with a measure of scorn but never their capabilities. Codebreaking provided a mass of material on several of the points which were most fundamental and problematical for British intelligence in the Middle East: the enemy's order of battle and dispositions and the movement of its formations and units. Although on occasion codebreaking also helped to determine the genuine strength of Turkish formations and units, particularly by solving the official strength or hospital returns of Turkish commands, the problem of determining the true fighting strength of Turkish units and formations was never satisfactorily solved. The material provided through cryptanalysis also demonstrably shaped three of the four major British offensives in Palestine and Iraq during 1917. Despite this advantage, General Murray's attack on Gaza in March 1917 was abortive. In Iraq between January to March 1917, conversely, a knowledge of Turkish strength and dispositions provided by codebreaking helped General Maude to achieve a major victory. Codebreaking also shaped General Allenby's triumph in Palestine of November 1917. It revealed the enemy's reaction to the British breakthrough, its plans for counterattack – and the weak spot in its line. This was precisely where he threw his reserves. Altogether, in this theatre during 1916–18, codebreaking was as useful a source of operational intelligence for the British Army as was ever Ultra during the Second World War.

1

Message from G.H.Q., Egypt to G.O.C. Force D. Repeated C-in-C India and War Office,[2] 3 January 1917

I A 2838.

Very secret.

We have received information from absolutely reliable source giving as follow Enver's orders to Khalil.[3]

Officer commanding 6th Army.

English have not brought important reinforcing units to Irak, according to latest aeroplane observations. 6th Army therefore, in my opinion, will have sufficient forces to pass to the offensive as soon as 14th Division arrives, provided situation at Baghdad is favourable. Offensive to be undertaken in Irak will otherwise remain exposed to danger. Inform me please as soon as possible how such can be carried out, and what help is required by 6th Army, especially if any heavy artillery is needed.

Copies to: Sent to:–

    M.I. 1   D.M.1.

                                M12 & b

                                ~~M13 & b~~

                                ~~D.M.O.~~

                                ~~M.O.2. & a & c~~

WO 106/1511

2

From Director of Military Intelligence to Caucasus Military Agent and Major Rowlandson[4]

SECRET

(No. 27483, cipher.)   4th January, 1917.

We have absolutely reliable evidence that the Turks intend to launch an offensive against Force "D".[5] Enver suggests, provided the situation in Baghdad is favourable, that this should take place as soon as 14th Division arrives. He asks what help Khahl (sic) required and if heavy artillery is needed. Please telegraph last definite locations of each regiment of 14th Division and of units Hamadan and Rowanduz fronts.[6] It seems possible that 37th Regiment and 1st and 2nd Machine-gun Companies have been sent to Hamadan to replace a division which may be withdrawn, as weather conditions might enable smaller force to hold the passes on the Hamadan–Baghdad road.

2.   Presume snow in on Hamadan front, which is referred to in Caucasus Military Agent's No. 673.

Repeated to Basra and India.

Sent to
D.M.I.
M.I.2 & b.
~~M.I.3.& b~~
D.M.O.
M.O.2. & c.
M.O.2. A
India Office

WO 106/1511

3

**Message from G.H.Q., Egypt to Director of Military
Intelligence, 5 January 1917**

I.A.2844.
Information from an absolutely reliable source indicates that 12,000 is maximum total strength of Turkish HEDJAZ Expeditionary Force at MEDINA. Composition of force unchanged consisting of Regiments 42, 55, 130, 1 battalion 29th Regiment, and other oddments such as gendarmerie, camel corps etc.

They are short of winter clothing, and there were 1200 sick in hospital and (?100) wounded at the end of last month.

Copies to: M.I.(1)   Sent to:–

                                  D.M.1.

                                  M1.2.&b.

                                  ~~M1.3.&b.~~

                                  ~~D.M.O.~~

                                  ~~M.O.2. &.a.&c~~

WO 106/1511

4

Excerpts from the Intelligence Diary of the Egyptian Expeditionary Force

13/10(1916) ("32 wireless messages sent by the enemy were intercepted and decoded at G.H.Q. on 12th and 13th Oct." – deleted) We have received a large number of reports from an absolutely reliable source giving certain Turkish identifications. The units mentioned in these, as forming part of the Expeditionary Corps have nearly all been identified before, either from documents or by contact after the KATIA operations.[7]

Amongst new units are

2nd Hejin Regt ? Circassion Irregular Cavalry, at BITTIA, 8 miles W of ARISH

3rd Cavalry Divn at JAFFA-GAZA

Depot regiment – Bethlehem – ASARIJE

Machine Gun Battalion – AIN KARIM

KAKULE ? Column – HAFIR (AUJA)

Mining detachment – EL ARISH

In a lengthy message from KRESS VON KRESSENSTEIN,[8] detailed instructions are given with a view to facilitating relations between Austro-Germans, of the PASHA formations[9] and the Turkish Lines of Communication.

The centre of enemy concentration has definitely shifted

from SINAI to S.SYRIA. G.H.Q. is to be at JERUSALEM also H.Q. of 3rd Division. 32nd regiment at JERICHO 31st regt at RAMLEH and JERUSALEM. RAFA on 8/10 contained 400 troops 7 guns & 2 machine guns, 300 Syrian Camel Corps passed through these on their way to EL ARISH. A post has been established at SHEIKH ZOWEID.[10]

EL ARISH on 9/10 contained 1380 men. The 9 aeroplane hangars at FAGIRA have been removed. 1 aeroplane remains.

4/3 (1917) *TURKEY*

Information from an abs. reliable source shows that Turks in SW PERSIA on 2/3/17 believed that troops were being moved by Russians from that front to CAUCASUS.

SYRIA

These (sic) is absolutely reliable information that VON KRESS has informed his subordinate commanders that

(1) 4th Army[11] is to be so strengthened that after some time it will be able to drive English from Turkish soil.

(2) positions at GAZA, JEMAMA, TEL EL SHERIA and SABA are to be greatly improved (an unlikely line ? mentioned to conceal from troops that further retirement is to take place).

(3) SHELLAL is to be abandoned.[12]

ARABIA

An abs. reliable report states that the ARABS have cut the railway in two places at EL HAMRA and MATALI north of MEDAIN SALEH and that H.Q. of Composite force recently at MEDAIN SALEH are now at TEBUK.

5/3 *ARABIA*

An Abs. reliable report ("from DA" – deleted) states that JEMAL G.O.C. 4th Army at DAMASCUS has ordered G.O.C. HEJAZ Exp. Force at MEDINA to withdraw that force to PALESTINE. Move to commence at once. Holy relics books etc to be taken. Force to march along railway accompanied by maximum of 10 engines & 100 trucks for stores supplies etc. Reserve rations to be collected at

HADIYA & ELULA. Camels to be taken from AKINJE and Turkish Dromedary Regts. organized.[13]

13/3 *TURKEY*

An abs. reliable report states that the vanguard of the 13th Army Corps reached PAITAK PASS on evening of 12/3 and that the Army Corps are stopping on the SAMARRA line.[14]

14/3 *TURKEY*

An absolute reliable report states that Turks when evacuating right bank of TIGRIS lost 23 guns including 6 siege guns, 3 gunboats 1 steamer 6 barges & 4500 "healthy" prisoners.

15/3 *TURKEY*

A report from an abs. reliable source states

(1) The decision to abandon the DIALA line was taken in consequence of the complete breakdown of moral of the 18th Army Corps. It is indicated that TIGRIS force consists of 14th 51st & 52nd divisions.

(2) The detached force arrived MUSEYIB on night of 11th inst.

(3) The concentration of the 13th Army Corps was to be concealed and protected.

(4) 2 Divisions of 18th A.C. were on 14/3 west of TIGRIS and 1 Division East about 30 k.m. north of BAGHDAD.

22/3 *TURKEY*

Information from abs. reliable source that

(1) 18th A.C. was crossing at SAMARRA on 21st under great difficulties.

(2) Believing MOSUL in danger if he concentrates on left bank TIGRIS Corps commander suggests concentrating on right bank near BELED in anticipation of attack by SINDIE DELI ABBAS.

(3) Shortage of supplies still serious.

22/3 *SYRIA*

Information from an absolutely reliable source states that newly arrived troops at GAZA have no entrenching tools and have asked for 300.

23/3 *TURKEY*

Information from abs. reliable source indicates

(1) that 181st Regt. was expected to leave RAS EL AIN for MOSUL on 22/3/17 and that 31st Cavalry Regt was proceeding from FELUJA to SAMARRA with any unallotted troops and ammunition from RIMADIAH. [note 181st (twice repeated) may belong to 59th Division reported at MANISIA on 21/1/17]

(2) on 22/3 the 18th A.C. was crossing to left bank of TIGRIS. 1 Regt. of 52nd Division was being left on the right bank with (?) one regt of 51st Division. Two Regts at least were probably to be left on right bank as supplies are still at SAMARRA.

(3) on 23/3 orders were issued to ? SAMARRA to leave some unidentified unit or units on (?) right ("left", deleted) bank as 52nd Divn. was considered sufficient for left bank. The possibility of ("probability", deleted) an advance from both banks on 25/3/17 was indicated.

26/3 *MESOPOTAMIA*

Abs. reliable information indicates

(1) A Division was on 25/3 expected to reach MOSUL within next 6 weeks probably marching via NESIBIN.

(2) EUPHRATES flotilla at RIMADIA was on 22/3 short of coal. HIT mine could not supply enough.

(3) 14th Division was on 25/3 ordered to advance to the DEHLETAVE-KARNABIT line.

(4) ?18th Army Corps was to advance in SINDIA-DEHLETAVE direction.

(5) Flying Corps personnel to be transferred from HIT TO SAMARRA.

28/3 *SYRIA*

Abs. reliable information states

(1) 163rd Regt. advancing from MEJDEL to GAZA
53rd Div being concentrated at MEJEDL
79th Regt taking place of 162nd.

(2) 137th Regt. apparently arrived in RAMLEH area.

(3) Cases of typhus in RAMLEH area.

(4) 3rd Division from JEMAME, 16th from SHERIA & 3rd Cav Div from SABA moving towards GAZA.[15]

31/5 *SYRIA*

Abs. Rel. information shows that on 31/5/17 GOC IV Army informed ENVER Pasha, Vice Cinc at DARDANELLES that British forces had been much increased since 2nd battle of GAZA & that he expected them to attack, to meet which his present force on PALESTINE front was insufficient. He was therefore bringing mule mounted Reg. hitherto employed against brigands in ? HAUKHAN to this front, but had no other available reinforcements in IV army. He therefore requested

(1) Tranport of 26th Div. to IV Army to begin at once & at top speed.

(2) Reference (sic) over all other armies to be given to IV Army with regard to transport of guns & heavy artillery allotted to it but not yet arrived, also for transport of 4 infantry bns. from V Army & all unallotted troops for IV Army.

(3) That infantry regiment now stationed between KATIMA [?KATMA HAN] & the Lake, belonging to the 46th Div., destined for VI Army, might be given to IV Army.[16]

WO 157/709, 713, 715

5

Memorandum from Brigadier-General, General Staff, Intelligence, G.H.Q., I.E.F. "D" to Director of Military Intelligence, War Office, 20 February 1917

SECRET   No. Ig. (a)152/34
MEMORANDUM

In continuation of my Ig. (a)152/30 dated 22nd. January 1917 translations of the important Turkish 4 figure code messages

intercepted during the week are forwarded herewith; also a list of new groups identified.
Copy to:–
General Officer Commanding
Egyptian Expeditionary Force
(S.L.)

7328.	7742.
7333.	4743.
6533.	7668.
2239.	6972.

(1)   M.24.   From S.M.R. to S.T.K. intercepted 13th February 1917. 1049 MELONE   240 groups.
1.   There is an extraordinary quietness over the whole front.
2.   One enemy cavalry regiment appeared at 10 a.m. on the 29/11/32 (=11/2/17) coming out of the hills to the S.W. at AK TEPPE and entered GIRDARABAD 6 km. N.W. of AK TEPE and stayed there. A detachment from another cavalry regiment appeared at 1 p.m. yesterday 15 km. N.W. of AK TEPE and reconnoitred due S.W. in the direction of MUBAREKABAD. It was impossible to see where it went after ..... (a short phrase corrupt). The cavalry detachment which I reported in the neighborhood of AK TEPE in yesterday's report has not been seen again .....(?). The ..... who went out to destroy (?) this force have not yet returned.

ALI IHSAN.[17]

(2)   M.25.   From S. T. K. to S. B. A. intercepted 14th February 1917. 1557 APFELSINE (SMR) 12024.   148 groups.
..........(jammed..........*Answer*
Your order dated 9/2/17 was received on 10/2/17 and orders were given for the move of the whole 37th Regiment and on the same day I made the tactical moves (? ....jammed) ordered. To-day the 37th Regt. 37th Regt. (sic) is between SINNEH % and BIJAR (which is ...... 2 groups undeciphered, perhaps near some place) and its movements are being much hampered by the

heavy snow which is falling on all sides but it is expected that the head of the column will reach SINNEH % to-morrow.

ALI IHSAN.

% This cannot be taken as *absolutely* certain but it is practically so.

(3)   M.29.   S. M. R. to S. T. K. intercepted 14 – 15/2/17. 115 (MELONE) No. 12146.   160 groups.

VERY SECRET

In continuation of my cipher message of 28/11/32 (=10/20/17). The main body and rear guard has concentrated in SINNEH. One battalion of the 37th Regt. left SINNEH to-day for BANEH %. Another battalion, the M.G.'s and the regimental staff move off together to-morrow. The last battalion leaves BIJAR to-morrow and follows the rest. If it is decided to concentrate this Regt. on the BANEH % front, in order not to make too conspicuous its presence at BANEH % with the 44th and 11th Regiments (translation not absolutely certain) it will rest there two days and then march off again. Please send orders for its destination (?).

ALI IHSAN.

(% "BANEH" can only be said to be the likeliest place to be represented by this group 4478)
(S.L.)

(4)   M.31.   S M R to S T K & S B A intercepted 18/2/17 1605 (Melone) Nr. 356 – 13270   330 groups.

Nothing important to report yesterday in the 5478 and BIJAR Sectors. The DAULATABAD telegraph line has still not been repaired. The snowstorm which has been raging for the last week started again yesterday evening after two days intermission and it is snowing hard. The majority of the telegraph and telephone lines are down and the roads are blocked in many places. There has been no communications between ASADABAD and 5478 for 5 days. I am putting on labour corps men in hundreds every day to clear the road but have not yet heard that they have succeeded in clearing it. (short sentence not understood). I have ordered the last remaining battalion of the 37th regiment to move but expect it will be prevented by the snow. It is probable that the troops which are moving from SINNEH to 4478 (BANEH ?) have been delayed on the road. I have had no news of the battalion which I sent from here to BIJAR since UREVA (? KHURWAR). I am concentrating the H.Q. of the Cavalry Brigade and the 13th Cavalry at 5478 and relieving the 6th Division's battery which is at DAULATABAD. But owing to the storm this move has not been carried out and I have not got the orders through to DAULATABAD yet.

ALI IHSAN.

(5) M32 S M R to S T K, S B A intercepted 18/2/17.
Unfortunately the beginning of this message is lost and the remainder is very corrupt. The following however can be made out of it:–
"------- the line between KERIND and 2178 was broken by the storm ....

..... to prepare the 6th Division at once and if the 6th Division is taken from Persia it involves the necessity of being willing and ready to abandon all.

IWM, Sir Gerard Clauson Papers.

6

Translation of Intercepted Enemy Communication, November 1917

S.G. 1690.
To:– EL TINE.
From:– JERUSALEM. T.B.E. 1208 on 9th.

7 parts.
General Von Kress. As I observed from the telegram of your Excellency, you have to prepare to arrest the enormous might of

the enemy on the WADI KUSSIER and you are well aware what confidence the Fatherland places in your prudence and resolution. The danger that enemy fleet will accomplish anything important is not great, as you are full (sic) aware of the presence of numerous submarines off the coast.

Part 2

The distance of the van of the enemy infantry from JAFFA is at present 40 kilometres as crow flies, a distance which the enemy will not be able to cover in the next two or three days if he be opposed along the coast by a detachment of all arms, which need not be strong in numbers but must consist of picked men especially commanded by an energetic leader. The next position of the army must lie behind the ARABA and WADI SURAR Sector, its left wing in the district East of the railway station of WADI SURAR.

Part 3

I intend on 10th November the 53rd Infantry Division of the group ALI FUAD and the right wing of the 7th Army from the district of DAWAIME and the south to push a counter-thrust against approximately the line ARAK EL MENSHIYE – BIR SALEM and AWUKEL, and I anticipate that it will not only save the 8th Army from further harrying, but will bring about an appreciable lightening of the situation.

Part 4

I recommend to your notice again the blowing up of the railway and destruction of all bridges in the districts given up.

FALKENHAYN[18]

IWM, Guy Dawnay Papers.

7

Translation of Intercepted Enemy Communication, November 1917

S.G. 1691.
To: EL TINE.
From: JERUSALEM. 1350.
8th Army H.Q. Also for the group of ALI FUAD.

Firstly. Enemy position up to midday 9th: One weak group near the height of ASKALON. Strong infantry and cavalry forces on both sides of the railway especially however on the west side following the line up to the WADI HESI.

Secondly. The 8th Army will prevent with all his forces the advance of the enemy in the KUSSIER sector with its left wing resting on the railway.

Thirdly. Under the leadership of the 7th Army an attack group will be formed in which the units of the 7th Army at hand and the group of ALI FUAD, including the 53rd Infantry Division, will be included. The attack group is on 10th November to attack on a wide front on the line ARAK EL MENSHIYE – BIR SALEM – ABU GERAR.

To protect the southern flank of the attack group the 7th Army H.Q. is to utilise all units capable of taking part.

Fourthly. I base my expectations on the conviction that every commander and every man who is about to participate in this encounter is aware of its significance for the welfare of our beloved Fatherland.

MARSHAL VON FALKENHAYN[19]

End of Message.

IWM, Guy Dawnay Papers.

8

Translation of Intercepted Enemy Communication, November 1917

S.G. 1762.
To TEBUK.
From DAMASCUS.   T.B.E.   1530 on 9th.
To Shevket Bey, Line Commissaire General, at ULA on the line.

The situation on the SINAI front has become bad. TEL EL SHERIA and GAZA have fallen. All the provisions in the stations south of SARAR will be withdrawn to RAMLEH and the ammunition to TULKEREM*. Part of the troops are concentrating at NABLUS. KRESS has transferred his H.Q. to RAMLEH. Last night FUAD Bey sent for us and asked what would be the quantity of transport we could provide by using at the same time all the water, fuel and relief trains running on the stretch of line from TEBUK inclusive to MEDINA, i.e. all the engines and trucks used for daily local traffic. By using such words as "Fighting" and "carrying rails for repairs" he indirectly gave us to understand that an evacuation was probable. He says "This is merely a staff calculation and does not imply any intention", but I do not know exactly where the truth lies. We here shall reply according to the information at our disposal, but I beg you to investigate this question personally and send a report to G.O.C. SYRIA and W.ARABIA if necessary.
FERID your assistant

* Probably TULKERAM.

IWM, Guy Dawnay Papers.

9

Message from Brigadier-General G.P. Dawnay, B.G.G.S. for Major-General, Chief of the General Staff, Egyptian Expeditionary Force to G.O.C., Desert Mounted Corps, 10 November 1917

Latest information shows that enemy Headquarters moved back yesterday to RAMLEH and that part of the VIIIth Army appears to be concentrating as far back as NABLUS. The enemy is evidently in the greatest difficulty about transport to get his material away.

The XXI Corps should have its advanced guards near BEIT DURAS and ESDUD tonight, and will be ready to move on after you.

The moment we can get within striking distance of the railway at Junction Station, the whole of the enemy force which was originally engaged against our right flank north of BEERSHEBA will be in extreme difficulties, and it would seem possible that in this case the defence of JERUSALEM might become very difficult.

["be almost impossible" deleted].

[By aeroplane at 11.20]

IWM, Guy Dawnay Papers.

10

Translation of Intercepted Enemy Communication, November 1917

S.G. 1735.   16th November.

From KILKILIYE.

To JERUSALEM.   T.B.E. 1700. } 16th.
Intpd. 1816. }

YILDERIM.

Enemy cavalry has burst into JAFFA. Their strength is estimated at a Cavalry Brigade. On the rest of this front of the army about

5 cavalry regiments have been driven off. In front of the VIII Army at present are at least the 2 Cavalry Divisions and 1 infantry division its main body at EL KUBEIBE.

VON KRESS

IWM, Guy Dawnay Papers.

II

Message from Intelligence, G.H.Q., 1st Echelon to Colonel Nugent, Advanced G.H.Q., 21 November 1917

GOK to TUL KARIT and NABLUS from vgt location unknown aaa TBE 1600 21st aaa. 20 8th army army (sic) order no 18 aaa all attempts of the enemy to advance beyond the front of the 3rd and 22nd army corps have been repulsed aaa 3rd and 22nd army corps remain at their former posts aaa 3rd army corps had entrusted the 3rd Cavalry division with the protection of the roads leading through the mountains along the line SARIS-BIUKIN-ABUD aaa the covering advanced infantry detachment has been attached to the 3rd Cavalry division aaa connection is to be made with storm company 50 at TERRATA aaa. A field wireless station is to be detached to the 3rd Cavalry division the wireless station in JERUSALEM is detached for the 22nd army corps and the one in NABLUS for the 7th army headquarters aaa The divisional staff is now in BIR-EL-JET aaa The reserves of the 24th infantry division are to be concentrated as strongly as possible at and north of RAMALLA BIRE aaa. The 22nd army corps has also strong reserves behind its right wing aaa. Infantry regiment 72 is so to be disposed that its march to the north can take place without delay on the receipt of the order aaa. 7th army headqrs (sic) from this evening in NABLUS aaa FENSI.

IWM, Guy Dawnay Papers.

12

Translation of Intercepted Enemy Communication with further Annotations, November 1917

SECRET.

S.T. 1928.   25th

From DAMASCUS.

To TEBUK.   T.B.E. 1325 on 24th.

Intpd. 1010 on 25th.

G.O.C. 2nd Composite Force.

Situation on Palestine Front is as follows:–
The 8th Army under JEVAD PASHA's command is behind a line
from the source of the AUJA river which is North of JAFFA along
the wadi AUJA and the wadi ABDULJA.

The 7th Army under the command of FAVSHI PASHA has for
4 days been victoriously defending the fortified camp of JERU-
SALEM.

The enemy situation is one infantry Division with one or two
cavalry divisions north of the JAFFA-LUDD line against the 8th
Army.

4 infantry divisions and 2 cavalry divisions are in ? deep
formation attacking JERUSALEM.

I firmly hope that JERUSALEM will be a xxxxxx CHANAK.

G.O.C. Syria and Western Arabia.

[Handwritten note:

O. For information

ABDULJA = probably ABU LEJJA.   Apparently KRESS no longer
Commander 8th Army.

25/11/17   M A P Whitby Capt
                             for Major GSI

Later

Wireless Station UBG at TULKERAM sent closing down signal at
1306 today.]

IWM, Guy Dawnay Papers

13

Translation of Intercepted Enemy Communication, November 1917

To CONSTANTINOPLE
From DAMASCUS, working for H.Q. and L. of C. 4th Army.
Personal.
To ENVER PASHA Vice C-in-C.

Instead of the necessary measures for a serious defence of JERUSALEM being taken first the forces at hand were wasted by offensive operations, in the imaginary hope of indirectly saving JERUSALEM; this caused the fall of JERUSALEM. The (?material and) moral responsibility for it rests, in my opinion, with FALKENHAYN. I inform you that I can never pardon this man who was given the title of Pasha without deserving it.

AHMED JEMAL,
G.O.C. SYRIA and W. ARABIA.
Minister of Marine.

IWM, Guy Dawnay Papers.

Notes

Introduction

The editor is indebted to the copyright holders for permission to cite material from the following collections of private papers: the Imperial War Museum (the papers of Gerard Clauson, Guy Dawnay, General Horne, Walter Kirke, Lord Loch, Archibald Murray, C.R. Outen and P.G. Whitefoord), the Marconi Archives, the National Army Museum (Philip Leith Ross and Henry Rawlinson) and the United States Army Military History Institute (the A.L. Conger papers and Curriculum Archives). All ADM, AIR, CAB, MUN, T and WO files are held by the Public Record Office and L/MIL files by the India Office Library and Records. In both cases such material falls under Crown copyright and appears by permission of the Controller of Her Majesty's Stationery Office. All RG-9 files are held by the Public Archives of Canada, and appear by permission of that institution.

A complex specialist terminology is used in reference to signals intelligence. In modern parlance, that term – often called 'signal intelligence' – means any exploitation of all electronic emissions, of which one particular form is 'communications intelligence' – material acquired from the reading of encrypted messages. The latter term is also defined as 'cryptology', the study of the techniques of the defence of ('cryptography') or the attack upon ('cryptanalysis') secret messages. This modern teminology will be used in the commentary on these documents. However, that is not the case within the documents themselves because contemporary British figures did not follow this language. They used the phrase 'wireless intelligence', for example, to indicate all forms of exploitation of the external features of signals communication and the term 'cryptography' to mean all the matters covered by the modern terms 'cryptology', 'cryptography' and 'cryptanalysis'.

1 William F. Friedman, *Cryptography and Cryptanalysis Articles, Volume 1*, (Laguna Hills, Ca., 1976) p. 27.
2 See Bibliographical Essay.
3 Memorandum by E.T. Williams, undated but *c.* 1945, 'The Use of Ultra by the Army', WO 208/3575.
4 'The Strategical Side of I(a)', undated memorandum and no author cited but by GHQ Intelligence, Iraq, and *c.* early 1919 according to internal evidence, Leith-Ross Papers, National Army Museum, 8312–69–10.
5 Memorandum by G-2, G.H.Q., A.E.F., 15.6.19, *United States Army in the World War, 1917–1919, Volume 13* (Washington, 1948), p. 13.
6 Bibliographical Essay.
7 David Kahn, *The Codebreakers, The Story of Secret Writing* (New York, 1967) and John Ferris, 'Before "Room 40": The British Empire And Signals Intelligence, 1898–1914', *The Journal of Strategic Studies*, 12/4, (1989).

8　John Ferris, 'The British Army and Signals Intelligence in the Field during the First World War', *Intelligence and National Security, 3/4* (1988); Marcel Givierge, 'Problems of Code', in Friedman, *Cryptography and Cryptanalysis Articles*, op. cit., pp. 7–10.

9　Kerry, A.J., and W.A. McDill, *The History of the Corps of Royal Canadian Engineers* (Toronto, 1962); A. Lincoln Levine, *Circuits of Victory* (Garden City, 1921); John S. Moir, (ed.), *History of the Royal Canadian Corps of Signals, 1903–1961* (Ottawa, 1962); R.E. Priestley, *The Signal Service in the European War of 1914 to 1918 (France)* (Chatham, 1921); W. Arthur Steel, 'Wireless Telegraphy in the Canadian Corps in France', Chapters 1–11, *Canadian Defence Quarterly, Vols. VI–IX* (1928–1931).

10　Lecture by Blandy, 3.17, RG–9/111/C–1/3827.

11　Priestley, *Signal Service.* op. cit., p. 326.

12　Intelligence E (c) to G.S.I.e, 10.10.18, ADM 137/4701; W. Arthur Green, 'Wireless Telegraphy in the Canadian Corps', Chapter 8, 'Amiens, August 1918', *Canadian Defence Quarterly, Volume VIII, 1930–31*, p. 92. (The units of number and time cited in the latter source have been converted in order to allow direct comparison with that in the first source).

13　GHQ to First Army 'I', 6.1.18, RG–9/111/C–1/3827.

14　War Office to Treasury, 20.12.19, T 1/12462/2148.

15　William Friedman, *Solving German Codes in World War One* (Laguna Hills, Ca., 1977), pp. 78–79; Wayne G. Barker, (ed.), *The History of Codes and Ciphers in the United States During World War 1* (Laguna Hills, Ca., 1979), pp. 125–69.

16　Friedman, ibid. pp. 112–14; E.W.B. Gill, *War, Wireless and Wangles* (Oxford, 1934), pp. 22–26.

17　Barker, *Codes and Ciphers*, p. 19.

18　Marconi War History, Marconi Archive. German field codes were never solved through cryptanalysis within 36 hours; however, those used for traffic between spotting aircraft and artillery formations were. That fact and other details cited in this excerpt imply that these individuals specialised in the attack against such systems.

19　For codebreaking during the Great War in general, cf. Kahn, *Codebreakers*, op. cit.; for British signals intelligence in particular, cf. Ferris, 'The British Army', op. cit.

20　While the sources after November 1917 are thin, they indicate that the British did routinely intercept and solve German and Turkish operational traffic in the Middle East throughout 1918 ('Notes on Wireless Working by Corps W/T Officers, 4.18 and 6.18, WO 95/4476; War Office to GHQ Egypt, 25.7.18, WO 95/4370; Gill, op. cit., pp. 19–26).

21　Givierge, 'Problems', op. cit., p. 16–17.

22　Lecture by Major-General D.E. Nolan, 20.3.33. Curriculum Archives, 392–A–19. United States Army Military History Institute, Carlisle Barracks.

23　For a definition of 'Wave' messages and some examples of their nature, see 9th Corps Signals Order, 21.5.17, WO 95/845; Australian Corps Signals Log, 6.25 p.m., 11.20 p.m. and 12.35 p.m., 9.8.18, WO 95/986.

24　Barker, *Codes and Ciphers*, op. cit., p. 180; Steel, Chapter 6, pp. 365–66 and Chapter 8, p. 91.

25　Memorandum by I(e), 'Enemy Codes and their Solution', I.18, ADM 137/4660.

26　Givierge, 'Problems', op. cit., p. 17; Friedman, *German Codes*, pp. 79, 126; Barker, *Codes and Cipher*, p. 215. cf. *United States Army in the World War*, Volume 13, ibid, p. 42.

NOTES TO INTRODUCTION

27 Friedman, ibid.

28 Priestley, *Signal Service*, op. cit., p. 236.

29 Walter Kirke diary, entry 6.7.16, passim, Walter Kirke Papers, Imperial War Museum; notes for lecture by Kirke, 27.11.25, Walter Kirke papers, Intelligence Corps Museum; Charteris to MacDonogh, 5.7.16, WO 158/897; 2nd Army to Corps, 25.4.16 (erroneously dated '1915'), WO 95/637; memorandum by 1st Army, 27.10.16, WO 95/167; memorandum by German Wireless Intelligence Organisation, 20.1.19, WO 170/4268; Ferdinand Tuohy, *The Battle of Brains* (London, 1930) pp. 158–67; Priestley, *Signal Service*, op. cit., pp. 98–108.

30 Kirke diary, entries of August–December 1916 contain a wealth of material on this topic; ANZAC to divisions, 23.9.16, WO 95/980; memorandum by General Staff (Intelligence), 1.17, S.S. 537, MUN 4/3575; Priestley, *Signal Service*, op. cit., pp. 99–115. For the organisation of the German 'Arendt' service, cf. General Staff, 'Handbook of the German Army in War. April 1918', p. 119 (copy in Imperial War Museum).

31 Memorandum by Williams, 4.12.19, passim, T 173/22A. One member of the Arendt units recalled that Fullerphone traffic could be intercepted 'under certain circumstances' (Wilhelm F. Flicke, *War Secrets in the Ether, Volume 1* (Laguna Hills, Ca., 1977), pp. 34–35. He was correct: British technical experts concluded that Fullerphone traffic from poorly installed systems could be intercepted up to 60 yards from the line in question ('Report on Experimental Work', 12.12.16, AIR 1/864; cf. Steel, Chapter 6, p. 375, ibid). The system, moreover, had to be used properly in order to be effective. Fullerphones could not prevent telephone traffic from being intercepted; in one American division during 1918, however, Fullerphones were used as normal telephone sets. *United States Army in the World War, 1917–1919, Volume 3* (Washington, 1948), p. 215.

32 Tyler to Nolan, 7.3.18, A.L. Conger Papers, United States Military History Institute, Carlisle Barracks.

33 This form of signals intelligence could also produce unusual human consequences. A British radio operator and other rank noted that
'One of the most unpleasant experiences a Wireless Operator with the Artillery could have, was to listen to a German aeroplane – the wireless signal of which was most distinctive – *ranging on his own Battery!*
In Nov. 1917 I had this experience on a number of occasions. As I had a copy of the current German code, I was able to follow the progress of his 'Shoots' in complete detail! One would hear the succession of three dots (ie. morse code) – 'Fire!' & then about half a minute later over comes the shell into our Battery position. A minute or so later the correction was sent. Fierce arguments would arise with the gunners & bets freely given and taken as to what his target was! These were settled when the 'OK' signal came down – (Direct Hit)! These were seldom accurate, & the target was usually found to be a Gun Pit. I have a very vivid recollection of listening to a German aeroplane one morning, with his shells coming closer & closer to my dug-out, and then suddenly realising his target was *my Wireless Mast!'*
(Undated note by C.R. Outen, 'The German Method of Coordinating the Fire of Artillery by means of Wireless Signals', C.R. Outen papers, 74/25/1, Imperial War Museum.)

34 Lefroy to RFC Wireless, 16.5.15, passim, AIR 1/754/204/4/71. Material on the

319

sporadic work between the summers of 1915 and 1916 may be found in the Lord Loch papers, 71/12/3, Imperial War Museum; 'War Diary for Pack Set Wireless Telegraph Station', 26.5.15, WO 95/584; 6th Corps Intelligence Diary, 10.8.15, WO 95/767. For subsequent and more systematic developments in this field, cf. n. 37 below.

35 Barker, *Codes and Ciphers*, p. 195.

36 Undated and unsigned 'Resume' of Captain Bolitho's case before the Commission for Awards to Inventors, T 173/122.

37 Tuohy to GHQ Wireless, 13.10.16, AIR 1/996/204/5/1232; memorandum by GHQ intelligence, 18 May 1917, AIR 1/2141/209/1/52; 3rd Army wireless intelligence summary, 20 May 1918, AIR 1/996/204/5/1234. Ferdinand Tuohy, *The Crater of Mars* (London, 1929), pp. 132–48.

38 Tuohy, ibid, pp. 140–42. This statement is not so straightforward as it seems. The intuitive interpretation is that (a) signals intelligence reduced by 90 per cent the casualties which would have been inflicted by German artillery fire which (b) saved many lives. While these conclusions probably are true, neither can be demonstrated to be so. Perhaps, for example, the 10 per cent of bombardments which the British could not evade were the most devastating of the series. While this seems unlikely, the greater problem is – how many casualties would these 577 bombardments have caused had troops not taken cover? An entirely arbitrary guess is that these bombardments would have inflicted between 10,000–20,000 fatalities or between 20–40 per shoot. This, in turn, would have been a substantial contribution from merely one aspect of signals intelligence.

39 'Intelligence Lecture' undated but apparently 4.26, Major-General P.G. Whitefoord papers, 77/2/1, Imperial War Museum; Memorandum by 2nd Army, 11.11.18, AIR 1/2268/209/70/200. This appears to have been a conventional term for the inferences drawn from traffic analysis.

40 Memorandum 'Salonika 4' 15.2.17, passim, WO 157/753; memorandum by German Wireless Intelligence Organisation, 20.1.19, WO 170/4268. This was also true of Zeppelin call signs, which eased MI1(e)'s reconstruction of the enemy's order of battle.

41 Friedman, *German Codes*, p. 92.

42 Memorandum by I(E), 'Enemy Codes and their Solution', I.18, ADM 137/4660.

43 Friedman, *German Codes*, pp. 12–16.

44 ibid, p. 93.

45 German 9th Army to Group of Armies, German Crown Prince, 31.7.18 and memorandum by Ludendorff, 14.9.18, *United States Army, Volume 11* ibid, pp. 354, 428.

46 Memorandum by Ludendorff, 8.2.18, RG–9/111/C–1/3859; Ferris, 'The British Army', pp. 38–42.

47 There have been few studies of deception during the First World War: cf. Ferris, ibid and Yigal Sheffy, 'Institutionalized Deception and Perception Reinforcement: Allenby's Campaigns in Palestine, 1917–18', in Michael Handel (ed.), *Intelligence and Military Operations* (London, 1990).

48 Memorandum by German Wireless Intelligence Organisation, 20.1.19, WO 170/4268; GHQ France to Armies, 5.8.18, Guy Dawnay papers, 69/21/4, Imperial War Museum.

49 Rawlinson to Cavan et. al., 28.8.18, Henry Rawlinson Papers, National Army Museum, Volume 20.

50 Memorandum by German Supreme Headquarters, 14.9.18, *United States Army in the World War, 1917–1919, Volume 11* (Washington, 1948), p. 393.

51 Group of Armies, German Crown Prince, to Supreme Headquarters, 5.8.18, ibid; memorandum by Group of Armies, German Crown Prince, 5.8.18, *United States Army in the World War, 1917–1919, Volume 5* (Washington, 1948), p. 690.

52 Memorandum by Ludendorff, 18.8.18, *United States Army in the World War, 1917–1919, Volume 7* (Washington, 1948), pp. 811–12.

53 Memorandum by Ludendorff, 25.8.18, ibid.

54 Ferris, 'The British Army', pp. 41–42.

55 First Army to Canadian Corps, 24.7.18 and 25.7.18, RG–9/111/B–1/968; First Army Weekly Intelligence Reports, 27.7.18, WO 157/88, and 3.8.18, WO 157/89.

56 C.W.L. Nicholson, *Canadian Expeditionary Force, 1914–1919, Official History of the Canadian Army in the First World War* (Ottawa, 1964), pp. 389–90.

57 Ferdinand Tuohy, *The Secret Corps, A Tale of 'Intelligence' on All Fronts* (London, 1920), pp. 213–14.

58 Ibid, pp. 218–19; Marconi archive.

59 Memorandum by Second Army Intelligence, 1.12.18, AIR 1/2268/209/70/200; memorandum for Chief, Intelligence Section, A.E.F., 1.1.18, A.L. Conger papers.

60 Ferris, 'The British Army', pp. 32–34.

61 War Office, *Statistics of the Military Effort of the British Army During the Great War, 1914–1920* (London, 1922), pp. 169, 171–2.

62 Greene, Chapter 8, p. 91; Priestley, *Signal Service*, op. cit., pp. 190–92.

63 86th meeting of Bird committee, 1 May 1919, L/MIL 7/5467.

64 'Intelligence Corps-War Establishment', *c.* August 1917, passim, WO 158/962; G.S.I. to M.G.G.S., 4.11.18, WO 158/961; list of I(e) personnel in the Middle East on the 'Yinterim Code' system, 17.1.18, Gerard Clauson Papers, 80/47/2, Imperial War Museum; fragment listing names of I(e) personnel attached to GHQ Egypt, undated but probably summer 1917, Guy Dawnay papers, 69/21/2, Imperial War Museum.

65 'Historical Sketch of the Directorate of Military Intelligence During the Great War, 1914–1919', undated but *c.* 1919, WO 32/10776.

66 For the peak strength of the American codebreaking bureaus in Washington and the Western front (151 and 80 respectively), Barker, op.cit., pp. 22–23, 184–88, 201; for French numbers, cf. Givierge. op. cit., p. 16. Material for a provisional calculation of the strength of Room 40 is contained in Patrick Beesley, *Room 40, British Naval Intelligence, 1914–1918* (London, 1982) and ADM 137/4692–93.

67 Memorandum by 'C', 16.3.45, COS (45) 181 (0), CAB 80/92.

Chapter I: Field Telephones and Telegraphs

1 Field telephone and telegraph traffic carried via (a) an 'earth return' system (in which the ground was used as a medium of transmission), (b) 'earthed' circuits (where the wire was not insulated from direct contact with the ground) or (c) imperfectly insulated cables whose current leaked into the ground, could be intercepted in two fashions: through an earth 'pin' (a metal bar placed in the ground) or induction (long 'loops' of wire laid on the front line parallel to the enemy's cables). The danger of interception could be minimised although not certainly eliminated through the use of insulated cables, with an outer (metallic or

armoured) layer of steel, brass, enamel or lead. 'Pins' and 'loops' intercepted weak electrical currents originating from cables up to several thousand metres away and transmitted them by wire to an IT set. Here valve amplifiers boosted the strength of the currents so that operators wearing headphones could overhear the traffic. All messages were written down. Those in plain language and morse code were translated while those in secret code were despatched to the codebreakers.

2   From September 1915 until October 1916 the estimated size of the 'dangerous zone' rose steadily from 200 to 500 to 1,000 to 1,500 to 2,000 yards. (Lecture by 10 Corps Signal Company, 1.11.15, WO 95/875; entry 17.1.16, First Army War Diary, WO 95/161; Second Army to Canadian Corps, 6.2.16, RG 9/111/C-1/3867; memorandum by Director of Army Signals, GHQ, 16.2.16, WO 95/57). The estimate of 2,000 yards proved erroneous: in 1917–18 the British and German armies defined the dangerous zone as being 3,000 yards from the forward line.

3   The first elements of the Canadian Corps began to arrive on a quiet part of the First Army's front during 17–18 October 1916. In this case, German listening sets could have identified the redeployment of an entire corps virtually as its fighting units entered the trenches.

4   Despatch-rider.

5   Power-buzzer, an extremely robust, reliable and high powered signals system which worked through earth induction; hence, its traffic was almost certain to be intercepted by listening sets. They were primarily of use in trench warfare during 1917.

6   Artillery forward observation post. These posts posed an insurmountable problem for security. In order to correct artillery fire, observers had to communicate quickly and over field telephones. Such traffic was easily intercepted by the enemy.

7   Machine-gun.

8   Trench-mortar.

9   Royal Engineers.

10 The signals officer in charge of all communications on a brigade section of the front line.

11 The title, location or name of the units, formations or individual transmitting and receiving the message.

12 This document offers a generally accurate account of German practices, which might usefully be compared with British ones in three areas. First, points (a)–(g) of the German order of March 1916 were all fundamental to security against listening sets. Both in formulating and acting on such principles, the German Army was six months and thousands of lives ahead of its British counterpart. Second, by 1917 British and German practices were of similar quality, except that the Fullerphone gave Britain a notable edge. Third, during 1917–18 the Germans and the British used IT sets for different purposes and therefore in different fashions. The British assigned 2 IT sets to each corps, primarily to maintain signals security and secondarily to acquire tactical intelligence. Hence, these sets were placed under corps control. Beyond these functions, the Germans also appear to have used IT sets to acquire every scrap of information possible on the enemy's order of battle. Hence, the German Army maintained roughly twice as many IT sets per formation than did the British and kept them under a greater degree of central control. Each approach provided an effective means to meet differing needs.

13 Storage battery.

14 On the First Army front, near Vimy Ridge.
15 Location on a trench map.
16 Listening saps were the dugouts, usually in front of one's own trenches, from which IT sets worked. Nos 2, 5, etc., are different IT sections not of the Canadian Corps but of the British Army, which were numbered from 1 to about 80.
17 An overhead cable.
18 The pins for a single IT set covered a 600 yard perimeter.

Chapter II: Traffic Analysis

1 Reply.
2 Speak ——————— (the second word is uncertain).
3 Telephone immediately.
4 Not included in the original file.
5 Captain Lefroy was one of the British Army's few experts on wireless and the only professional military officer to rank among the leaders in British radio interception during the Great War. In 1915, profiting from the work of Captain H.J. Round, a Marconi Company employee and authority in radio technology who had just brought the British Army's direction finding up to the state of the art, Lefroy began to specialise in radio interception and traffic analysis. While the evidence is fragmentary, Round appears to have provided the equipment for interception and the techniques for direction-finding, while Lefroy devised the science of traffic analysis. In 1916–17 Lefroy established and controlled all aspects of the Army's signals intelligence service around the eastern Mediterranean basin and in the Middle East. In 1918 he lost responsibility for codebreaking in those regions but remained in charge of 'wireless intelligence' (radio interception and traffic analysis) until the Armistice.
6 Abbreviations for the German words 'chiffer' and 'ziffer', both meaning cipher. In the usage of the German Army, CHI messages usually referred to tactical traffic and ZIF to that regarding signals procedure.
7 Not included in the original file.
8 During the First World War, direction-finding was on the leading edge of the theory and practice of telecommunications. Precisely as its practitioners set to work, they were, in effect, conducting primary research into electromagnetics, and making basic discoveries which their theory could not explain. The unexpected variation in the bearings, especially at night, provided by any one intercepting station on any one transmitting station, which could change as much as 60 degrees, is merely one example of the problem. Such technical difficulties had serious practical consequences. How could commanders trust a source of intelligence which, on occasion, located German stations along the Western Front behind the British lines? It took extraordinary efforts to overcome these problems, led by some of the leading electric engineers on earth and the solution involved a great deal of redundancy. As Round wrote, 'With so many possible errors at night, it was never safe to have only two groups, in fact one gained a false confidence in the beautiful intersections made by using only two stations and only had occasional shocks when the German fleet was found to be well inland. A third station enabled one to know much more definitely if results were of value, and I personally preferred four, the last one being a check on the other three'. Three stations appear to have been the

norm accepted to provide an accurate fix. (Captain H.J. Round, 'Direction and Position Finding', *The Journal of the Institution of Electrical Engineers*, Volume 58 (1920), p. 238, passim; Round to The Royal Commission for Awards to Inventors, 20.12.26, War Office to same, 5.1.28, T 173/428.)

9   Naval Intelligence Officer.

10   The discipline of direction finding evolved with extraordinary speed during the war. In August 1914 literally no one on earth had expertise in the field. The first British practitioners had difficulty with elementary matters such as determining the frequencies used by enemy stations. By 1917, as a matter of routine, British traffic analysts provided a daily list of the callsigns and wavelengths used by every German radio station on the Western Front – indeed, on earth. By 1918 the Allies had one direction-finding station for every ten kilometers on the Western Front, while readings were on average accurate to about two degrees (or a circular error probability of some 800–1,000 metres) of the target. (Second Army Wireless Intelligence Summary, 21.6.17, WO 157/115). Definitive bearings were calculated on a 1/80,000 scale map, on which pins indicated the location of direction finding stations while protractors determined and coloured threads illustrated the angle of each individual bearing and their intersection near the location of the transmitter. (Booker, *Codes and Ciphers*, pp. 189, 205).

11   VI Corps Royal Artillery.

12   Possibly a misspelling for the German phrase 'beware of gusts of wind'.

13   These maps, which show the location of and the nature and volume of the inter-communication between the enemy's radio stations, are not included. For reproductions of such maps, cf. Green, Chapter Six, op. cit. pp. 367–68.

14   This comment shows that while a general change of call signs could temporarily confuse British traffic analysts, German signals personnel, like their British counterparts, quickly compromised the procedure.

15   *Difua* or *Divfunka*: German military abbreviation for 'Divisions-Funker-Abteilung' or Divisional Wireless Detachment.

16   The Intelligence and Operations staffs at a GHQ.

17   This was a function of the contemporary and primitive state of radio technology.

18   That is, of one's own field wireless stations, which might incidentally or as a matter of policy intercept enemy traffic.

19   Although this document was captured by the Eighth Army in Italy during 1945, it is authentic and contemporary.

20   This comment does describe with accuracy British practice until roughly July 1918. After this stage, in principle, British radio camouflage embraced both active and quiet sectors of the front. Why this report should have missed that change is unclear: perhaps the British Army did not always enact this principle or did so with great subtlety or, from the German perspective, had no quiet sectors.

21   This reference is mysterious. The British Army did not use directional transmissions during the Great War. This comment may stem from a German misunderstanding of the continuous wave and the trench set systems used by the British, or from the effect of drills used to ease communications and increase security, such as minimising the strength of wireless signals and the length of messages sent on the front line.

22   In signals deception, dummy traffic was the opposite of radio silence – wireless transmissions which were not related to any real military activity. The intention in

both cases was to maintain steady and stable levels of radio communication
across the front, so to break the connection between traffic and military actions.
The British do not appear to have created phantom armies through signals
deception.

23 This assessment was wrong. It indicates that the enemy grasped neither the
sophistication nor, perhaps, even the existence, of British operational deception and
also that German intelligence underestimated its enemy – an error which the
British did not make. The approach favoured by the Germans – which they had
frequently used on the Eastern Front – was central to Meinertzhagen's classic
deception campaign in Palestine. He might well have used it again had the war in
the west continued into 1919. The transmission of messages which the enemy was
intended to read, with the hope of specifically misleading rather than generally
confusing it, had also intermittently been adopted by British forces on the Western
Front during 1916, but with little success. Indeed, there is as yet no evidence to
suggest that this technique worked for anyone on that front, although it did prove
effective elsewhere. In any case, as Document Three of Chapter Five shows, during
1917 the head of secret intelligence at GHQ France, Colonel Drake, deliberately
rejected the use of this most precise form of deception. Since Drake already had
some experience in the practice of deception, his decision cannot simply be
discounted as an amateur error. He knew that deception could have unpredictable
and even counter-productive consequences. He opposed this technique because of
the problems involved in its use and of the operational circumstances of the
Western Front. In essence, he wrote, successful deception through this means must
sometimes involve the transmission of genuine messages; otherwise, over the long
term, a competent intelligence service – such as Germany possessed on the
Western Front – will discover one's use, aims and means of deception. Either
circumstance may compromise one's real intentions and in a disastrous fashion.
Against an able enemy, Drake argued, the risks were not worth the rewards. The
British Army, moreover, could launch major attacks in only a few different places at
any one time on its fifty-odd mile front. While no single attack could be guaranteed
to smash the enemy, Britain could switch large forces from one sector to another so
as to mount a rolling campaign. To deliberately mislead the enemy through this
means of deception might, therefore, hamper instead of assist British operations. It
could prevent Britain from attacking in one of the few sectors possible, precisely
because that was where the enemy would expect an assault. Meinertzhagen could
adopt this approach in Palestine because the enemy's intelligence services were
incompetent and one attack could settle the battle. In Drake's view, neither
condition held true on the Western Front. This approach was conservative, perhaps
excessively so; it was not illogical.

Chapter III: Aircraft Intelligence

1 Individual radio interception stations specialised in the traffic either of the enemy's
artillery/aircraft or field stations. I(z) was the British title for the 'Artillery
Aeroplane Wireless Section' and I(y) for the 'Field Wireless Section'. I(y) may be
the origin for the latter British codeword 'Y', to refer to all forms of signals
intelligence acquired in the field.

2 AG, Adjutant-General; QMG, Quarter-Master-General; DAS, Director of Army

Signals; G.O.C., L.of C. Area, General Officer Commanding, Lines of Communication Area.

3   Major-General Royal Artillery, the senior artillery officer in a corps.

4   Brigadier-General General Staff.

5   That is, during 1918 – unlike the previous eighteen months – the radio traffic of the German Air Force was not a certain indicator of the operational intentions, concerns and deployments of the German Army. Contrary to the analysis put forward in Document 14, however, that development was not simply the product of German signals security, but of the complex interaction between communications, security and operations. The following assessment is true not merely for the Germans but generally so for every army on the Western Front. During 1916–17 artillery was the dominant arm but could be brought effectively to bear only through the constant registration and correction of individual guns. This could best be done through aerial spotting. In 1916 and the first half of 1917, however, the Germans had few spotting flights and artillery groups equipped with and trained to use wireless. Naturally, these scarce resources were concentrated in the main area of operations, which in turn betrayed German intentions and capabilities. Under these circumstances camouflage was difficult to establish. Active sectors could not be concealed amidst a high and constant level of wireless activity. By mid 1917, however, the Germans had spotting airplanes equipped with wireless everywhere along the front – these did not automatically have to be massed in the main sectors of operations. This produced a degree of natural camouflage. German attempts to mask the concentration of their artillery spotting aircraft through artificial camouflage, however, by and large failed during 1917, because their signals security was inadequate. By early 1918, conversely, German signals security became sufficiently good to achieve this end. Simultaneously, changes in the use of artillery altered the role of spotting aircraft. A central means to cover one's intentions in 1918 was to conceal the deployment of artillery to the attack front until at least 24 hours before an assault was launched. This was done through an increased use of predictive fire and the silent registration of targets. Once that became the norm, changes in aircraft spotting and its concomitant radio traffic were no longer necessary before launching a major attack. In any case, some spotting could still be conducted in advance at the site of an actual operation because this would be occurring everywhere along the front.

6   Continuous wave, one of the two main radio systems in use during the Great War. 'Spark' sets worked through electromagnetic radiations which overlapped on a wide band of frequencies and produced continual interference of sets. This was the only type of system available in 1914–16, and that most commonly used until the armistice. Continuous wave sets used a thermionic valve ('diode' or 'vacuum tube') and worked on more narrow frequencies, which reduced the mutual interference of stations. Such sets were adopted in 1917 and increasingly common in use until the Armistice.

7   That is, during March and April 1918 the location of a single German squadron had twice indicated the approximate site (although not the time and sequence) of crucial German attacks and therefore might do so again. While correct in principle – the discovery of real indicators for the enemy's actions is or primary importance in intelligence – this assessment was somewhat naive in practice. Although attacks were launched near to Lille and St. Quentin, between them, squadrons based in

those areas could have spotted effectively for super heavy artillery everywhere on the British section of the German front.

Chapter IV: Signals Security and Cryptography

1 The use of enlisted signals personnel to encipher and decipher messages was contrary to standard British practice; such work was usually done by staff or regimental officers. This unusual change in procedure, which lasted until September 1918, was produced by the rise of radio. Few British officers were skilled in the use of either of the standard cipher systems of the Army, the Playfair or the Field cipher. All British radio operators could be more easily trained in the use of these systems than could every British officer. The German Army adopted the same procedure for a slightly different reason, on the grounds that if radio operators handled enciphering and deciphering, they could check the accuracy of every message before transmission and avoid the need for the repetition of messages.

2 The B.A.B. was 'corrected' through a primitive form of superencipherment. As I(e) noted, this system was 'transparent and as used is not likely to cause the enemy more than temporary delay in solving' (Wright to Henderson, undated but c. September 1918 according to internal evidence, ADM 137/4701).

3 A list of code names for military units, formations and geographical locations.

4 Diagram excluded.

5 Diagram excluded.

6 The *Schlüsselheft* (or, as Allied cryptanalysts entitled it, the Three Number Code) consisted of a basic book (or 'base') and the *Geheimklappe* superencipherment system. The base was common to every unit in the German Army, while every division had its own *Geheimklappe* key which was changed every day. This is a classic example of how poor usage can wreck cipher security. On literally the day it was first used, on 10–11 March 1918, a German operator sent an identical message in this code and in another which the Allies had previously solved. Thus, Allied codebreakers immediately discovered part of the vocabulary of the base, which in turn quickly allowed them to determine its structure and the fact that it was defended by a superencipherment system. Without this initial compromise, cryptanalysis would have been far more difficult. Then, in its first few weeks of use, the *Geheimklappe* was not used in about 50 per cent of the messages sent in the *Schlüsselheft*. Allied codebreakers could discover when this was the case, presumably by determining whether the groups whose meaning was known were being used as, according to previous experience, they should have been in military messages. When this was not the case, the *Geheimklappe* was obviously being applied. Codebreakers could use the encoded but not superenciphered messages to solve much of the base by analogy (cf. n. 14, Chapter Seven). Simultaneously, the increasing volume of basic code groups whose meaning was known provided a foundation of comparison which allowed Allied codebreakers to determine the nature of the superencipherment system. Once these mistakes had occurred, even scrupulously proper use by German operators could not prevent rapid inroads into the Three Number Code. The daily change in *Geheimklappe* key could be determined through a relatively simple process of trial and error conducted against messages regarding whose content one could make educated guesses, such as those likely to have been sent in stereotyped form. Once the *Geheimklappe* key had been

327

determined in a single case, the superencipherment could be stripped off every message sent in that key (ie. by every radio station transmitting tactical traffic within a single division). This in turn immediately provided a true reading of the code groups whose meaning already had been determined and exposed the rest of the code to continued solution. Within two weeks of its introduction, much of the basic code and the *Geheimklappe* system had been reconstructed. Yet this was in formal terms a sophisticated means to defend tactical traffic. Properly handled, it should have remained impregnable for a far longer period. After 25 March 1918, when copies of the basic code book were captured, the system as a whole was defended only by a simple encipherment process.

7 Conventionally, in military cipher systems, before transmission and after reception, a message was written out in the form of a matrix (for example, a five by five letter square) in order to carry out both enciphering and deciphering.

8 A group conventionally used to indicate 'full stop'.

9 In transposition ciphers, the order of letters in a plaintext message are rearranged. In substitution ciphers, conversely, each letter in the alphabet is replaced by some defined combination of letters or figures (a 'cipher alphabet'). In simple substitution ciphers, only one such cipher alphabet is used, producing a monoalphabetic rather than a polyalphabetic system.

10 These principles are derived directly from Auguste Kerckhoff's classic study, *La Cryptographie militaire* (Paris, 1883).

11 The additional letters needed to ensure that the number of letters in a message would fit the cipher square exactly.

12 Enemy airplanes.

13 The code consisted of groups of two letters used by or with the RAF or, as a remote possibility, the American Air Force.

14 Because even before a single group was solved, direction finding and traffic analysis would show which stations were using this code and for what purpose. This would be obvious with a code used between aircraft and ground stations.

15 The maximum number of groups possible in a two letter code – 26 letters X 26 letters = 676.

16 These represented letters and were used to spell words which were not in the vocabulary of the system. In this code, certain groups represented words unless they lay between the groups 'Spell' and 'Cease Spell', in which case they designated letters. Once this system was discovered, the identification of the groups for 'Spell' and 'Cease Spell' would immediately betray the location of letters (which could be quickly solved) and, as a bonus, also the meaning of several words.

17 These groups could wreck the security of an entire system. These were easily identifiable, frequently repeated and served one function only in messages. They immediately identified numbers which were a weak point in all front line codes and, in this case, also compromised the meaning of certain words.

18 The maximum number of groups available in this code – 3 letters X 26 letters X 26 letters = 2028.

19 Abbreviation for 'Unabhorchbare Telegraph' (or 'untappable telegraph'). The Utel operated on the principle of the Fullerphone. It entered general service in the German Army during early 1918 about 14 months after the Fullerphone achieved that status for the British.

20 Under this older German procedure, when a controlling station wished to transmit

a message to all its sub-stations, it would make a 'general call'. Its sub-stations in sequence would immediately send their own call signs, indicating their readiness to receive the message and the structure of communications and command for an entire formation.

21 Here the original German document, as against the British commentary, begins.

22 Allied cryptanalysts entirely reconstructed the *Schlüsselheft* within two weeks of its introduction and solved over half of messages sent in the system. While the evidence regarding the *Satzbuch* (or, as Allied codebreakers termed it, the Three Letter Code) is less certain, until May 1918 it appears to have been broken as easily as any code of 1917. Thereafter, according to American sources, the *Satzbuch* was never solved in any sector before operations began, at which time rapid reconstruction became possible. Although after May 1918 the Americans never solved the Satzbuchen used on their front, the French and/or British may have done so, since they engaged the Germans rather more often than did the Americans. Neither the Gedefu nor the War Ministry code were solved by the Allies. However, the ADFGVX cipher used for purposes similar to those of the Gedefu was broken 10 times during 1918.

23 Minenwurfer=mortar, Artillery Survey=flash spotting and sound ranging. In these instances, as with corrections for artillery fire, the need for rapidity in the transmission of information overrode that for security.

24 Disused lines and even metallic pipes laid underground might be sufficiently close to cables in use to pick up electrical currents through induction and sufficiently leaky to provide an echo which, in turn, the enemy's IT sets could intercept. In this fashion, disused cables running perpendicular to the front might also pick up traffic from brigade or divisional headquarters behind one's own dangerous zone. From spring 1917, this was the best means by which IT sets could acquire intelligence of operational rather than tactical value. For two examples of such practices see Green, Chapter 6, op.cit. p. 374.

25 The final portion of this memorandum, describing the *Geheimklappe* system, has been omitted. It is reproduced in Friedman, *German Codes*, pp. 104–110.

Chapter V: Signals and Operational Deception

1 Group system. Under this system, for technical reasons (such as keeping sets on their assigned frequencies in order to minimise their mutual interference) all wireless sets in a formation worked under the supervision of a Control Station. This system provided obvious opportunities to the enemy's traffic analysts. While this danger could be reduced by having Control Stations as far as possible contact their subordinate sets by telephone rather than radio, careful monitoring of the drills used to govern communication within a formation still could allow traffic analysts to derive useful inferences from the use of the group system.

2 If one could connect individual radio stations to their callsigns, much of the enemy's pattern of communications could easily be reconstructed and thus its order of battle, structure of command and dispositions. The 'basic call' system was a means to increase signals security in this sphere without hampering communications. Under this, the most secure procedure regarding call signs devised by armies of the Great War, each station received a basic call which was changed routinely through a simple encipherment process. The French and Germans

adopted this system at some stage before the British did so. By March 1918 GHQ issued a list of four letter basic calls to replace the old three letter station calls (see Document Three, Chapter One). The list itself would be completely replaced every 14 days while all call signs were to be changed every four days. The nature of this system is uncertain; it appears never to have been used. In May–June 1918 the British Third Army tested another four letter call system, perhaps a variant of the earlier one. The rest of the Army apparently retained the three letter call system, although these call signs were at least changed every day. By July 1918 a modified version of the four letter call system was introduced throughout the Army. A list of basic calls was provided for the use of all radio stations down to brigade headquarters. This list was changed every month while each callsign was modified every day. Although that system was better than the older one, during its study by the Third Army the Germans had reconstructed it (see Document seven, Chapter Two). This procedure was compromised even before it was introduced into general service and thus an entire failure. Nor did the four letter call system apply beneath brigade headquarters. By early September 1918, however, another version of the basic call system was introduced to overcome this problem. Every British division was ordered to select call signs for the stations attached to its units from the same fixed list of two letter calls and to reallocate these signs every five days. In theory, since the stations within each British division would have exactly the same call signs, traffic analysts could distinguish neither one formation from another nor determine any of their boundaries. It is uncertain whether this system worked effectively. Even if it did so, the insecurity of the four letter call system would have negated much of its value. (Ist Anzac Corps Circular Order No. 106, 19.11.17, WO 95/984; GHQ to Armies, 23.3.18, WO 95/369; Third Army to Corps, 8.5.18, WO 95/370; Third Army to GHQ, 6.7.18, WO 95/371; Australian Corps Wireless Section War Diary, general entry for June 1918, WO 95/1010; Director of Army Signals to Deputy Director Signals of Armies and the Cavalry Corps, 10.7.18, ADM 137/4700; memorandum by GHQ Intelligence, August 1918, Ie/1647/2, 'System of Allotting Code Calls', RG–9–111–B–1/2260; Third Army to Corps, 9.9.18, WO 95/372).

3   The effect of deception is difficult to establish even in well documented cases, which the two instances in the text are not. Hence, the following analysis is of a provisional nature. In Documents Five and Six, the aim was to conceal a change in British strategy and the time and sequence of British operations. GHQ intended to switch much of its weight from the Fourth Army on the southern edge of its line to the First and Third armies on the centre of the British front (the Albert-Lens axis). Three major attacks would then be launched in the following sequence – first, near the junction of the First and Third armies in central Flanders, second, by the Canadian Corps (which would be transferred from the Fourth Army's command) in north-central Flanders, third, by the Australian Corps on the Fourth Army front. Throughout the preparatory period of the next week, the Germans expected attacks by 20 divisions everywhere along the British front but could not determine the locations, sequence or time of the operations. While inconclusive, the evidence suggests that the Germans realised the Canadian Corps had left the Fourth Army, but could not determine the new location of that formation until it entered the front line. The attacks of the First and Third armies on 23 August and of the Canadian Corps on 25 August achieved complete operational surprise, while that of the Australian Corps on 28 August achieved tactical surprise. (Memoranda by German

Supreme Headquarters, 18 and 25 August 1918, Group of Armies Boehn, 24.8.18, *United States Army in the World War*, 1917–1919, Volume 7 (Washington, 1948), pp. 811–14.)

In Document Six, the aim of deception was deliberately to draw German attention to the First Army and away from the Fourth Army. During the next 10 days the Germans did regard the front of the First and Third armies as being the most likely area for attack, because the British were known to be strong in that sector, which, moreover, had been for several weeks the centre of British operations. From a German perspective, this also seemed the most obvious and dangerous place to attack. During the period covered by the schedule of deception, however, their concern about the First Army did not rise, nor do they seem to have swallowed the rumour about American troops. None the less, the Germans still recognised that attacks could occur anywhere and remained confused regarding British intentions. Their grasp of Allied and especially British dispositions was grossly inaccurate – by 6 September, for example, the Germans had 'located' 25 per cent of the Allies' divisions in the wrong place. The Fourth Army's attack of 18 September on St. Quentin achieved operational surprise. (ibid, memoranda by Supreme Headquarters, 9.9.18, 15.9.18 and Group of Armies Boehn, 7.9.18, 20.9.18, pp. 819–21, 828, 832; and *United States Army in the World War, 1917–1919, Volume 11* (Washington, 1948), pp. 381–415; British General Staff, Ia/56138, 21.11.18, 'German Appreciation of the Allied Order of Battle', German Fourth Army, No. 6449, 6.9.18, General Horne Papers, Imperial War Museum, 73/60/1).

In both cases German assessments of British operational intentions and capabilities were often badly wrong and almost invariably imprecise: they indicated that anything and everything might happen, and simultaneously. Consequently, the Germans were in general confused – they could not determine where or when a British assault would fall and with what strength. Yet the nature of their confusion was not directly parallel to the schedule of British deception. Between 15 August to 20 September, for example, the Germans invariably expected a major attack around Ypres. Yet the British did not plan to do so and did not even attempt to make the enemy expect an assault in that sector, although they had done this before 8 August. Conversely, the Germans do not seem to have believed and acted on many specific aspects of the British deception campaign. Altogether, the evidence suggests that British deception failed to mislead the enemy in a specific fashion but did, along with security, engender confusion in German minds. This led the enemy to waste its reserves across the front and to fall victim continually to surprise, which harmed German morale and eased the success of British operations. On the other hand, deception as against security might not have been necessary to produce this result.

4 Brigadier General, Intelligence, ie. the officer in charge of intelligence at GHQ. Meinertzhagen was intended to be the Army Security Officer.

5 Camouflage officers were in charge of physical camouflage.

6 Major-General, General Staff, ie. the chief of staff at an Army headquarters.

7 The emphasis on providing false information to one's own troops is characteristic both of operational deception and of the First World War where prisoners were continually captured and very often provided accurate information to both sides. This problem was addressed by two divergent strategies – training one's personnel not to provide any information when captured and ensuring that any intelligence they did provide would be misleading.

8   In 1919, GHQ Intelligence in Iraq noted that under existing procedure, the Intelligence branch provided and distributed codes while the Operations branch controlled cipher officers. The latter were typically 'junior regimental officer(s) unfit for field service, ignorant of cryptography, and consequently not in a position to know all the dangers of carelessness in the matter of encipherment'. In order to establish 'strict cipher discipline', a single Intelligence officer (trained by and cooperating with I(e)) should control the users of ciphers, while I(e) should prepare codes and determine the principles to govern their use. GHQ Intelligence also noted

> ... that breaches of cipher rules are committed from ignorance rather than from carelessness. It is very desirable that every officer, and especially Staff Officers, should receive in peace time more training than hitherto in the mechanism and the practice of the various cipher systems. Then, when ignorance can no longer be an excuse, the strictest cipher discipline should be exacted.

('The Control and Safeguarding of Codes and Ciphers', undated and no author cited, but *c.* 1919 by internal evidence, Leith-Ross Papers, 8312–69–10, National Army Museum). Between 1919–39, the Army ignored recommendations such as these; between 1939–41, consequently, its performance in these areas was extremely poor. By 1942, when its practice finally became professional, it followed the path suggested in 1919. (John Ferris, 'The British Army, Signals and Security in the Desert Campaign, 1940–42', in Michael Handel (ed.), *Intelligence and Military Operations* (London, 1990)).

9   This was one of the most common and peculiar fallacies about signals security: that the more radio messages transmitted, the less the problem of security, because the sheer volume of traffic would overwhelm any interception service. In fact, an increase in signals traffic creates additional but by no means insurmountable problems for the enemy. Once a signals intelligence service has overcome these problems, the greater the volume of traffic, the greater the amount of information which it can provide.

10 It was extremely difficult although not impossible to intercept field telephone traffic across a water barrier.

Chapter VI: Codebreaking: Organisation

1   In January 1917 there were about 125 German radio stations on the Western Front, and by August almost 700 of them (Friedman, *German Codes*, p. 65).

2   A rank for officers in the Intelligence Corps, a major source of manpower for British Army intelligence in the field.

3   The British and American codebreaking bureaux worked in roughly similar ways, although their internal structures were not entirely identical. Hence, the following description of American practices can be used to illuminate the general procedure of the British code and cipher department. First, operators at radio monitoring stations took down in longhand the groups contained in intercepted messages. Such material was immediately despatched to the codebreakers – in the American case, to the Adjutant's (or 'outer') office of the Radio Intelligence Section at GHQ. Here a cipher clerk, using the known external characteristics of messages, such as signals procedure, differentiated German from Allied traffic; German Naval, Diplomatic

and Colonial Office messages (which were despatched for cryptanalysis to Washington) from Army traffic; the code from the cipher traffic of the German Army. All material in the last category was sent to the analytical (or 'inner') office, which was divided into three main departments – 'Goniometric' (direction finding), 'Cipher' and 'Code'. The Goniometric Department provided information of direct relevance to cryptanalysis – it could determine the units or formations with which specific radio sets worked and thus indicate the cryptographic system their operators would use. (In the British case, this department also carried out traffic analysis against the enemy's spotting aircraft.) The nature of the internal organisation of the Goniometric Department is unknown. That of the Cipher Department is uncertain. Its personnel may have been divided into three sections, to deal with the two main cipher systems used on the front and miscellaneous ones; alternately, and more probably, they may all have attacked material from each and every cipher system as the need arose. Cryptanalysts could switch from one enemy cipher to another at a moment's notice without undue confusion. The structure and mode of work of both the British and American cipher sections may, in fact, have been similar to that of the cryptanalytical bureau in Iraq, discussed in Document Four. The Code Department was subdivided into four functional divisions – one each for Three Letter, Three Number, Aviation and Meteorological codes. The Aviation Division attacked not the codes used by artillery spotting aircraft but rather by the enemy's 'Giant' aircraft. The Three Letter and Three Number divisions were each sub-divided into two groups – specialising in the different sectors held by two enemy armies, both of which used different Three Letter codebooks. (In the British and probably in all cases, individual codebreakers worked on only one system at a time, in order not to confuse the processes of association between groups and parts of speech which underlay this work.)

Material sent to the Code Department was received by another cipher clerk who (working from the external features of messages and direction-finding reports on the location of stations) allocated it to the appropriate division and/or sector group. He further divided traffic in Three Letter and Three Number codes into sub-sectors representing a divisional front (each enemy division used different Three Number codebooks, while useful analogies might be drawn between events on so small a line and the content of traffic in Three Letter codes). He then arranged the messages chronologically by time of interception and produced what might be called a standard copy of each one. Several monitoring stations might easily intercept the same transmission in whole or part, while German radio personnel often repeated individual messages up to six times. Thus, there could be several duplicates of individual messages, some of which might contain obvious corruptions or gaps – for example, if several intercepts taken at roughly the same time and from the same station were identical except for a few groups (or even just digits or letters within groups) in one case. Since corrupt groups could not help and might impede cryptanalysis, they were so far as possible weeded out. In such instances, the clerk produced the standard copy by adopting the reading provided either by the majority of the intercepting personnel or by the most reliable or experienced of individual operators. Any cases of uncertainty about the correct group were noted on the standard copy, which was the basis from which codebreakers worked. The intercepts were then placed with meticulous accuracy onto a stencilled sheet, and distributed to the codebreaking divisions or sector groups. These sheets were kept in loose leaf binders, with individual messages and/or pages being identified by letters or numbers. The codebreakers recorded in indices of various forms the page location of all individual encoded groups, their frequency of recurrence and their position in each message. In the latter case, the Americans devised an elaborate formula to show the total frequency of recurrence of each individual group, and its number of occurrences as the initial, second, interior, penultimate and final group of messages, and the number of times it was repeated within an individual message. All groups were entered by alphabetical order in a book, entitled 'The Bible', alongside their known or suspected plaintext equivalents. 'The Bible' also included a list of the plaintext words or phrases which, according to experience with earlier systems, were likely to be found in the code. Codebreakers used this list as a tool to jog their memories when gauging the probable meaning of groups. (Friedman, *German Codes*, pp. 9–11, 18–25; cf. Document Two, Chapter Seven.)

4   Administrative personnel freed codebreakers and traffic analysts purely to attack the enemy's systems. The former fell into three main groups.

(a)   'Interpreter clerks' worked in the radio interception section. They intercepted and translated the enemy's plain language transmissions, particularly of its artillery-spotting aircraft, and probably also participated in traffic analysis.

(b)   'Cipher clerks' carried out the functions described in Note 2, ibid. They may also have translated traffic in codes which had been solved and, as a very remote possibility, participated actively in cryptanalysis.

(c)   The remaining personnel – clerks, assistant administrators, batmen, drivers and 'women' – carried out less skilled supporting services.

5   Lieutenant G.G. Crocker, an officer of MI 1 (b) in London. The author of this unsigned letter was Gerard Clauson, chief of British military codebreaking in Iraq during 1917 and in the Middle East in 1918. Subsequently, he joined the Colonial Office. During the Second World War he was, among other things, that department's expert on cryptographic security.

6   Special Service Officers, the title for the counter-intelligence and human intelligence personnel of the British Army in Iraq.

7   Campbell Thompson believed that the keys for the German double transposition cipher were derived according to a fixed system from some phrase, which he had discovered; that by comparing this phrase to keywords previously solved, one could calculate the system used to derive them and then solve every new key immediately through this means rather than by attacking the crytogram letter by letter. Apparently, Campbell Thompson's hunch was correct. According to American codebreakers, the German double transposition cipher used on the Western Front was 'normally based on numerical keys derived from key-words or phrases usually of some length; but the actual key-words or phrases were never recovered'. (Barker, *Codes and Ciphers*, p. 214.) While seemingly odd, this was simply a variant of a standard means of organising and distributing a military cipher system. No evidence suggests that Campbell Thompson's approach ever worked against the double transposition system used in the Middle East.

8   Direction-finding.

9   This is the best documented case from the First World War of the relations between British radio intercepting and codebreaking personnel, signals and staff officers. It shows the strains and delays which could arise from the complicated

lines of bureaucratic demarcation about signals intelligence. The relevant personnel were Lefroy, Clauson, Colonel W.F. Beach, the Director of Intelligence, GHQ,
Mesopotamian Expeditionary Force, General Stanley Maude, the Army Commander and Lieutenant J. Coxon, the commander of the 'Special Wireless Section'
(SWS) in Iraq. Under the Army's system, the signals branch ran the technical side
of interception while the intelligence branch determined its application and
exploitation. In effect, two distinct chains of command each controlled one half of
the work. Neither Clauson nor Coxon commanded the other, yet signals intelligence could only function effectively if each was competent and both cooperated.
Clauson was directly responsible to Beach and Lefroy, and Coxon to the Signal
Officer-in-Chief and Lefroy, but also guided by Beach in his intelligence functions.
This system could work effectively if all personnel cooperated, which they generally
appear to have done. When they did not, the only means to coordinate them were
Lefroy (who appears to have had but a loose supervisory function), Maude and
authorities in the War Office. Under this system, if two Lieutenants could not
cooperate, adjudication between them might have to be made by generals. Until
mid 1917, normal radio stations conducted all interception in the Iraq theatre.
Coxon and some of his personnel arrived there during May 1917. In late June,
Coxon and Beach (with Maude's personal approval) determined locations for
intercepting stations. For unknown reasons, tension soon arose between the
protagonists. The only certain fact is that Coxon, unlike wireless officers already
present, failed to overcome the unusually difficult problems of radio reception in
Iraq. Over July and August, Beach frequently discussed with Coxon the latter's
'weekly report' on radio interception, while Coxon requested increases in his
personnel and equipment. His first section began to work formally only on 15
August (three months after it had arrived) by which time Beach was discussing the
matter with Clauson. By late August Coxon pressed his case with Maude in person.
On 20 September Maude ruled that the SWS should have the establishment of a
WOG in Europe, which may indicate that Coxon had demanded a larger strength
than this. When Coxon apparently protested, the Military Intelligence Directorate
at the War Office was contacted and by mid October it was decided to relieve him.
At this stage, the 'First (Australian and New Zealand) Wireless Signals Company'
began to intercept enemy traffic, which it continued to do alongside the SWS until
the Armistice. Lefroy arrived at Baghdad to take over Coxon's work in late October
and on 4 November the latter was formally relieved, ostensibly on grounds of
health. (Director of Signals, Mesopotamian Expeditionary Force, War Diary,
entries 25 May and 3 June, 1917, WO 95/4985; Intelligence Diary, GHQ, MEF,
25–26.6.17 (WO 157/800), 18 and 31.7.17 (WO 157/801), 15 and 22–25 August
1917 (WO 157/802); Operations War Diary, GHQ, MEF, 3 and 20 September
1917 (WO 157/803) and 7–10 and 13 and 27 October 1917 (WO 157/804);
Wireless Press Section War Diary, entry 4.11.17 (WO 95/5001); First Anzac
Wireless Signals War Diary, entries Oct. 1917, passim (WO 95/5001).

10 Colonel C.N. French, a senior figure in the Military Intelligence Directorate in
London.

11 The location of MI 1(b) in London, which both attacked the Turkish and German
ciphers used in the Middle East and also trained and loosely supervised the British
personnel attacking these systems in Iraq and Egypt.

12 Telegraphic address of the Directorate of Military Intelligence, London.

13 Colonel W.F. Beach, Director of Intelligence, GHQ, Iraq.
14 Colonel W.H. Jeffrey, the head of the codebreaking section of the Indian Army.
15 As a result of these decisions, Clauson became head of codebreaking and Lefroy of Wireless Intelligence in the Middle East – respectively, 'I(e)1' and 'I(e)2'. (Intelligence Diary, GHQ, MEF, 23.12.18, WO 157/818).

Chapter VII: Codebreaking: Techniques

1 This undated memorandum is one of the technical papers referred to in Documents Four and Five, Chapter Six – probably the latter.
2 Direction Finding Officer.
3 Clauson was correct to link his own success in cryptanalysis to the inadequacy of enemy cryptography. On the Western Front, where the Germans used a similar double transposition system but changed the keys every day, allied cryptanalysts rarely penetrated it – and only when German personnel made fundamental errors such as forgetting the second transposition (Booker, *Codes and Ciphers*, p. 214).
4 Signals Service, ie. messages relating to its technical performance.
5 The *Asienkorps* (also known as the German Asiatic Column and Pasha 11), a German infantry brigade with the supporting arms of a division attached to the Yilderim Army Group, the Turkish reserve force developed for use against the British in summer 1917.
6 Quartermaster General of the Turkish Sixth Army – presumably part of the German staff organisation attached to that formation.
7 Commander of the German detachment on the Euphrates River, which was the area where the Yilderim Army Group was originally to be deployed.
8 Khalil Pasha, commander of the Turkish Sixth Army, which included its forces in Iraq.
9 Presumably a cryptographic system used for traffic between the Turkish commands involved with the Yilderim Army Group. In September 1917 the Second and Fourth Armies (respectively in the Caucasus and Palestine) although not the Sixth Army were ordered to 'exchange daily war reports' with the Yilderim Army Group. (C.C.R. Murphey, *Soldiers of the Prophet* (1921) pp. 178–79). The Sixth Army did not regularly use this system.
10 In this context, 'decipher' means 'cryptanalytical solution'.
11 In the German language, the letter's 'h' and 'k' invariably follow 'c', just as 'u' does 'q' in the English language.
12 This document is one of two surviving and complementary treatises on the solution of German Army codes during the First World War. Comparison with the other one, which refers primarily to the codes used in 1918 (Friedman, *German Codes*, op. cit.), indicates that the basic principles and techniques outlined by Document Two were applied with success until the Armistice.
13 Commanding Officer.
14 Wireless telegraphy station.
15 'Where is evening report?' This message and most – in fact, probably all – of those cited elsewhere in Document Two are solutions of actual German messages. Throughout this document only complete sentences and some military phrases have been translated. The aim has been to achieve not a literal but a clear translation. I am indebted to Anne-Marie Link for most of the translations, and to

Professor Frank Eyck for confirming several of the rest. Unfortunately, a definitive translation is surprisingly difficult to provide. These messages are sometimes enigmatic because their authors had to emphasise brevity and to use codes with limited vocabularies under emergency conditions; moreover, they were referring to situations known to the recipient. Many German words are spelled incorrectly, because of mistakes on the part of German operators, British intercepting personnel and/or British typists. On occasion, this renders the meaning of words uncertain. The document, moreover, does not always place the initial letters of German nouns in the upper case. Sometimes this creates the possibility of confusion between nouns and verbs and hence the sense of a message itself. The translations, then, may not be perfect, but they do illustrate the sorts of material provided by codebreaking on the Western Front during 1917. While their content often seems trivial, traffic of this sort provided useful information on the enemy's order of battle and sometimes its operational intentions. In June 1918, for example, French codebreakers solved a German message which read merely 'Expedite supplies of ammunition, if not observed, even by day'. This information allowed the French to detect and smash a major assault on the Chemins des Dames (Givierge, 'Problems of Code', op.cit., p. 17). Conversely, the messages of February 1917 did reveal the German decision to retreat to the Hindenberg Line, but had little effect on military operations. After some initial reserve – codebreaking, after all, had not provided high-level intelligence to GHQ France since November 1914 – GHQ did believe these statements, which were corroborated by several different sources. It did not act effectively on them, however, and perhaps could not have done so. While the evidence is too fragmentary to permit a conclusive statement, it appears that codebreaking provided material of greater operational value during 1918 than in 1917 – not because German cryptography became worse but because the Germans used radio more often. Excluding the material about the Hindenberg line, most of the surviving solutions of German radio traffic in British records from 1917 refer to the actions of battalions, and rarely to those of regiments and divisions – and even then only during tactical emergencies. Perhaps half of the surviving solutions from 1918 refer to the actions or intentions of regiments and divisions, and, in a few cases, to those of corps. As a further complication, however, some of the material from 1918 probably came from plain language transmissions, and one can rarely determine whether and when this is so. Such material stands to the credit of signals intelligence but not of codebreaking.

16 How is the situation there?
17 'First principles' is the attack on a cryptographic system regarding which ones knows nothing. 'Analogy' is an attack on a system of which one knows an earlier variant and/or the general content of messages being sent and/or the usual form of such traffic.
18 Three radio messages sent, four received.
19 Cipher message 17 to KS not understood.
20 Radio message 1806 dealt with.
21 Who sent Radiomessage 1037?
22 To Division 105, Evening Report 18–2–17. (1) From 10.25 this morning until 3.30 this afternoon 40 heavy calibre rounds on mapsheet M2 mapsquare 5209. (2). Enemy flier activity small, five fliers over Sector 5A. (3) Weather good, clear

visibility. (4 to 7) Nothing. (8) 2 non commissioned officers and 7 men badly
wounded, 10 men lightly wounded (9 to 10) nothing. Signed Battalion 11/316.
23 2 sent, 5 received.
24 Regiment b, Evening Report b.
25 20 to 30 rounds.
26 5 to 8 nothing.
27 From 4 in the evening to five in the morning.
28 Send a soldier to KW immediately.
29 Please ( ) batteries.
30 Radiomessage ——— cannot be understood.
31 2 sick men on station.
32 Increased radio readiness, pay good attention.
33 This is uncertain.
34 Weather report of 26–12–17. Ground wind 100,0,6: two hundred, zero, eight, five
hundred, zero, twelve: one, five, zero, zero, Barometer 03,6. Humidity 92 per cent.
Air pressure, 171,30.
35 News or propaganda messages sent in morse code over radio by press agencies or
by government controlled stations.
36 i.   A and B Companies. Hundred eighty thousand captives, hundred (sic. – a
word may be missing in the original) guns; on one day 16,000 men and four
hundred guns. Gemona has fallen.
ii.   Number captured on Izonzo has risen to 60,000 men and 450 guns.
37 ——— (perhaps misspelling for 'first') Reserve Pioneers 13. Water level 6 o'clock
evening. Overstream 4; understream 3.65 metres.
38 Before eight o'clock at night.
39 Front and rear terrain.
40 25 rounds on sector.
41 Little flier activity during evening period.
42 Where are current station reports from points . . . etc?
43 C.O.S. is the call sign of a ship that finds itself in the greatest danger. (Presumably
this is an example of a dummy message.)
44 Which radio frequency is the station using?
45 Where is evening report?
46 30 rounds on trenches to the west of ———.
47 Enemy artillery activity less than on previous evening.
48 Greatest gas readiness.
49 Inform Regiment that enemy is in our forward trenches.
50 3. Connnection available. 4. Visibility obscure. 5. Nothing.
51 Brigade. Situation quiet. Signature C.O.
52 Between Point L and K on mapsheet.
53 Fliers activity lively on both sides.
54 Crew healthy. Codebooks received.
55 Sweeping fire on the rear uqv (plural).
56 (There is obviously a spelling error in the original for 'fuer': the sentence may be
read either as 'Send a firewagon immediately one light and 2 ric' or 'Urgent a
wagon for a light and 2 ric'.)
57 How goes (an obvious spelling error, perhaps 'Vorprufung', 'preliminary examination'?).

58   To middle C.O. please send Regiment morning report.

59   To middle regiment. Moderate (----fire (----calibre. CO.O. -rlp house 2. Without change. 3. present. 4. dark. 5. without news. 6. c-o-1-d. 7. without change. C.O.

60   Trench strongpoint: 12 officers-32 non-commissioned officers--292 men casualties: 2 men heavily wounded.

61   Where are requisitions?

62   Between Red and Blue C and D on mapsheet VD 36 C (1:10,000).

63   Wind direction between North-East and East, C.O. North and South, fire falling on sector right and left.

64   From 12–1–18 barrage fire red, annihilating fire green etc etc ——— signal flare.

65   To Group Thomas. Situation. Enemy in sector E and left sector invaded. (The following sentence is corrupt: there are two plausible meanings – 'Our artillery fire toward line of poplars (or 'Pappleschnur', a place name?) falling short' or 'Our artillery should shortly fire in direction line of poplars'.)

66   Group. Around 6 o'clock the infantry will counterattack at the line of poplars. Necessary supporting fire will be requested.

67   To Group D. Shots toward the line of poplars are still falling too short. To prevent own damage (word missing in original) had to be unconditionally increased, according to the testimony of our infantry officer.

68   To 32nd Infantry Division. From stormtroops three black and four red. Leader healthy and an Englishman wounded in the leg captured. Battle Battalion 177.

69   Group Thomas. Strong concentration of troops at Moulinruine. One can count upon an attack.

70   Schwytz cuts the Vaux woods. Schubert.

71   Regiment Caesar. Two battalions will be relieved the night of 21–22.

72   Sector E. Is the relief of Batttalion 231 accomplished? How are things with the first Battalion 230? 99 Reserve Infantry Brigade.

73   To Regiment Schaakolz. Immediate reinforcement. Otherwise position indefensible.

74   Be ready to move with all equipment at 2 o'clock. I am sending three people. Do not give a clear text.

75   To First Guard Division. Outpost position overrun with troops, 5 machine guns, 5 mortars taken. Contact right and left (? not successful) until tonight. Second Guard Reserve Division.

76   8.30 this morning withdrew Regiment Bremen to Irles. The advance posts of the guard remain to secure our lines. The advance posts have to stay with the guards. Safeguard the endangered right wing without reinforcing the outposts. Machine guns which are not required with the outposts to withdraw. 2 F Sector Battalion 11 Ferdinand.

77   Station ready to move 4 o'clock tomorrow with entire infantry equipment to Moslains. Approach order. Lieutenant Muhlank.

78   Heller is not coming, since the store wagon is going to Templeux.

79   When are our provisions coming? We have nothing more.

80   Dismantle during the night. Wagon there at 6 o'clock. Sergeant-Major Deter.

81   Close station. Collection tomorrow morning. Welp.

82   VP to await dismantling hourly, according to orders from C.O.

83 LD dismantles tomorrow. (Second sentence incomprehensible.) 7.30 vehicle. 9 o'clock Equancourt Church.

84 Deputy Officer Remagen. Immediately move Army-Command radio.

85 Lieutenant Hein. Dismantle tonight. Car 7.30 east exit Fins-Gouzencourt. Lieutenant Cullman.

86 Station dismantles at 12 o'clock. Reerect at Caudry around 8 o'clock.

87 ——— (spelling error; word uncertain) try, which should be repeated 4 o'clock, will be repeated today at 10 o'clock.

88 Division staff withdrew morning. 111 Infantry Division Detachment Bernstorff. Orders regarding disbandment from 203. March destination for second Bicycle Battalion 1 Bellingcourt.

89 14 Hussars. Enemy occupied Ham. Cavalry of the 35th Infantry Division is going to Aubigny and Bray St. Christophe. Hussar battle station 13 inform 11th Infantry Division. Some cavalry 221 Infantry Division at Forest. Cyclists in batttle with enemy cavalry. 11th Infantry Division retreats to Etreillers over Roupy. Inform where right and left join. 221 Infantry Division.

90 To C.O. Immediately clarify position of Brigade. The English shall soon be in Bullecourt. If necessary, immediately counterattack. Brigade.

91 Division Messines. Morning Report. No contact with C.O.6. Relief completed smoothly. Brigade Messines.

92 Division. Reinforcements urgently required on the whole line.

93 The position for the new batteries is on the Zonnebeke-Droogenbroodhoek road.

94 It was intercepted, that tomorrow the English intend to attack on a broad front.

95 Battalion 3 Bavarian Reserve 5 to march from Paschendael to North Regiment. The remainder to advance in prepared position. Brigade.

96 Sector North Bavarian Regiment 5 is counterattacking from Paschendael to Zonnebeke. One Bavarian Battalion has in any case advanced to Droogenbroodhoek and is ready for counterattack. Brigade.

97 Gas attack not 1.30 but 3.30.

98 Forward line is under harassing fire, infantry requests harassing fire at the cemetery.

99 Immediately report position of your front line. Frontline is to push immediately into old line.

100 Frontline 895 recovered. Main line of resistance in our hands. Casualties unknown. Urgent ammunition for light machine guns.

101 From 8.30 to 11 gas stand-by. Own gas firing.

Chapter VIII: Codebreaking in the Middle East

1 Maxwell to Kitchener, 11.12.15, untitled volume, Archibald Murray papers, Imperial War Museum.

2 The address shows that the message was solved by codebreakers attached to the Egyptian Expeditionary Force. It demonstrates the standard distribution list between commands for cryptanalytical material acquired in the Middle East.

3 Enver Pasha was the Turkish Minister of War and the dominant figure in Turkish strategy. This solution refers to one of the best documented and most illuminating cases of the effect of cryptanalytical intelligence on British operations during the Great War. (Unless otherwise specified, codebreaking is the source, either

definitely or almost so, for all of the intelligence cited below.) The context was a debate between Turkish commanders about their future strategy in Kurdistan (the territory between Mosul, Diabekir and Lake Van) and Iraq. Ultimately, Enver authorised two different and major offensives – against both the Russians in Kurdistan and the British in Iraq. Turkish forces in the latter theatre would be increased by approximately 50 per cent in strength. Khalil Pasha, in turn, proposed to have his existing formations on the Tigris River fronts, the XVIII Corps, simply hold down the British forces before them. Meanwhile, his reinforcements would form a new corps and, assisted by the XIII Corps on the Hamadan front, launch a surprise attack through eastern Iraq and south eastern Persia in order to encircle and annihilate British forces in Iraq. Altogether, during December 1916–January 1917, several Turkish commanders urged different lines of policy. The debate swayed to and fro, involving changes in aims and means. In Kurdistan and Iraq, the Turks were reorganising their divisions, corps and armies in order to support two distinct operations. Through codebreaking, the British were privy to much of this debate, which was not entirely a blessing. They could read only 'a random selection of secrets' (Ralph Bennett, *Ultra and Mediterranean Strategy* (New York, 1989), p. 44) – that part of the debate which was conducted over radio, intercepted and solved. Some messages took longer to break than others – thus authentic but outdated statements of Turkish intentions were received after subsequent messages (which reflected current Turkish aims) had been solved. Given the nature both of the source and the issue, this information was extremely difficult to assess, a problem increased by the apparent fact that GHQ in Iraq had never before had to analyse such reliable yet complex information on enemy strategy. Experience could not guide its judgements.

On 31 December 1916, an 'absolutely reliable source' informed GHQ Intelligence in Cairo that two new Turkish divisions were being formed in Kurdistan. British authorities expected these formations to support a force of cavalry which was currently pushing the Russian VIIth Caucasian Corps under General Chernozubov back from Mosul toward Persia. This conclusion was not surprising, since the Turks were involved in heavy operations against all the Russian forces south of Lake Van. On 3 January 1917 'very reliable information' confirmed that these two new divisions would be created and form the Eighth Wing Army under Khalil's command. GHQ Intelligence in Iraq found this command structure 'peculiar', since the Second Army had hitherto run the battle against Chernozubov's forces, but took it to mean that for unknown reasons, Khalil would be involved with these operations. At this stage codebreaking was providing confusing information about which specific corps, divisions and regiments Khalil would command. Ultimately, the British realised that the Turks had removed the old divisions from a corps in Kurdistan hitherto attached to the Second Army – but the III Corps, rather than the Eighth Wing Army – given this corps control over different divisions and transferred what had become an entirely new formation to Khalil, leaving virtually all of the old III Corps except its title in Kurdistan.

Until this stage, the material provided by codebreaking had as much confused as clarified the situation for the British. Document One, however, finally allowed them to overcome most of this problem and to assess Turkish capabilities and intentions with accuracy. This message demonstrated that the Sixth Army would launch a major attack against British forces in Iraq but did not clearly state where, when, or in what strength. Two simple indicators, however, the movement of the 14th Division (and of any other formations or units which could definitively be linked to it) and of Turkish artillery would reveal the time and the place of the attack. Document One immediately led the War Office to expect a Turkish assault in Iraq. GHQ Intelligence in Iraq, however, wavered between this possibility and that of an operation against Chernozubov. It requested the date on which Document One had originally been transmitted. That is, it questioned whether this order might not have been superseded. Its views may have been reinforced by a near contemporary solution (the date of receipt by GHQ Iraq is uncertain) which showed the Turkish intention to launch a general offensive in Kurdistan, involving an unknown degree of cooperation with some indeterminate elements of the III Corps. GHQ Iraq may also have doubted that Enver would divide very limited Turkish resources against two completely different objects. In any case, GHQ Iraq obviously did not expect the operations in Iraq planned by the Turks, and cryptanalytical intelligence was necessary to eliminate the danger of being caught by strategic surprise. Against this, although these operations were intended by the Turks, they were in the end never executed. Intelligence revealed a might have been which never happened.

GHQ Iraq, however, quickly concluded that Khalil intended to attack on the Tigris River front by early February with between 2 and 4 divisions, each possessing approximately 5,400 men. This assessment was marked by some degree both of uncertainty and error. The uncertainty stemmed from two factors. First, the British could not be certain whether another corps might assist the attack of the III Corps. While cryptanalytical intelligence did not suggest that this would be so, neither did it deny that possibility. Hence, the British had to determine whether the worst case might be the real case. In particular, they believed – reasonably enough in principle – that the Turks might leave only a small force on the Hamadan front and redeploy the two infantry divisions of the XIII Corps to support the III Corps. Second, the British could not determine with absolute certainty the number of the second division attached to the III Corps. While this was expected to be the Fourth Division in Kurdistan, some intelligence indicated that this might also be the Sixth Division, currently attached to the XIII Corps. Hence, the minimum strength of the attack would be two divisions, if only the III Corps was involved; three, if the Sixth Division was in fact attached to the III Corps and the remaining division of the XIII Corps was used in the operation; or, as an outside possibility, four, if the III Corps consisted of the Fourth and 14th Divisions and both formations of the XIII Corps were used in support. Beyond this, the British could not certainly determine the rifle strength of any of these formations. The figure of 5,400 men was simply an educated guess. The material provided by codebreaking could not resolve these tangled and important points; hence, the British assessments had to include a sizable margin for error.

GHQ Iraq, moreover, misunderstood Khalil's intentions – and not unnaturally. In order to reach the jumping off point for Khalil's attack, the elements of the III Corps would have to pass close to the Tigris River front, which obviously was a possible target for the Turks. Khalil's projected course of operations, moreover, was almost certainly unworkable. GHQ Iraq could not expect an enemy to adopt so risky a strategy, which, paradoxically, was almost the only factor which might have allowed this operation to succeed – assuming that the British could not learn of it in time. Had Khalil executed his intentions, however, codebreaking would probably have compromised the secrecy on which its success relied. Furthermore, the British misunderstood Khalil's intentions precisely because they understood better than he the military realities in Iraq. By the time the 14th Division did arrive, the Turks were being crushed on the Tigris River front. Khalil then altered his intentions and switched this formation to that sector, but too late in the day to matter. Thus, although GHQ's assessment of the danger was in one sense wrong and in another imprecise, these problems proved in practice to be of minor consequence.

Throughout January 1917, all sources of intelligence available to the British were trained on Turkish movements in Kurdistan and Iraq. While the British could not definitively follow the deployment of the 14th Division, snowfalls could be expected to prevent its rapid movement, and by 30 January they learned that neither it nor the Fourth Division, nor either formation of the XIII Corps, had yet left the Kurdish or Hamadan fronts. By 16 January 'highly reliable' sources also indicated that sizable reinforcements of Turkish artillery would reach Iraq by early February; these sources determined in complete detail the strength and movements of these batteries over the next two weeks. (Daily Summaries of Intelligence, Mesopotamian Expeditionary Force, 3.1.17, 4.1.17, 5.1.17, 6.1.17, 12.1.17, 18.1.17, 30.1.17, WO 157/795; GHQ, EEF Intelligence Diary, entry 31.12.16, WO 157/711; Government of India Weekly Intelligence Letters, #1, 2 and 3 of 1917, 2, 9 and 16 January 1917, WO 157/823).

Precisely as this intelligence was first received, Maude had commenced a series of set-piece attacks which, between December 1916 and February 1917, smashed the Turkish forces on the Tigris River front. Maude, as one of his corp commanders later wrote, 'framed his plans with the intention of defeating the enemy's forces before they could be reinforced and of inflicting such blows on the Turks that their morale would be lowered for the future. This could only be attained by hard fighting, seeing that his opponents were flushed with their successes at Kut, and were confident that their own fighting powers far surpassed ours'. (C.E. Caldwell, *The Life of Sir Stanley Maude* (London, 1920), p. 266). As all his sources of information demonstrated – and here codebreaking provided less important material than did combat troops – Maude possessed a sizable numerical advantage on the Tigris front. This ultimately proved to be approximately 3.5 to 1 (45,000 to 12,000) in fighting men and two to one in guns. He correctly expected to crush this enemy so long as it was not reinforced. The latter, however, could easily be done. The III Corps could have doubled Turkish strength on the Tigris River front; indeed, these forces and perhaps some artillery might have reached the front in time to matter had they begun to move in early January. Had they done so a stalemate could easily have ensued on that front.

Here codebreaking provided precisely the intelligence which Maude wished to know, although rather late in the day. According to the procedure outlined in Document Four, Chapter Six, Maude himself would have seen the important solutions, especially since this notorious centraliser, by his own admission, 'did most of the General Staff work himself'. (Caldwell, *Maude*, p. 292). This material showed that the enemy intended to reinforce the theatre and to attack British forces somewhere in Iraq. Given the terrain, the distances and the weather involved, that attack could not happen for some weeks, and its time and place would be signalled by the movement of the 14th Division and of Turkish artillery. Codebreaking, that is, informed Maude after he had formulated his plan of campaign but while he was only beginning to execute it that (a) the enemy had both the intention and the ability to reinforce the Iraq theatre, (b) the projected attack in the Caucasus would occupy reinforcements which otherwise might have reached Iraq, (c) he would have advance warning of the time and place of the operation in Iraq and probably of any Turkish redeployments to the theatre and, ultimately, (d) that these reinforcements could not reach the front in time to forestall his own operations. All this provided a guarantee that his attritional operations of January–February 1917 could succeed and if so would have valuable strategic consequences. On the other hand, this intelligence merely confirmed the wisdom of a campaign which Maude had already launched and eliminated any uncertainty about Turkish intentions and capabilities.

Any more precise account of the effect of this intelligence on Maude's actions during January–February 1917 must be speculative and rest on a judgement of Maude's personality and the use of conditional logic. However, the information on Khalil's intentions could only have been of great significance had Khalil been able to act upon them, which he was not. Given Maude's numerical superiority on the Tigris River front and his own skill as a commander, he was bound to break the enemy – unless he had lost his nerve because of uncertainty about Turkish intentions and capabilities (which does not seem likely). Hence, this intelligence simply increased Maude's certainty and confidence, made it unnecessary to keep large reserves in hand to deal with unexpected enemy actions and marginally hastened the success and lowered the cost of his set-piece battles on the Tigris. An able commander received first-rate and surprisingly precise intelligence of the enemy's capabilities and intentions from codebreaking which was assessed tolerably well. Since these intentions were never executed and probably never could have been, however, Maude did not need to act on this knowledge or change in the least his present course of operations.

During Maude's subsequent operations between 17 February to 11 March, when his forces smashed the Turkish defences and captured Baghdad, codebreaking revealed the Turkish debate regarding whether or not to despatch reinforcements to Baghdad and demonstrated that none could arrive immediately (GHQ, EEF Intelligence Diary, 18.2.17, 27.2.17 (WO 157/712) and note 17, below). No doubt this information shaped Maude's belief that he could safely seize Baghdad and pursue the Turkish forces further north, and the War Office's willingness to authorise this action, which it had initially regarded as being rather risky. Codebreaking may also have affected Maude's actions during this period in another way. According to Ferdinand Tuohy, *The Crater of Mars* (London, 1929) pp. 164–65, following Maude's breakthrough at Shumran, British codebreakers solved a message from 'Nazim Pasha, commanding the retreating Turkish Sixth Army' which stated that Turkish forces could not hold the Diala lines, the last possible defensive position before Baghdad; and that this news led Maude to drive forward energetically. In general, Tuohy is a very reliable witness and in this case an informed one – he visited Iraq several months after these events. There are, however, some errors in his account – Nazim Pasha, for example, did not command the Sixth Army, while Touhy's account of the War Office's attitude toward an advance on Baghdad is distorted. Moreover, the content of a Turkish message solved after Maude had captured Baghdad (see Document Four, 15.3.17) is roughly similar to that described by Tuohy: possibly he confused the date (and therefore the effect) of a specific solution. In any case, the official intelligence files –

which provide a reasonably good although not perfect record for codebreaking during this period – neither confirm nor contradict Tuohy's account. This, however, does not necessarily invalidate it. As matters stand, the truth in this case is uncertain.

4   The British liaison officers with Tsarist forces in the Caucasus and Persia. They were expected to acquire information from Russian sources so to trace the movement of the 14th Division and to determine whether other forces, particularly from the XIII Corps, might be despatched from those regions to Iraq. Thus, material acquired from codebreaking was guiding the collection of intelligence in general on the enemy's operational intentions and reducing the possibility that Turkish redeployments could catch the British off guard.

5   The Indian Army title for British and Indian forces in Iraq, which was being replaced by the term 'Mesopotamian Expeditionary Force'.

6   The Russo-Turkish fronts in Kurdistan and on the borders between Iraq and Persia.

7   The battle of Romani in July–August 1916, the last Turkish offensive into the Sinai desert.

8   Kress von Kressenstein, a Bavarian Colonel attached to the Fourth Army. Formally the chief of staff of the VIII Corps, in practice also the commander for many sizable Turkish military operations.

9   Pasha I, a German force of machine guns, heavy artillery, anti-aircraft guns and mortars supporting Turkish forces in Palestine. Not to be mistaken for Pasha II (cf. note 5, Chapter Seven).

10 This intelligence corroborated material from other sources and demonstrated the location of the enemy's new centre of strength. In context, this revealed that the enemy had switched at least temporarily to a defensive posture in Palestine.

11 The Turkish force defending Palestine.

12 This was a detailed and generally accurate statement of the Fourth Army's intentions. However, the authoritative and unambiguous declaration of intent in (1) was misleading. The Fourth Army was not a leading priority for Enver Pasha; whatever its commanders might have wished, they were not significantly reinforced before autumn 1917. They may have realised this fact and have made this declaration simply so to boost the morale of their officers. In any case, this misleading declaration did not hamper British actions. More significantly, the British appear to have doubted one of von Kressenstein's statements and thus misunderstood Turkish intentions. The commentary after (2) indicates that the Intelligence Branch at the Egyptian Expeditionary Force did not expect the Turks to hold a line between Gaza and Beersheba. This assessment was wrong. Until November 1917, that remained the main Turkish line of defence. The British may have doubted the accuracy of von Kressenstein's statement because the defensive system along this line during March 1917 – which consisted of a few strongholds, with sizable reserves placed 10–15 miles to the north – was patently flawed. As events turned out, however, this misinterpretation (and the misleading nature of the information in note 13 below) had no ill effects. British commanders may have underestimated the Turkish determination to hold their existing positions in the Hejaz and Palestine and overestimated the ease with which the enemy could be driven back. The first British attack on Gaza, however, was a bold and rational gamble which almost succeeded. In these cases, a first rate source of intelligence

provided material on the enemy's intentions which was generally accurate but in two ways misleading and in a third proved open to misinterpretation. None of this, however, harmed a plan of campaign which was based on an accurate enough grasp of the enemy's capabilities on the front line.

13 About five weeks earlier, a 'very reliable source' (codebreaking) had indicated that the forward elements of the Hejaz Expeditionary Force (HEF) were withdrawing to Medina (Daily Summary of Intelligence, Mesopotamian Expeditionary Force, 25.1.17, WO 157/795). Hence, the material of 5 March fits British perceptions of the likely future of the HEF. On 6 March General Murray, the commander in Egypt, noted that the operational failure and the imminent withdrawal of the HEF was 'now obvious. It is naturally of vital importance, in view of the source from which our information has been obtained that no premature announcement of any kind should be made on this subject either in the Press, in Parliament, or elsewhere. In fact, for the moment, the less said about it the better ... we should in all probability be deprived of an invaluable source of information by any premature talk on the subject'. (Chief Egyptforce to War Office, 6.3.17, WO 158/605). These assessments were rational but proved wrong for reasons which could not be foreseen. The Turks did not act on Jemal's specific declaration of intent. While the HEF maintained a purely defensive position, the Turks continued to hold Medina until the end of the war.

14 The material between 13 to 23 March pertains to the period following Maude's capture of Baghdad. These documents (and other solutions in Government of India Intelligence Reports, Nos. 10–16, 8.3.17–19.4.17, WO 157/824) show that throughout March–April 1917, codebreaking continually informed Maude of the enemy's strategic intentions, for example, that the two halves of the Sixth Army (the XVIII Corps on the Tigris and the XIII Corps in northeastern Iraq), were withdrawing in order to unite in north-central Iraq, of the proposed lines of retreat and interim defensive positions of these corps, of the poor morale and supply situation of the XVIII Corps, and of the miniscule level of reinforcements being despatched to the theatre. While some of this material merely confirmed that derived from other sources, codebreaking provided an unmatched and first rate picture of the chaotic state of the enemy army and of its intentions. This knowledge presumably shaped the determined pursuit by which Maude sought to smash the XIII Corps or at least to prevent its junction with the XVIII Corps. These operations, however, were unsuccessful.

15 These solutions traced Turkish reinforcements to the front two days after the failure of the first British attack on Gaza. At the time it would have been unclear whether this was a temporary or permanent deployment. It proved to be the latter.

16 Jemal Pasha. This message revealed part of the Turkish debate about its future strategy, and Jemal's perceptions obviously would have interested the British command. The degree to which his demands were met also provided several indicators by which to gauge Turkish strategic priorities, the importance which Enver attached to the security of Palestine and the chances for British success in that theatre. The full extent to which the British solved other messages pertaining to Turkish strategic intentions and capabilities throughout the rest of 1917, such as the role of Yilderim Army Group, however, remains uncertain. Definite proof about this matter would shape one's assessment of British strategy in the Middle East during 1917. The only sure evidence on this topic comes from Iraq. In the spring

and summer of 1917, codebreaking accurately determined where any new Turkish offensive in Iraq would be launched, provided information which led the British to conclude correctly that the enemy hoped to despatch the Yilderim Army Group to Iraq and also traced its efforts to build a logistical base along the Euphrates River. One of Maude's last actions during 1917 was to establish a powerful defensive position precisely where the Yilderim Army Group planned to attack. (Document One of Chapter Seven; EEF Intelligence diary, entry 4.6.17, WO 157/716; Robertson to Maude, 30.8.17, L/MIL 5/738). In the Iraq theatre, codebreaking allowed the British to place the Yilderim Army Group in check even before it reached the board. Ultimately, however, that formation was despatched to the Palestine front.

17 Ali Ihsan, commander of the XIII Corps in northeastern Iraq. These messages were transmitted and solved during Maude's breakthrough to Baghdad. They demonstrated that the XIII Corps was preoccupied with its own front and that the only Turkish reinforcement which might have allowed the Turks to hold Baghdad against a British assault could not arrive in time to do so.

18 Field Marshal Erich von Falkenhayn, previously commander-in-chief of the German Army and presently commander of the 7th and 8th Armies of the Yilderim Army Group, which now controlled Turkish and German forces in southern Palestine. The Fourth Army, based in Damascus, controlled the rear logistical network.

19 Documents Six, Seven and Eight illuminate the effect of cryptanalytical intelligence during the third battle of Gaza. By 9 November 1917 the Turkish defences on the Gaza-Beersheba front had broken but Allenby's attempt to annihilate the foe had failed. At this point codebreaking informed him of a fleeting opportunity to exploit his breakthrough. It demonstrated that the Fourth Army was both preparing for a general withdrawal from southern Palestine and suffering from immense transport difficulties. It revealed Falkenhayn's operational intentions – to hold a defensive position north of Beersheba, strip his centre of troops and concentrate his forces on the Mediterranean coast for a desperate counterattack. The discrepancy between the intentions of von Falkenhayn and of the Fourth Army also showed that the enemy's counsels were divided. Allenby immediately acted on this knowledge. He believed that von Falkenhayn's intention could not be executed: as one of his senior staff officers wrote, Allenby did 'little more than give a contemptuous glance over his shoulder at his great opponent's threat', (Archibald Wavell, *Allenby, A Study in Greatness* (London, 1940), pp. 220–22). Allenby merely alerted his troops already along the coast (including a small reserve force) of the attack. The latter did indeed abort – but to the British surprise, von Kressenstein disobeyed his instructions and advanced toward Beersheba. In this sector of the front, cryptanalytical intelligence about the enemy's intentions had actually proven counterproductive. This action shows one of the classic problems involved in the use of cryptanalytical intelligence. It also played straight into Allenby's hand. For on 9–10 November Allenby concentrated his forces in the centre of the line – which he knew was the weak point in the enemy's front – and drove north to seize all of the Plain of Philistia including Junction Station, thus cutting railway communications between Jerusalem and Damascus. This stroke worked exactly as Allenby had intended. It broke the enemy's army into two pieces, both of which had to withdraw immediately so as to avoid annihilation – a problem increased by von Kressenstein's attack. It magnified

the logistical difficulties for the Turkish forces in central Palestine which, in turn, crippled their defensive capacity over the next month during the battle for Jerusalem. Finally, it created problems of supply which ensured that any Turkish forces operating below northern Palestine must fight in two isolated groups. Altogether, on 9–10 November cryptanalytical intelligence gave Allenby the opportunity to use his resources with their greatest effect, which he did. Conversely, under the circumstances he most likely would have won the battle without the advantage of intelligence while his victory did not annihilate the enemy.

20   Documents Ten, Eleven and Twelve show how, during the first (and unsuccessful) British assault on Jerusalem, codebreaking frequently revealed the enemy's order of battle and dispositions and also its assessments of British strength, locations and intentions.

Bibliography

MANUSCRIPT SOURCES

Imperial War Museum, London
Sir Gerard Clauson Papers
Guy Dawnay Papers
National Army Museum, London
Philip Leith-Ross Papers
Public Archives of Canada, Ottawa
RG–9
Public Record Office, Kew
ADM 137 War Histories, 1914–1918
AIR 1 Air Ministry Correspondence
WO 95 War Diaries, 1914–1918
WO 106 Directorate of Military Operations and Intelligence Papers
WO 157 Intelligence Summaries, 1914–1918
WO 158 Military Headquarters Papers, 1914–1918
WO 170 War Diaries, Mediterranean, 1939–1945

BIBLIOGRAPHICAL ESSAY

The only bibliographies which are directly relevant to a study of British military intelligence during the Great War are Michael Occleshaw, *Armour Against Fate, British Military Intelligence in the First World War* (London, 1989) and Wesley Wark, 'Intelligence Since 1900' in Gerald Jordan, (ed). *British Military History: A Supplement to Robin Higham's 'Guide to the Sources'* (New York, 1988). Occleshaw is valuable, if incomplete regarding signals intelligence. Wark is of rather limited value, although the section on human intelligence networks is useful.

While the literature on British military intelligence between 1854 and 1914 is reasonably good, much work remains to be done. The best study is William Carpenter Beaver II, 'The Development of the Intelligence Division and its Role in Aspects of Imperial Policy Making, 1854–1901' (Oxford DPhil thesis, 1976). Other good general accounts are Christopher Andrew, *Secret Service, The Making of the British Intelligence Community* (London, 1987) and Thomas G. Fergusson, *British Military Intelligence, 1870–1914, The Development of a Modern Intelligence Organisation* (London, 1984). B.A.H. Parritt, *The Intelli-*

gencers, *The History of British Military Intelligence Up to 1914* (1971) retains some value; Jock Haswell, *British Military Intelligence* (London, 1973) does not. Useful studies of specific issues, British signals intelligence among them, include John Ferris, 'Lord Salisbury, Secret Intelligence and British Policy Toward Russia and Central Asisa, 1874–78' in B.J.C. MacKercher and Keith Neilson (eds), *Go Spy the Land* (forthcoming) and 'Before "Room 40": The British Empire and Signals Intelligence, 1898–1914', *The Journal of Strategic Studies*, 12/4 (1989); Nicholas Hiley, 'The Failure of British Espionage Against Germany, 1908–1914', *The Historical Journal*, 26/4 (1983) and 'The Strategic Origins of Room 40', *Intellligence and National Security*, 2/3 (1987); Peter Morris, 'Intelligence and its Interpretation: Mesopotamia 1914–1916' in Christopher Andrew and Jeremy Noakes (eds), *Intelligence and International Relations 1900–1945* (Exeter Studies in History, No. 15, 1987), and 'British Secret Service Activity in Khorassan, 1887–1908', *The Historical Journal*, *XXVII* (1984); Adrian Preston, 'British Military Policy and the Defence of India: A Study of British Military Policy, Plans and Preparations During the Russian Crisis, 1875–1880' (University of London Ph.D. thesis, 1966), and 'The Eastern Question during the Franco-Prussian War' in Jay Atherton (ed.), *Historical Papers, 1972* (Canadian Historical Association, 1972). George Armand Furze, *Information in War: Its Acquisition and Transmission* (London, 1895) and General Wolseley, *The Soldier's Pocket-Book for Field Service* (1886: fifth edition) are useful sources on contemporary views of military intelligence.

The literature on British military intelligence during the First World War is uneven. It has also progressed in a peculiar fashion. During the interwar years, many reliable and important works on the topic were published. Among the most accurate and valuable, and certainly the best written, are Compton Mackenzie's accounts of his experiences as an intelligence analyst during the Gallipoli campaign and chief of British counter-intelligence at Athens during 1916–17: *Gallipoli Memories* (London, 1930), *First Athenian Memories* (London, 1931) and *Greek Memories* (London, 1939). George Cockerill, *What Fools We Were* (London, 1944) is a trustworthy and illuminating memoir by a leading figure within the Military Intelligence Division (MID) in London; George Aston, *Secret Service*, (London, 1920) is an informed – perhaps demi-official – account of rather mixed value, but flowers bloom alongside the weeds. John Charteris, *At G.H.Q.* (London, 1930) is an apologia and not a particularly accurate one; read with reserve, however, it contains useful material. Decades later, Richard Meinertzhagen, *Army Diary, 1899–1926* (London, 1960), provided an important and reliable account of intelligence and deception. John Lord, *Duty, Honour, Empire: the life and times of Colonel Richard Meinertzhagen* (London, 1971), competently elucidated this theme. James Marshall-Cornwall, *Wars and Rumours of Wars* (London, 1984) provided what may prove to be the last memoir of an army intelligence officer from the Great War. While worth reading, his assessment of the relationship between Haig and Charteris is open to question. Alice Ivy Hay, *Valiant for Truth, Malcolm Hay of*

Seaton (London, 1971) is a useful if anecdotal account of the MID and especially MIı(b) at work.

During the interwar years, several accounts were published by veterans of the signals intellligence service of the British Army. These works retain fundamental importance and are quite accurate regarding matters with which their authors had direct experience. They include E.W.B. Gill, *War, Wireless and Wangles* (Oxford, 1934), Captain H.J. Round, 'Direction and Position Finding', *The Journal of the Institution of Electrical Engineers* (London Volume 58, 1920), pp. 224–257, and Ferdinand Tuohy, *The Secret Corps, A Tale of 'Intelligence' on all Fronts* (London, 1920), *The Crater of Mars* (London, 1929) and *The Battle of Brains* (London, 1930). The last three books, one of which is a collection of factually based short stories, are repetitious but remain among the most important works on British military intelligence as a whole during the Great War. Much valuable information on signals intelligence is also contained in two demi-official accounts of British and imperial signals services – R.E. Priestley, *The Signal Service in the European War of 1914 to 1918 (France)* (Chatham, 1921), and Major W. Arthur Steel, 'Wireless Telegraphy in the Canadian Corps in France', Chapters 1–11, *Canadian Defence Quarterly*, Volumes 6–9, 1928–1931, especially Chapter 6, 'I Toc and Policing Work', Volume 7, 1929–30.

Increasingly, however, this topic was ignored by historians. The Official Histories of the British Army, for example, rarely referred to intelligence, even though their chief editor, General James Edmond, was extraordinarily well informed on the topic. To a large extent, between the 1930s and the 1960s the matter was forgotten. The main exceptions were three semi-official histories, Kerry, A.J. and W.A. McDill, *The History of the Corps of Royal Canadian Engineers* (Toronto, 1962); John S. Moir (ed.), *History of the Royal Canadian Corps of Signals, 1903–1961* (Ottawa, 1962); and R.F.H. Nalder, *The Royal Corps of Signals, A History of its Antecedents and Developments (circa 1800–1955)* (London, 1958). While derivative of Green and Priestley, these works referred in detail and with accuracy to signals intelligence on the Western Front.

Since the 1960s, a scholarly literature has slowly emerged on British military intelligence during the Great War. No account, however, deals thoroughly with the whole topic, and none has the general value of Ralph Bennett's *Ultra in the West* (London, 1979) and *Ultra and Mediterranean Strategy* (New York, 1989) or Patrick Beesley's *Room 40, British Naval Intelligence, 1914–1918* (London, 1982). The best recent general studies are Major S.R. Elliot, *Scarlet to Green* (Toronto, 1981) and Occleshaw, *Armour Against Fate*. These works clearly describe the process by which intelligence was collected and assessed at all levels of command and, to a lesser extent, illuminate its use. Occleshaw is uneven, his methodology sometimes naive and on occasion his assessments are questionable to a spectacular degree. As a whole, however, his account is accurate and ranks alongside the works of Tuohy as the best introduction to the topic. Elliot's analysis is short but excellent. While specifically of Canadian military intelligence during the First World War, that service reflected British practice and experiences. Indeed, the various studies of Canadian military intelligence are fundamental sources for British intelligence on the Western Front.

There are few useful accounts of the effect of intelligence and deception on specific British military operations. The main exceptions to this rule are Richard Popplewell, 'British Intelligence in Mesopotamia, 1914–16' and Yigal Sheffy, 'Institutionalized Deception and Perception Reinforcement: Allenby's Campaigns in Palestine, 1917–18' in Michael Handel (ed), *Intelligence and Military Operations*, (London, 1990); John Ferris, 'The British Army and Signals Intelligence in the Field During the First World War', *Intelligence and National Security*, 3/4 (1988); David French, 'The Origins of the Dardenelles Campaign Reconsidered', *History* (1983), and 'Sir John French's Secret Service on the Western Front, 1915', *The Journal of Strategic Studies*, 7/4 (1984). Popplewell, ibid., has superseded Morris, 'Mesopotamia', op. cit. David French, 'Watching the Allies: British Intelligence and the French Mutinies of 1917', paper presented to the Fourth International Conference on Intelligence and Strategy, United States Army War College, May 1989, is an interesting account of an important form of intelligence – on one's allies rather than enemies. This topic requires more study than it usually receives. In 1917, for example, the 'first problem' of the intelligence section of GHQ, American Expeditionary Force, was to acquire intelligence on 'the political and economic situation of France, England and Italy, as well as Holland, Switzerland and other Allied, neutral and enemy countries of Europe' (Memorandum of Chief of G–2–A, G.H.Q. A.E.F., 8.6.19, p. 22, *United States Army in the World War, 1917–1919, Volume 13* (Washington, 1948).

A small but important and reliable literature discusses the work and worth of the main sources of intelligence for the British Army during the Great War. Peter Mead, *The Eye in the Sky: history of air observation and reconnaissance for the Army, 1875–1945* (London, 1983), E.H. Hahn, *The Intelligence Service Within the Canadian Corps* (Toronto, 1930) and John R. Innes, *Flash Spotters and Sound Rangers, How They Lived, Worked and Fought in the Great War* (London, 1935), are the best studies of aerial reconnaissance and photography, artillery intelligence and the collection of intelligence on the battlefield proper. Guy Hartcup, *The War of Invention, Scientific Developments 1914–18* (London, 1988) includes useful accounts of the development of all the technical sources of intelligence. The literature is particularly good about the agent networks of the British Army. Among other studies, see French, 'Intelligence Service' and Andrew, *Secret Service*, pp. 195–259 for the networks in western Europe; Andrew, op.cit. pp. 297–325 and Keith Neilson, '"Joy Rides"? British Intelligence and propaganda in Russia 1914–1917', *The Historical Journal, Volume XXIV* (1981) for those in Russia; H.V.F. Winstone, *The Illicit Adventure: the story of political and military Intelligence in the Middle East, from 1898 to 1926* (London, 1982), for those in the Middle East. Richard

Popplewell, 'British Intelligence and Indian Subversion, The Surveillance of Indian Revolutionaries in India and Abroad, 1904–1920' (University of Cambridge PhD, thesis, 1988) is an excellent study of British human intelligence in general during the Great War.

The literature is weak regarding the signals intelligence service of the British Army. Elliot and Occleshaw include short but useful and reliable discussions on the topic. 'Nigel West' (Rupert Allason), *G.C.H.Q., The Secret Wireless War, 1900–1986* (London, 1987) offers a section derivative of Nalder – and thus ultimately of Priestley – judging by the text. Most other recent studies have entirely overlooked this matter. The main exceptions are Ferris, 'The British Army', French, 'Intelligence Service', Wing Commander M.T. Thurbon, 'The Origins of Electronic Warfare', *Journal of the Royal United Services Institute, Volume 122* (1977) (an incomplete but reliable account of radio interception in the BEF during 1914) and W.J. Barker, *A History of the Marconi Company* (London, 1970), (a useful although not exhaustive account of radio interception and direction finding). These works can be supplemented by Gill, Green, Tuohy, Priestly, Round and David Kahn, *The Codebreakers, The Story of Secret Writing* (New York, 1967), (which includes an accurate and excellent account of British codebreaking on the Western Front). There is no systematic study of the problems of signals security and communications – for examples of this sort of work for other armies and periods, cf. John Ferris, 'The British Army, Signals and Security in the Desert Campaign, 1940–1942', in Michael Handel (ed), *Intelligence and Military Operations*, and 'The British "Enigma": Britain, Signals Security and Cipher Machines, 1906–1946', *Defence Analysis, 3/2* (1987) and H.C. Ingles, 'Tannenburg – A Study in Faulty Signal Communications' (1929) in William F. Friedman (ed.), *Cryptography and Cryptanalysis Articles, Volume 1* (Laguna Hills, Ca., 1976). No historian has assessed the work of MI1(b) or MI1(e); while ample evidence survives on the latter organisation, the former may well remain forever in the shadows.

Some of the small but useful literature on the signals intelligence services of other armies in the Great War illuminates the British experience. David Shulman, *An Annotated Bibliography of Cryptography* (New York, 1976) has an excellent general bibliography, albeit rather weak on the British side. Kahn, op.cit., is the standard survey of military codebreaking, and an excellent one, with an important general bibliography. English translations of two important articles, Marcel Givierge, 'Problems of Code' and 'Problems of Code (continued)' (1926) (originals in *Revue Militaire Française*, June–July 1924), can be found in Friedman, *Cryptography and Cryptanalysis Articles*, ibid. A short but well-informed and useful account of German military signals intelligence on the Western Front is contained in Albert Praun, *German Radio Intelligence* (paper prepared for Historical Division, Headquarters, European Command, United States Army, undated but post-1945). Wilhelm F. Flicke, *War Secrets in the Ether, Volume 1* (original date of writing uncertain, but post-1945)

(Laguna Hills, Ca., 1977) is more problematical. Flicke was a veteran of German military signals intelligence during the First and Second World Wars. Much of his book is of questionable reliability: however, his account of the interception of field telephone traffic and of the signals intelligence service of the French Army on the Western Front (purportedly based on material captured from French archives during 1940) are generally accurate. Two contemporary reports written by signals intelligence personnel of the American Army on the Western Front have been published: William Friedman, *Solving German Codes in World War One* (Laguna Hills, Ca., 1977: copy of a memorandum written by Friedman *c.* 1919) and Wayne G. Barker (ed.), *The History of Codes and Ciphers in the United States During World War One* (Laguna Hills, Ca., 1979: a 'sanitized' edition of an internal history written by members of the United State's Army Security Agency during 1946). These accounts are reliable and also illuminate the practices and experiences of their French and British counterparts – especially the latter, since the signals intelligence of the American Army was based largely on the British model.

Index

ARMY RECORDS SOCIETY
(FOUNDED 1984)

Members of the Society are entitled to purchase back
volumes at reduced prices.
Orders should be sent to the Hon. Treasurer, Army Records Society,
c/o National Army Museum,
Royal Hospital Road,
London SW3 4HT.

The Society has already issued:

Vol. I:
The Military Correspondence of
Field Marshal Sir Henry Wilson 1918–1922
Edited by Dr Keith Jeffery

Vol. II:
The Army and the
Curragh Incident, 1914
Edited by Dr Ian F.W. Beckett

Vol. III:
The Napoleonic War Journal of
Captain Thomas Henry Browne, 1807–1816
Edited by Roger Norman Buckley

Vol. IV:
An Eighteenth-Century Secretary at War
The Papers of William, Viscount Barrington
Edited by Dr Tony Hayter

Vol. V:
The Military Correspondence of
Field Marshal Sir William Robertson 1915–1918
Edited by David R. Woodward

Vol. VI:
Colonel Samuel Bagshawe and the
Army of George II, 1731–1762
Edited by Dr Alan J. Guy

Vol. VII:
Montgomery and the Eighth Army
Edited by Stephen Brooks